Morning Glory

365 Devotionals like no other!

Dr. Sheila Hayford

Book Title: Morning Glory

365 Devotionals like no other!
Copyright © 2016, 2017 by Dr. Sheila Hayford
2017 Edition
Published By: Dr. Sheila Hayford, What A Word Publishing and Media Group
http://www.whatawordpublishing.com
Email: info@whatawordpublishing.com
ISBN: 978-0-692-85237-8
All rights reserved. No part of this book may be reproduced or transmitted in any form or by any means without written permission from the author, Dr. Sheila Hayford. Permission Requests should be addressed to: info@whatawordpublishing.com
You may also contact the author via the Publisher's website by visiting http://www.whatawordpublishing.com
Book is available for sale at www.whatawordpublishing.com, various online merchants including at www.amazon.com, retail stores, and via direct sales.
* "The Sermon of the Shoes" ©2007 by Dr. Sheila Hayford. Excerpt from "W.A.W. - What A Word – Inspirational Words for Everyday Life Here on Earth" Used with permission.
**"Sermonette: Turning Water into Wine ©2011 by Dr. Sheila Hayford. Excerpt from "Turning Water Into Wine" Used with permission:
Scripture verses are from the King James Version Translation of the Bible unless otherwise indicated.
New International Version (NIV)
Holy Bible, New International Version®, NIV® Copyright ©1973, 1978, 1984, 2011 by Biblica, Inc.® Used by permission. All rights reserved worldwide.
This book is intended to be used as a spiritual guide from a Christian perspective. For your specific needs, seek expert professional advice.

Printed in the United States of America.

$\mathcal{T}$his book is dedicated to:

- Dr. Diane Komp, Professor of Pediatric Hematology-Oncology, whom I first met at Yale University New Haven Hospital in New Haven, Connecticut. My life was literally changed when I met you through our highly respected friend, Dr. Robert LaCamera. Thank you for being my friend, mentor, spiritual mother and for believing in me and God's work in me

- Dr. Robert LaCamera, a highly renowned role model in personal and family life and highly regarded in town and gown life. Your leadership has changed my life and countless others for eternity. Who would have thought that God would have such an enjoyable fulfilling career for me as a Pediatrician, allow me the grace to share my lifelong love of reading and writing and help others do the same? There is still much more work to do. Let us advance in our calling and not grow weary. For as the book of Galatians Chapter 6, verse 9 reads, "And let us not be weary in well doing: for in due season we shall reap, if we faint not."

  Dr. Sheila Hayford.

Acknowledgments

I would like to acknowledge and thank the many partners, businesses, organizations and individuals I have collaborated with over the years. Together we play our part in the betterment of society for the glory of God. It would more than fill this book if I were to name each one of you. God sees, knows your commitment and service and will reward us beyond our imagination. It is a pleasure to share the featured businesses and organizations with our readers. Thank you for your commitment and hard work.

Dr. Sheila Hayford.

Foreword

The first three months of the year in the United States of America celebrate the African-American experience: The Reverend Dr. Martin Luther King, Jr. Holiday in January, Black History Month in February and Women's History Month in March. And so it is fitting to pause and reflect on the challenges facing African Americans and society at large in the 21st century. Yes, there has been a lot of progress; desegregated schools, African-Americans in the work force and positions of authority and the right to vote politically. However, challenges remain. We read about police racial profiling, brutality against many African-American men, black on black violence, the disintegration of the nuclear family, division, name calling and the stereotyping of our fellow human beings. Economic, educational, racial and social disparity in many areas continues.

As a society, we have our part to play by becoming socially responsible and contributing to the welfare and dignity of the human race. However, we must never lose sight of our individual responsibilities. So what does God have to say about what is going on in this world? Is everything doom and gloom? To the contrary! The Lord Jesus tells us in John Chapter 8, verse 36 that whomever the Son (Jesus Christ, the Son of God) has set free is free indeed. True freedom is not just the absence of physical, mental or spiritual bondage; true freedom is a state of spiritual, physical and emotional wellbeing in the fullest sense. It is the freedom to be our truest self and to achieve our fullest purpose in life. And it starts with the gift of life we are given each day by God. The devotionals in this book are inspiring, challenging and life changing. As we discover more of God, we discover more of ourselves and the changes we need to make in order to live out our authentic God given life. I so enjoyed writing this book and my prayer is that we will jump-start each day with a devotional, in prayer, spending personal quiet time with God. And then, go forth and change our world!

Dr. Sheila Hayford.

January 1
It Is Our Time

Deuteronomy Chapter 1, verses 6-8:

The Lord our God said to us at Horeb, "You have stayed long enough at this mountain. Break camp and advance into the hill country of the Amorites; go to all the neighboring peoples in the Arabah, in the mountains, in the western foothills, in the Negev and along the coast, to the land of the Canaanites and to Lebanon, as far as the great river, the Euphrates. See, I have given you this land. Go in and take possession of the land the Lord swore he would give to your fathers - to Abraham, Isaac and Jacob - and to their descendants after them." (NIV)

Prayer: Dear God; we thank you for the gift of life and for allowing us to enter into this New Year, a year filled with hope and possibilities. Empower us by your Holy Spirit and enable us to achieve your will in and for our lives. As we remember your faithfulness in years past, we lovingly entrust ourselves to you. In Jesus' Name, Amen.

It is a New Day and a New Year! What are your expectations? It is easy to get comfortable with the status quo because change may be uncomfortable or at times unpleasant. Doing what you have done every day becomes a habit and habits may not always be easy to break. The Lord God was speaking to the people of Israel through the prophet Moses. God had led them in the wilderness in what could have been a very short journey. They murmured, they complained, and at times, they were stubborn. God was very patient with them but even God had had enough. "You have been here long enough. It is time for you to advance!" God was saying. What is it that God has called you to do? How long will you keep circling around the same habits, the same people, the same places? Sometimes you have to break camp with the familiar to attain the unfamiliar. It is our time to fulfil our destiny. God has more than enough for each one of us. I am determined this year with God's help to advance in my God given destiny. I will possess my God given land and the inheritance that is mine in Christ. God is saying to us: "It is your time. Go get yours!"

© By Dr. Sheila Hayford.

January 2
My Help Comes From The LORD

Psalm 121, verses 1-7:

I lift up my eyes to the mountains - where does my help come from? My help comes from the LORD, the Maker of heaven and earth. He will not let your foot slip - he who watches over you will not slumber; indeed, he who watches over Israel will neither slumber nor sleep. The LORD watches over you - the LORD is your shade at your right hand; the sun will not harm you by day, nor the moon by night. The LORD will keep you from all harm - he will watch over your life; the LORD will watch over your coming and going both now and forevermore. (NIV)

Prayer: Dear heavenly Father; we love you! Thank you for the gift of your Son, Jesus Christ and for the provisions you have prepared for us ahead of time. Forgive us where we have been doubtful or fearful. Forgive us of all sin. Help us to believe your Word, enable us to obey you and to live wholeheartedly for you. And as we experience your provision may we boldly declare: My help comes from the LORD, my life belongs to God, and my joy remains in God. In the Name of Jesus. Amen.

What beautiful, reassuring words of encouragement! Is your money short? Is your body in need of healing? Do you feel emotionally drained? Do you need personal spiritual revival? What is your challenge? You see, before you ask a person for help that person must not only be willing to help you, he or she must be CAPABLE of helping you. Your friend may empathize with your challenge but may not be in a position to help you. Not so with our God. We are reminded that HE, the LORD GOD, is the maker of heaven and earth. He is therefore the ultimate in authority over the affairs of men. Some years back the Lord God gave me specific instructions and promised me that if I would obey Him I would be His responsibility. At the time, I believed God but could not have imagined how serious God was when He said that. As I obeyed God I saw God fight my battles and win in His time and of His choosing. When I went to God in prayer, I would remind God that I was His responsibility, be specific about my need and watch God supernaturally provide. When I was unfairly treated I watched in amazement as God refused to allow some to see the light of day, called some over to their eternal destiny and made me feel like I was His favorite. The truth of the matter is this; through our Lord Jesus Christ, all who are adopted into the family of God are God's children. God is a good Father. He will watch over your life and take care of you. All you have to do is to believe what He says and do what He asks you to do. Your challenges will become your stepping stones, memorials of a faithful God.

© By Dr. Sheila Hayford.

January 3
God Is Love

1 John Chapter 4, verse 7:

Beloved, let us love one another: for love is of God; and every one that loveth is born of God, and knoweth God.

Prayer: Dear God of love: Thank you for loving us so much that you sent your Son, the Lord Jesus Christ, to die for our sins and bring us back to a right relationship with you. Thank you that we can now call you our Father. Forgive us when we say we love you but do not show kindness to our neighbor. Forgive us when we act out of selfishness or vain glory instead of being motivated by your love in everything that we do. Empower us by the Holy Spirit to truly walk in love. Let us bring you a Father's joy and not heartache. In the Name of Jesus we pray. Amen.

I love how simple God makes this command and so very practical. God is love and expects His children to demonstrate His character. Talk is cheap if it is not accompanied by corresponding actions. God wants us to love everybody, just as God does. Not only does God expect us to love our family, our friends and our co-workers, but also to love strangers and our enemies. Impossible in our own strength; maybe. You see, loving family and friends comes easy to most. However, loving someone who means you no good takes the power of God. Look at the Lord Jesus Christ hanging on the cross unjustly, having endured a sham trial, and yet asking God to forgive those who had placed him there. Jesus Christ showed us the ultimate sacrifice of love. Yes, the sacrifice of love because loving your enemies goes against the carnal fleshly desires of revenge and hatred. As Christians, we are witnessing an even more troubling scenario. We see believers in Christ fighting each other over the traditions of men. Remember the words of Jesus in the John Chapter 13, verse 35: "By this will men know that ye are my disciples if ye have love one to another." If you cannot love your fellow man whom you can physically see, how can you proclaim God's love while disobeying God's love command? "Beloved, let us love one another: for love is of God; and every one that loveth is born of God, and knoweth God."

© By Dr. Sheila Hayford.

MICHAELANGELO HAIR DESIGNS, INC
696 North DuPont Highway
Dover, DE 19901

We take Beautiful Hair to a Higher Level!

We are open Weekdays and on Saturdays
by Appointment.
Walk-ins also accepted subject to availability.
Our DAY SPA is open for your special event.
Call (302) 734-8343 today and see why we have
Generations of Satisfied Customers Since 2004!

January 4
Childlike Or Childish?

1 Corinthians Chapter 3, verses 1-6:
And I, brethren, could not speak unto you as unto spiritual, but as unto carnal, even as unto babes in Christ. I have fed you with milk, and not with meat: for hitherto ye were not able to bear it, neither yet now are ye able. For ye are yet carnal: for whereas there is among you envying, and strife, and divisions, are ye not carnal, and walk as men? For while one saith, I am of Paul; and another, I am of Apollos; are ye not carnal? Who then is Paul, and who is Apollos, but ministers by whom ye believed, even as the Lord gave to every man? I have planted, Apollos watered; but God gave the increase.

Prayer: May the words that we speak and the meditation of our hearts be acceptable in your sight, dear Lord Jesus, our Rock and our Redeemer. Amen.

Childishness in an adult is very unattractive. As an adult you are expected to take responsibility for your actions, to teach others through your years of experience and as a Christian to grow in your faith and knowledge of the Holy Scriptures. "Grow up!", the Apostle Paul was saying, "you are supposed to act better." Childlike faith on the other hand is very attractive to God. Children are supposed to trust their parents and believe that whatever their parents say or ask them to do is for their own good. A baby is helpless without the parents. If the parents fail to feed the baby daily, the baby may not live. God is our father. We owe our very lives to God. We freely enjoy the air He allows us to breathe. Whatever gifts and talents we have comes from God. When we come to God in childlike faith, with love in our hearts, we bring Him joy. God delights in doing good to us out of His great love for us. Just look at all God has manifested to us through Jesus Christ. Do we delight in God?

© By Dr. Sheila Hayford.

January 5
Exercise Your Happiness Right

John Chapter 6 verse 24:
"Hitherto have ye asked nothing in my name: ask, and ye shall receive, that your **joy may be full**."

Prayer: Dear God: Forgive me when I have allowed myself to be discouraged by all the negativity that seems to be in the headlines. Help me to remember that I am a pilgrim on this earth heading for my everlasting home with my Savior, Jesus Christ. Enable me to share the good news of salvation with others as I live as salt on this earth. In Jesus' Name, I pray. Amen

There seems to be an orchestrated attack on joy these days. You turn on the television and the headlines are filled with news of violence, hurt, and cynicism. A young boy sharing his future aspirations is told by some not to set his goals too high. A newly wed gushing with joy is told by some married couples that her marriage has a fifty percent chance of making it. "Says who?" you might ask. Good question! You see, your life views are shaped by your beliefs. If you believe in the Lord Jesus Christ, the one who came to give you the abundant life, then you are poised to live your life with the unlimited power of God and the resources we have in Christ in God. When the naysayers see only doom and gloom, you see the power of God available through prayer to change things for the better. We know sin is still at work in this world. However, each of us will personally answer to God. And God, who is the righteous judge, will do what is right. So let us exercise the joy that is ours in Christ. It is going to be a good day because God lives. And, through Christ, I live victoriously. Hallelujah!

© By Dr. Sheila Hayford.

January 6
The Heart of an Overcomer:

John Chapter 16, verse 33:

In this world you will have trouble. But take heart! I have overcome the world.

Prayer: Dear Lord Jesus; how we love you! I am so grateful and thankful that you are our perfect example and that you would never ask us to do anything without giving us the power to do so. Enable us to look beyond any challenges to you. Let us trust Your Word and the Holy Spirit to transform our perspective, our situations and us. Enable us to live victoriously by giving us victory over sin, satan and all evil. May we renew our mind with and correctly apply your Holy Scriptures so that our lives will bring glory to our heavenly Father, God Almighty. Amen.

What is the Lord Jesus really saying to us? Is the life of a Christian always supposed to be full of trouble, or at the least, drama? Whenever I see the word 'trouble' I can usually replace it with the word 'challenge' or 'challenges'. So the text would be understood as: In this world you will have challenges. But take heart! I have overcome the world. Now I can relax! It means WHATEVER situation or challenge I am facing I can <u>always</u> have the victory. So how does victory in our challenges look like? It is victory God's way, in God's timing, and of God's choosing. When Joseph was going through all the earlier challenges that we read about in the Book of Genesis, it did not look anything like victory because in the eyes of men it seemed evil had gained the upper hand. But in God's eyes, every time Joseph refused to yield to sin, Joseph was victorious. Every time Joseph refused to give in to bitterness and unforgiveness, Joseph was victorious. And when Joseph was promoted to second in command to King Pharaoh, Joseph's overcoming victories were manifest to all. And who got all the glory? God. For ultimately, that is what our lives are all about; living lives that are glorifying to God.

© By Dr. Sheila Hayford.

January 7
Light and Darkness

I John Chapter 1, verse 5:

This then is the message which we have heard of him, and declare unto you, that God is light, and in him is no darkness at all.

Prayer: Dear Lord Jesus: Thank you for bringing your light to mankind and redeeming us from the power of sin. Thank you for giving us the Holy Spirit to guide and direct us and to empower us to live for you. May your light shine unhindered through us. We love you. Amen.

We know light drives out darkness; thus we are told not to curse the darkness but to shine the light. The focus in many instances is on the physical aspects of light and darkness and the evil that seems more prevalent in society these days. However, God, who is more concerned about the heart or the inward appearance of a person, gives us His spiritual perspective of light and darkness. His Son, Jesus Christ says in John Chapter 8 verse 12, "I am the light of the world. Whoever follows me will never walk in darkness, but will have the light of life." In Jesus Christ is light and no darkness. In other words, the Lord Jesus is pure, without sin and provides light, illumination and clarity to the spiritual truths of God. Sin, on the other hand, is characterized as spiritual darkness. As believers of Christ, what does God see when He looks at us? It all depends on our level of obedience to God. When we walk in love and obedience to the principles of God, yielding to the direction of the Holy Spirit within us, the light of God is reflected through us. That light permeates the darkness of sin and draws others to the God we serve. The kingdom of God advances as the powers of darkness fall to the power of God. Are you making the difference you want in your home, your church and your community? In the words of Isaiah Chapter 60 verse 1, now is the time to "Arise, shine, for your light has come, and the glory of the Lord rises upon you."

© By Dr. Sheila Hayford.

January 8
The Sermon of the Shoes: It Is In The Material*

Luke Chapter 6, verse 45:

A good man out of the good treasure of his heart bringeth forth that which is good; and an evil man out of the evil treasure of his heart bringeth forth that which is evil: for of the abundance of the heart his mouth speaketh.

Prayer: Psalm 51, verse 10: Create in me a clean heart, O God; and renew a right spirit within me. In Jesus' Name, Amen.

I tend to see God in the ordinary. As I was preparing my clothes and accessories for church the next day I noticed the pair of shoes I wanted to wear felt tight. I placed the shoe stretcher in the shoes expecting them to open up the next day as my other pair of shoes had done. The next morning the side of the shoes where the shoe stretcher had been was cracked. "Why, Lord," I asked, "When the other shoes responded so well?" God the Holy Spirit replied, "It is in the material." The other pair of shoes was made from leather that was pliable in the hands of the shoe stretcher. The shoes that cracked were made of manmade material that did not respond well to pressure. As you read these inspirational and sometimes thought provoking words, it is my prayer that you will be pliable in the hands of Almighty God whose desire is to stretch us and not crack us. Enjoy!

*Used with Permission ©2007 By Dr. Sheila Hayford.

January 9
The Dream

Genesis Chapter 31, verses 4-6:
And when his brethren saw that their father loved him more than all his brethren, they hated him, and could not speak peaceably unto him.

And Joseph dreamed a dream, and he told it his brethren: and they hated him yet the more. And he said unto them, Hear, I pray you, this dream which I have dreamed:

Prayer: Dear Lord God; Thank you for the many ways you reveal yourself to mankind through our Lord Jesus Christ. We pray for the wisdom and discernment that comes from the Holy Spirit. In the Name of Jesus. Amen.

Joseph was a God ordained visionary and one of the ways God revealed God's plans as well as God's purpose for and to Joseph was through dreams and the interpretation of dreams. God also spoke to Father Abraham about significant events in Abraham's life through dreams. It is important to know that dreams do not always originate from God so we must always apply the discernment of the Holy Spirit to any dream, especially if someone says they had a specific dream that concerns us. Here are a few points so consider when it comes to dreams:

1. The Originator of the Dream. In other words, is this dream consistent with God's Words and God's plan, using the Holy Bible and the Holy Spirit as our guide. 2. The Purpose of the Dream. Sometimes the Holy Spirit will show you in a dream events and other things that you would never otherwise know in the natural. This may be to warn you, show you what you need to do that you would not do otherwise, who you should or should not collaborate with and what is going to happen as it affects you. At other times, God will reveal His future plans for you to give you direction, guidance and hope. 3. The Timing of the Dream. Is the dream concerning your current situation, or like Daniel, is God revealing to you what will happen in the future? 4. The Sharing of the Dream. Joseph assumed everyone would be excited and happy about his dream. As such, he was indiscriminate as to who he shared his dream with. His dream still happened but it might have occurred with less drama if he had not shared it with his brothers. When God gives you a vision, be wise and discerning with your dream. Sharing what is

precious to you with mockers and haters is not a good idea. The goal of sharing your vision or dream is not to try to impress others but to flow with God's plans for the dream. 5. The Fulfillment of the Dream. If God blesses you to see the fulfilment of the dream, your obedience to God will play a big part in seeing the fulfillment of that dream. If the dream is to be carried out by someone else, as in the case of King Solomon building a temple for God, do your part like King David did to bring about a successful accomplishment of the dream. And always give thanks and glory to God before, during and after the manifestation of the dream.

© By Dr. Sheila Hayford.

January 10
One Touch Down Away

Matthew Chapter 24, verse 13:
But he that shall endure unto the end, the same shall be saved.
Prayer: Dear God: In the midst of all the challenges and tests of life, help me finish my race with excellence and joy. In the Name of Jesus I pray. Amen.

It was the Super Bowl 50 football game and the eyes of the world were on both teams. The Carolina Panthers had played superbly during the regular season. I would pray for their victory and they came through winning the NFC Championship. Their wins in the regular season were impressive. Their margin of victory was usually very wide and usually occurred early. They had lost only one game during the regular season and were projected to win against the Denver Broncos with whom they were playing in the Superbowl.

As God would have it, I was in attendance at a Super Bowl event when my home team at the time, the Washington Redskins, were playing against the Denver Broncos. The Denver Broncos started that game ahead by ten points but then the Washington Redskins came back to win the game 42 to Denver's 10. In the 2016 Super Bowl, dubbed Super Bowl 50 because of the history of the Super Bowl, Peyton Manning with the Denver Broncos had expressed some sentiments about a possible retirement after the season. Manning was a great football player and the talk was that many were sorry to see him retire in a game many predicted the Carolina Panthers would win. Both teams had worked hard during the year, mostly unnoticed by many Super Bowl viewers during the regular football season. Now they were on the world stage and it was their time to shine.

What happened next was very strange. The Super Bowl began with the usual festivities. Then the game began. The Denver Broncos were quick to score but as I mentioned earlier I had seen teams come back and win the Super Bowl so I was not that concerned. What beat the imagination was the unravelling of the Carolina Panthers on the world stage. They were a younger team but young teams have won Superbowl games so their performance could not be attributed to age alone. They fumbled the ball, could not score and played terrible. They were only one touchdown away to come back and win the game but somehow they could not get it together. And so the unlikely team at the time, Denver Broncos with Peyton Manning won Superbowl 50!

What has this to do with our spiritual journey? Everything! In the book of Hebrews, we are told there is a great cloud of witnesses cheering us on in this game of life. It may be a game but this is no ordinary game. For the battle is between God and satan. Through the Lord Jesus and the power of the Holy Spirit, we have everything that we need to win. How are we performing? Remember, those who started well, but did not play well do not win the race. Those who persevered, even when it seemed the odds were against them and others were predicting their early demise, won the race. The Scripture tells us that the one who endures to the end will be saved. What a sobering lesson! May we each be a winner in our Super Bowl race here on earth!

© By Dr. Sheila Hayford.

BERINGSON REALITY
MollyB.com
CALL MOLLY and DICK
443-366-0990
Husband and wife Team
Licensed in Delaware and Maryland

January 11
Associations

I Corinthians Chapter 15, verse 33: Do not be misled: "Bad company corrupts good character." (NIV)

Prayer: Dear Lord God: Thank you for the wisdom, discernment and sanctified common sense of the Holy Spirit that is mine through Jesus Christ. Help me live my life in obedience to your Word, yielding to the Holy Spirit. In Jesus' Name, Amen.

If you add a negative to a positive, it subtracts. Those you choose to associate with influence your life. If you multiply a positive with another positive, you have rapid or accelerated multiplication. We can easily understand how this principle works in the Mathematics class but sometimes fail to apply it practically in life. If your friends show you by their actions that they mean you no good, why would you still hang out with them? For if you do, the fault is not only your friends, the fault is partly yours. It may be that you have convinced yourself that you are deserving of their actions, or that you are not worth better. Maybe you are afraid of being alone. Maybe you are scared of changing your familiar environments. Whatever the reason, God does not want you to live beneath who you are in Christ. The devil wants you to have an identity crisis. Satan, the ultimate in misery loves company. However,

God has given every human being a choice of where to spend eternity. Our Lord Jesus Christ paid the penalty of the sins of humanity on the cross. When we confess our sins to God, repent of them, believe and accept the Lord Jesus into our life as our Lord and Savior, God gives us the gift of the Holy Spirit and a new life in Christ in God. Victory in living is guaranteed if we live God's way and in God's will. Will we sometimes fail in our desire to live right all the time? Yes. Nevertheless, the work of Jesus Christ on our behalf to pay the price for our sins is for all time; past, present and future. So let us decide that we will not live beneath our God given inheritance in Christ in every area of our lives. Let our advisor be God the Holy Spirit and let us take counsel from those who seek our best. Does that mean we will not have friends who are different from us, or who may be facing challenges? No! We all have our individual challenges to deal with. The Bible clearly tells us in this verse that bad company ruins good morals. Thus, our closest friends will not be those who mock or despise our faith but those who provoke us to good works and right living by the power of God. God will not go against any individual's free will.

How we conduct ourselves matters to God. Does it matter to you?

© By Dr. Sheila Hayford.

January 12
Flavorless Christians

Matthew Chapter 5, verse 13:

Ye are the salt of the earth: but if the salt have lost his savour, wherewith shall it be salted? it is thenceforth good for nothing, but to be cast out, and to be trodden under foot of men.

Prayer: Dear Lord Jesus: Help us allow our beliefs in you and Your Word to transform our behavior. Help us to be the salt you have appointed us to be on this earth as we yield our lives to the Holy Spirit. In your Name we pray, Amen.

It was an election year at the time and the politicians were all out in full swing. Some who had supported Biblical standards of morality for years suddenly changed their positions to ones at odds with God's standards for holiness. I expected an outcry from Christian leaders, many of whom had publicly supported these candidates. I expected the Christian believers to stand up for God's ways. In my discussions with fellow believers asking them to vote their Christian conscience when it came to Biblical standards, I was told by some I was being too fussy, that we just "had" to re-elect certain candidates and many other excuses. God's word says God's judgment will be on any nation or people who rebel against God's laws. Christians began to be persecuted more prominently for not offering certain services because of their religious convictions and were considered intolerant because they stood up for their beliefs. The Christian values in a flavorless Christian society were being trampled upon. We must ask ourselves: Is our political affiliation more important than our Christian witness? Does God have the first priority in our decision making? And we must ask the Holy Spirit to help us make the right choices in life. Hell is a real place. Can Christians afford to be flavorless while people are entering an eternity in hell daily?

© By Dr. Sheila Hayford.

January 13
Corporate Prayer, Forgiveness And Communion Day

Mark Chapter 15, verses 25, 26:
And when ye stand praying, forgive, if ye have ought against any: that your Father also which is in heaven may forgive you your trespasses. But if ye do not forgive, neither will your Father which is in heaven forgive your trespasses.

Prayer: Dear Lord God, forgive us for the many times we have asked your forgiveness while harboring unforgiveness in our hearts towards our fellow man. Help us to repent and take the command of forgiveness by the Lord Jesus Christ seriously. Enable us to walk in love and refuse to allow any bitterness in our lives. We pray in Jesus' Name, Amen.

It is amazing how fellow born again believers can attend church services and events and not be on talking terms with a believer in the same or other congregation for years. And then take communion while harboring unforgiveness. It might be the reason the Apostle Paul says in the book of 1 Corinthians Chapter 11, verse 30 that some are sick, weak or have died. If the Lord Jesus Christ forgives us in spite of what we did to him on the cross of Calvary, do we have any right to hold unforgiveness against another person? I suggest that we each set aside a day a month for Corporate Prayer, Forgiveness and Communion where we take time to make it right with those we have offended or who have offended us. Will everyone willingly grant your request for forgiveness? Maybe not, but you will have done your part and exercised your clear conscience towards God in that respect.

If you would like to take the pledge for Corporate Prayer, Forgiveness and Communion for you, your family, your church and your organization here it is:

Corporate Prayer, Forgiveness and Communion Day Pledge:
I pledge by the power of God the Holy Spirit to walk in forgiveness even as my Lord Jesus Christ has forgiven me. I know it is not easy and that it may go against my natural instinct to seek immediate or long-term revenge or redress of an issue. However, I believe the Word of God that tells me I can do all things through Christ who strengthens me. I make the conscious decision to forgive ALL who have wronged me and I seek forgiveness from those I have wronged. So help me, dear Holy Spirit. In the Name of Jesus, Amen.

If you would like to let us know you took the pledge and would like to share the Corporate Prayer, Forgiveness and Communion Day Pledge with others visit forgivenesspledge.org. God thanks you!

© By Dr. Sheila Hayford.

January 14
A-Mail – God's Angel Mail

Genesis Chapter 28, verses 12, 13:

And he dreamed, and behold a ladder set up on the earth, and the top of it reached to heaven: and behold the angels of God ascending and descending on it. And, behold, the Lord stood above it, and said, I am the Lord God of Abraham thy father, and the God of Isaac: the land whereon thou liest, to thee will I give it, and to thy seed;

Prayer: Dear Holy Spirit: Thank you for the wonderful ways you give us understanding. We understand that God's holy angels are sent by God to minister to us. Help us to be diligent in prayer. In Jesus' Name. Amen.

We have heard of postal mail, e-mail and now we have the word of God telling us about God's angel A-mail. We should put our requests in prayer to God and trust that God will send us answers with the messengers God has appointed. Remember the words of the Apostle Paul when he tells us to be careful how we treat others as some have entertained angels unawares. Are you overlooking God's answers to your prayers? Are the words that you speak consistent with the answers you want from God? Are you encouraging God's holy angels to work on your behalf as needed and to request help from God's angelic hosts when needed? Thank God for A-mail. Use it for the glory of God!

© By Dr. Sheila Hayford.

January 15
Priceless Moments

Luke Chapter 1, verses 13, 14:

But the angel said unto him, Fear not, Zacharias: for thy prayer is heard; and thy wife Elisabeth shall bear thee a son, and thou shalt call his name John. And thou shalt have joy and gladness; and many shall rejoice at his birth.

Prayer: Dear God of the seemingly impossible; Thank you for giving us the opportunity to pray and ask seemingly incredible prayers and then witness the amazing results of answered prayer. May your Name be forever praised! In the Name of Jesus, we pray, Amen.

I had spent about an hour thanking and meditating on God answering my prayer, an answer that seemed so unlikely in the natural. During the day I thought, "I spent the whole hour being thankful for that one answered prayer when I could have prayed about other things." The Holy Spirit assured me my prayer time was about the time I had spent with God and not necessarily the prayer topics. When we spend quality, precious time with family and good friends, we are sometimes hard pressed to say exactly what we talked about. However, we always remember that we had a great time, great fellowship, great food, who we met and so forth. Why? It was their presence and the times shared together that mattered. Through the Lord Jesus, we are now a part of God's family. Take the time to "hang-out" in God's presence. God will reveal Himself to you and you will be energized and refreshed by the Holy Spirit. And that, I say, is priceless!

© By Dr. Sheila Hayford.

January 16
Too Much!

2 Peter Chapter 1, verses 3, 4:
According as his divine power hath given unto us all things that pertain unto life and godliness, through the knowledge of him that hath called us to glory and virtue: Whereby are given unto us exceeding great and precious promises: that by these ye might be partakers of the divine nature, having escaped the corruption that is in the world through lust.

Prayer: Dear God; Thank you for the gift of Jesus Christ, through whom we have everything that we need and then some to share. Help us not to be selfish. In Jesus' Name, Amen.

God has blessed me in Jesus Christ – TOO MUCH! Think of what this verse is saying. EVERYTHING we need that pertains to life and godly living is available to us through the Lord Jesus Christ. And so if we lack anything needed for life or godly living it is not God's fault. How do we access what is ours through the Lord Jesus Christ? The same way we receive salvation through the Lord Jesus Christ. It is by faith, believing what the Word of God says and then taking the corresponding action by speaking and living in obedience to God. Simple? Yes. Easy? No. Worth it? Absolutely!

© By Dr. Sheila Hayford.

January 17
Your Prayer Force

Esther Chapter 4, verse 16:
Go, gather together all the Jews that are present in Shushan, and fast ye for me, and neither eat nor drink three days, night or day: I also and my maidens will fast likewise; ...

Prayer: Dear Lord God: I remember the many times I have called on you in prayer and the many miracles you have wrought in answers to those prayers, large and small. Now is not the time to be weary or slack in prayer for there is yet much work to be done. Help me to be faithful in prayer and see your mighty hand at work, as believers exercise our God given dominion on this earth. In the Name of Jesus we pray. Amen.

Prayer is the lifeline to call for God's intervention. It is amazing as we read the Holy Bible how many times God worked miracles in answer to prayer. Queen Esther and her maidens prayed and fasted for God to intervene in the diabolical plot by Haman to destroy all the Jews. In response to their prayers, God delivered the Jews, a nation was saved and Haman was hanged on the gallows he had prepared for the Jews. With such history on God's side, we should turn to God in prayer with more fervor and frequency. We do not necessarily have to be kneeling to pray to God for prayer is ultimately having a conversation with God. Of course, the situation we are praying about will affect the way we pray. Intense challenges require intense prayers. In the case of Queen Esther, it was important for her to have her maidens, Mordecai and the Jews praying for the deliverance of the Jewish people, and that included Queen Esther whose life was also at risk.

Remember, the Name of Jesus is the name that is above all names. Calling on the Name of Jesus brings the Lord Jesus on the scene. Who greater to be on your side? No one!

© By Dr. Sheila Hayford.

January 18
Pray for your Enemies

Romans Chapter 12, verses 18, 19:
If it is possible, as far as it depends on you, live at peace with everyone. Do not take revenge, my dear friends, but leave room for God's wrath, for it is written: "It is mine to avenge; I will repay," says the Lord. (NIV)

Prayer: Dear Lord God: Help me be at peace while I trust in you. Thank you that the life I now live is my gift to you. Enable me by the power of the Holy Spirit to make you happy. In Jesus' Name, Amen.

When you pray for your enemies you are praying for yourself. For when you forgive your enemies you are asking God to forgive you. That is not to say that God will not judge your enemies on your behalf. What you are doing is releasing God to work on your behalf. Listen to the words of Jesus on the cross: Father, forgive them for they know not what they do. For indeed, how could anyone think they could fight against

God and win? The devil found that out the hard way. We have time on this earth to make sure we do not go the way of the devil for no matter what evil is done, God knows how to work all things out in the life of a born again believer for good. So it becomes a trust issue. Will we trust that God knows what is best for us? Do we trust that God has our best interest in every circumstance? Do we trust that God will always have the last word in eternity? If we can look at life with God's perspective, we will realize this life is short compared with eternity and too short to live a miserable unforgiving life. Let your enemies see you happy, fulfilling your destiny in Christ in God. They will have to answer to God just as each of us will. What say ye?

© By Dr. Sheila Hayford.

January 19
Do Not Withhold Good

Proverbs Chapter 3, verse 27:
Do not withhold good from those to whom it is due, when it is in your power to act. (NIV)

Prayer: Dear God: We know that all good things come from you. Please help us show our appreciation and love to you by living a life in which we submit everything, including our finances, to your divine authority. In Jesus' Name we pray, Amen.

We often think of this verse in terms of our relationship with our fellow man. While that is true, this verse also applies to our relationship with God. The Bible tells us that God will not withhold any good thing from those who love Him. He is the one who blesses us with the power to get wealth whether it is through our job, family business, or using our unique creativities. In the Old Testament, the Israelites were commanded to give a tenth or a tithe of their income to God. In the New Testament, the Lord Jesus in chiding the Pharisees in Luke Chapter 11 verse 42 did not chide them for tithing. The Lord Jesus said that in addition to tithing they ought to practice justice and live lives consistent with the love of God. When we receive our pay from our work, we have an immediate opportunity to do good to our God by not withholding the tithe that is due Him. We must trust God to fulfill his promises to us concerning our tithing in the book of Malachi Chapter 3 verses 10 to 12. Make your heavenly Father glad!

© By Dr. Sheila Hayford.

January 20
You Give Them Something to Eat

Matthew Chapter 14, verse 16:

Jesus replied, "They do not need to go away. You give them something to eat." (NIV)

Prayer: Our heavenly Father, forgive us when we have shirked our responsibility and given excuses to justify our position. Help us realize that many times you want us to be participants in the miracles of provision. Enable us to trust you entirely. In Jesus' Name we pray, with thanksgiving. Amen.

What does the Lord Jesus mean in this verse? First, let us look at the context in which he spoke. The Lord Jesus had just heard the news about John the Baptist and so he went by boat for some private time. But when the crowds heard of this they followed him by foot. The Lord Jesus did not send them away even though he must have been sad about what had happened to John the Baptist. He did not nurse his private pain but had compassion on the crowd and took care of the needs of the crowd. Jesus healed the sick among them. It was now evening time, they were in a remote village and the disciples asked Jesus to send the crowds away so the people could get some food to eat. It is in response to this that the Lord Jesus replied, "They do not need to go away. You give them something to eat." Jesus is saying, **"You take responsibility for their well-being."** And so today Jesus is saying to the C.E.O. of the company, "you take responsibility for the well-being of your employees." To the Father, Jesus is saying, "you take responsibility for the welfare of your wife and children." To the Teacher, Jesus is saying, "you take responsibility for the educational well-being of your students." To the Presidents and World Leaders, Jesus is saying, "you take responsibility for the well-being of the citizens in your countries." What happened when the disciples brought the five loaves and two fishes, which was all they had, to Jesus? Jesus gave thanks, broke the loaves and gave them to the disciples. The loaves became part of God's miracle of multiplication, the crowds were fed and everyone was satisfied.

© By Dr. Sheila Hayford.

January 21
Street Language?

Acts Chapter 2, verses 6, 7, 8:
Now when this was noised abroad, the multitude came together, and were confounded, because that every man heard them speak in his own language. And they were all amazed and marvelled, saying one to another, Behold, are not all these which speak Galilaeans? And how hear we every man in our own tongue, wherein we were born? Parthians, and Medes, and Elamites, and the dwellers in Mesopotamia, and in Judaea, and Cappadocia, in Pontus, and Asia, Phrygia, and Pamphylia, in Egypt, and in the parts of Libya about Cyrene, and strangers of Rome, Jews and proselytes, Cretes and Arabians, we do hear them speak in our tongues the wonderful works of God.

Prayer: Dear Holy Spirit: I love spending time in your presence. You are such a great teacher. Help me to be teachable. In Jesus' Name, Amen.

It was so funny. I heard what sounded to me like God speaking. There was no profanity, no evil words, but it sounded like street language. I had "prided" myself on knowing how to hear from God because God saved me through Jesus Christ in my teenage years. So I said to the Holy Spirit, "I have never heard you speak like that." To which God replied, "Yeah, I can do that vernacular thing too!" (Paraphrased) I laughed audibly. It was like an earthly father trying to prove to his children that he could be "cool" too. God, however, does not have to prove Himself. God is God, and as we read in the verses above, <u>God speaks to us in language we understand</u>. I had just experienced a fun teachable moment with God.

© By Dr. Sheila Hayford.

MR. INCOME TAX

Personal & Business Taxes; Great service at the best price!

Individual Tax preparation starting at $50!!! ***

*** 1040EZ preparation with up to 3 W2 forms.

OPEN YEAR ROUND

We offer the following services:

- Tax preparation for any year, any state
- Business Taxes for LLC, S-Corp, C-Corp and Partnerships
- 1099 forms for Contractors
- Audits (Federal and NC)
- Accounting for small businesses
- Free estimates and consultation (1st 30 min.)
- "Notary Public and much more!"

4008 Capital Blvd Suite 104-B, Raleigh, NC 27604
Tel: (919) 526-4829 (919) 827-8477

Hours: Jan - Apr: every day 10am to 9pm; May - Dec: Mon-Fri 11am to 7pm or by appointment"

January 22
Allow God to be God

Acts Chapter 10, verses 13, 14, 15:

And there came a voice to him, Rise, Peter; kill, and eat. But Peter said, Not so, Lord; for I have never eaten any thing that is common or unclean. And the voice spake unto him again the second time, What God hath cleansed, that call not thou common.

Prayer: Dear heavenly Father; help me not let the traditions of men negate the power of the Cross. In Jesus' Name, Amen.

It must be humorous to God how we sometimes try to put God in a box. We pray and expect God to give us what we want the way we want it, even if God's way will give us the same end result. Here is Peter, the disciple of Jesus, being asked to kill all manner of animals for food. Peter, as one of Jewish ancestry in the Bible, was aware of the rules and regulations concerning clean and unclean in the Old Testament. When the Lord Jesus came in the New Testament, He established the new order of the Holy Spirit. In John Chapter 15, verse 3 the Lord Jesus says we are made clean by the words that He speaks. If food is blessed in the Name of Jesus, it is to be eaten with thanks and without guilt or condemnation. If God has blessed the food, whether it be pork, vegetables or some exotic food, who is the man that would dare to call what God has cleansed unclean?

© By Dr. Sheila Hayford.

January 23
Desperation

Matthew Chapter 9, verses 20-22:

And, behold, a woman, which was diseased with an issue of blood twelve years, came behind him, and touched the hem of his garment: For she said within herself, If I may but touch his garment, I shall be whole. But Jesus turned him about, and when he saw her, he said, Daughter, be of good comfort; thy faith hath made thee whole. And the woman was made whole from that hour.

Prayer: God of all hope; what a beautiful story of faith, compassion and love. Help those of us who call ourselves Christians to follow the example of our Lord Jesus by extending compassion and love to others. In Christ's Name. Amen.

Desperation can cause some to become indiscriminate. The woman with the issue of blood had run out of options. She had spent all her money on doctors the previous twelve years and instead of getting better she was getting worse. She heard the Lord Jesus was coming to town and figured He could heal her. But there was one major obstacle. At that time she was considered unclean because of her affliction. How could she get to Jesus? She came up with a plan. She would quietly touch the hem of Jesus' garment and by faith receive her healing. She was not looking to be in the limelight. However, her faith got the attention of the Lord Jesus. She received her healing and in the process became an example of trusting God despite the odds. Fretting about your present circumstances without considering the future implications of your present actions is a mistake. This woman's desperation led her to a simple act of faith. And that simple act of faith turned her circumstances around. Her advice to us today would probably be: Have faith in God, no matter what!

© By Dr. Sheila Hayford.

January 24
You Are Loved

Jeremiah Chapter 31, verse 3:
The Lord hath appeared of old unto me, saying, Yea, I have loved thee with an everlasting love: therefore with lovingkindness have I drawn thee.

Prayer: Dear Lord God; thank you for your love, expressed to mankind through your Son, Jesus Christ. Help me never to take your love for granted. In Jesus' Name. Amen.

Many times when we see individuals acting out we are told they are looking for attention. Why would a person indulge in actions that are self-destructive to themselves or destructive to others? While there may be many reasons, we do read about some who grew up in an unloving environment. They do not feel love for themselves and often go looking for love in the wrong places. Hurting people sometimes project their negative thoughts on others and hurt others in the process. However, there is good news and the news is this: EVERYONE is LOVED BY GOD! And this love is everlasting. Nothing you have done, are doing or will ever do will change God's love for you. You do not have to earn God's love because you could not, even if you tried. All you have to do is to receive God's love, expressed to man through His Son, the Lord Jesus Christ. Invite the Lord Jesus into your heart and begin your love journey with God today.

© By Dr. Sheila Hayford.

January 25
Lovely Thoughts

Philippians Chapter 4, verse 8:
Finally, brethren, whatsoever things are true, whatsoever things are honest, whatsoever things are just, whatsoever things are pure, whatsoever things are lovely, whatsoever things are of good report; if there be any virtue, and if there be any praise, think on these things.

Prayer: Dear heavenly Father, may my thoughts be pleasing to you. In Jesus' Name. Amen.

What are you thinking? Is it in line with Philippians Chapter 4, verse 8? If it is not, you need a soul transformation to change your ways of thinking and to renew your mind with the word of God. It seems sad that some will pay good money to listen to trash talk. Some will leave the TV on and listen to whatever program is on their favorite channel. What you hear can affect how and what you think. Take control of the environment God has given you each day.

© By Dr. Sheila Hayford.

January 26
Give God

Psalm 37, verse 4:
Delight thyself also in the Lord: and he shall give thee the desires of thine heart.

Prayer: My heavenly Father; I love you and want to fulfill my call. Help me by the power of the Holy Spirt. In the Name of Jesus. Amen.

Give God what God wants:
- your praise,
- your worship,
- your obedience,
- your tithe
- your life

And God will give you what you want.

© By Dr. Sheila Hayford.

January 27
Misguided

Luke Chapter 21, verse 8:
And he said, Take heed that ye be not deceived: for many shall come in my name, saying, I am Christ; and the time draweth near: go ye not therefore after them.

Prayer: Dear Lord Jesus, the Way, the Truth and the Life. We love you and accept you as our Lord and Savior. Amen.

Why take heed? There are some who say that all religions lead to God. Is that theory or is that fact? As Christians, what does the Lord Jesus say? The Bible warns us not to be deceived when many come claiming to be the Christ. In the Greek, "khristos" means "anointed one" and in Hebrew Christ can be translated to mean "Messiah. So take heed when you hear someone other than the Lord Jesus Christ claiming to be the Anointed Messiah, the Christ. God gives each of us the free will to choose or accept the Lord Jesus Christ. Take God at His Word today!

© By Dr. Sheila Hayford.

January 28
You Are Lord!

Revelation Chapter 19, verses 4-5:
The twenty-four elders and the four living creatures fell down and worshiped God, who was seated on the throne. And they cried: "Amen, Hallelujah!" Then a voice came from the throne, saying: "Praise our God, all you his servants, you who fear him, both great and small!" (NIV)

Prayer: O Lord God, you are great and mighty! We revere you and join your marvelous creation in praising you for you are worthy of our worship. Glory be to your holy name! In Jesus' Name we pray. Amen.

The book of Revelation is a fascinating book in which the Apostle John was given glorious visions of God's heaven. What amazing insights we are given of worship at the throne of God! The angels cover their faces as they worship a holy God. God in all His power issues decrees concerning the earth and they are carried out by faithful angels. How amazing that man gets to worship this Holy God! As King David asks in the book of Psalms, "What is man that thou art mindful of him?"

Through the Lord Jesus Christ we can boldly enter God's throne room and, by the power of the Holy Spirit, offer praise and worship to God. But worship is not just an occurrence; the worship of God is a lifestyle.

I have found strength and a new positive perspective in life's challenges when I decide to worship God in spite of the challenges. What started out as a concern of mine paled in comparison to who my God is. My declaration of God's provision and power caused me to sing with joy. My heavenly Father must have been happy as He turned my situation around in better ways than I could have ever imagined. Yes, God, You are Lord indeed!

© By Dr. Sheila Hayford.

January 29
Wedding Feast: A Table Prepared

Matthew Chapter 22, verses 3-5:
And sent forth his servants to call them that were bidden to the wedding: and they would not come. Again, he sent forth other servants, saying, Tell them which are bidden, Behold, I have prepared my dinner: my oxen and my fatlings are killed, and all things are ready: come unto the marriage. But they made light of it, and went their ways, one to his farm, another to his merchandise:

Prayer: Dear God; Wow! You have already planned for our wedding feast with our Lord Jesus Christ. Thank you. Amen.

The Lord Jesus used this parable to teach an important truth. God has prepared a wedding feast. We know by reading the Bible that Jesus Christ is referred to as the bridegroom of the body of believers who make up the church. These believers have accepted the Lord Jesus as Savior and Lord. The invitation to accept the Lord Jesus and partake in this wedding feast is given to all. However, many in the parable made light of the invitation and felt they had more important things to do. As we read the parable further we see that the Lord Jesus was relating this parable to himself. The Lord Jesus is coming again to take his bride to be with him and we are looking forward to the Wedding Feast. Will you accept his invitation?

© By Dr. Sheila Hayford.

January 30
At Rest

Matthew Chapter 11, verse 28:
Come unto me, all ye that labor and are heavy laden, and I will give you rest.

Prayer: Dear Lord Jesus; give us your peace in the challenges and tests of life. There are things in life we may not fully understand and situations we wish would be different. Help us submit to you in all things and invite others to experience your rest. Amen.

Rest in a busy world takes advance planning. There seems to be so much confusion, restlessness and hopelessness in the news that you almost have to tune out some of the news. What is Jesus saying to us? First; that the Lord Jesus knows a lot about our earthly world. There were real life issues on the earth in the days Christ lived on this earth but we never read of Jesus being stressed out. There were times he would go out alone or with his disciples to pray or to teach. Jesus could sleep in the ship in the midst of a storm while his disciples were panicking. What Jesus wants us to have is the assurance, confidence and peace in God that comes from a right relationship with him.

Cast all your anxieties and cares on Jesus and he will give you peace. Not the absence of challenges, not a withdrawal from society, not laziness or sluggishness, but the peace of God that keeps us calm and at rest irrespective of life's pressures.

© By Dr. Sheila Hayford.

January 31
Planning for Eternity

Isaiah Chapter 57, verse 15:

For thus saith the high and lofty One that inhabiteth eternity, whose name is Holy; I dwell in the high and holy place, with him also that is of a contrite and humble spirit, to revive the spirit of the humble, and to revive the heart of the contrite ones.

Prayer: Dear Lord God; it is easy to be so caught up in the daily tests of life. But this life is really about getting to our eternal destination through Jesus Christ. Your love respects the free will of each person. We willingly ask the Holy Spirit to help us make the choices here on earth that will lead us to an eternal future with you. In Jesus' Name. Amen.

Eternity can seem so abstract in a society that is always advertising something you "need" to buy now, whether it be clothes, shoes, etc. So how do we plan for eternity? The answer is: consciously. Just as one would make plans to take a special vacation, ridding oneself of unnecessary spending distractions, so we need to consciously consider our life, or relationship with Jesus Christ and the path we need to follow by the Holy Spirit that will lead us to an eternity with God. This verse reminds us that God is holy and makes Himself known to those who come to him in true repentance and humility.

© By Dr. Sheila Hayford.

February 1
The Answer Is From The Lord

Proverbs Chapter 24, verse 12:

If you say, "But we knew nothing about this," does not he who weighs the heart perceive it? Does not he who guards your life know it? Will he not repay everyone according to what they have done?

Prayer: Dear Lord, we resist the temptation to be wise in our own eyes because you search and know the hearts and motives of all men. Help us to acknowledge Your Sovereignty in the affairs of men and to walk humbly with you. In Jesus' Name with thanksgiving, Amen

The implications of the stunning "shock" of the Presidential elections in the Unites States was beginning to manifest. A successful businessman and political novice, Mr. Donald Trump had just defeated an experienced political former First Lady of the Governor of Arkansas, former First Lady of the White House, former New York State Senator and former Secretary of State, Mrs. Hilary Clinton. The campaign was long, nasty at times and so much was at stake. The people had spoken and in addition to Mr. Donald Trump's victory, the Republicans had won control of the House and Senate. Many cheered, many were stunned that their candidate has lost the election, and worldwide it seemed the polls and sources many had placed their trust in were being shaken. So what were some of the lessons I learned from President-elect, Mr. Donald Trump? Here they are:

<u>7 Lessons I learned from President-elect, Mr. Donald Trump:</u>

1. Know Yourself. Mr. Trump worked under his father before he assumed ownership for what is now a very successful business empire. He is very involved in real estate and has many properties. Mr. Trump knows he is a builder, one who has created many notable buildings.
2. See the problem as your opportunity. As Mr. Trump crisscrossed the United States during the campaign, he met many disenfranchised individuals and communities; some had worked at manufacturing companies that had closed down, others had their jobs shipped overseas, others were grappling with crime and hopelessness in their cities. For some these problems may have seemed insurmountable, but Mr. Trump recognized he

could use his building and business skills to help create jobs and an atmosphere that could make it easier for companies and individuals to create jobs. And many bought into his vision.

3. Be fearless. When Mr. Trump's opponents said negative things about him, he did not cower. It emboldened him to go on the offensive. It is not acceptable for Christians to be "scared" about sharing our faith. We have the good news of salvation that many are seeking. And we have the command of the Lord Jesus to evangelize. So like the Lord Jesus, we must be about our heavenly father's business.

4. Believe the impossible and let your critics motivate you to go further. When many pollsters wrote off Mr. Trump's candidacy at the beginning of the campaign, Mr. Trump told his supporters, he was going to win the Presidency and he was going to win big. And he delivered.

5. Learn your life's lessons. Yes, the Lord God allows us to experience challenges and tests in life but these are not meant to crush his children. Mr. Trump had some business losses, bankruptcy, marriage challenges in his life journey but he did not allow that to be the end of his story. He used them as steps towards a greater purpose.

6. Prioritize. The lack of focus has derailed many plans. The Lord Jesus knew His mission on this earth and fulfilled it. Mr. Trump was on a mission to be the next President of the United States. He had to realign his business responsibilities, campaign schedules and family responsibilities in the right order to achieve his desired goal.

7. <u>Believe and Speak</u> the desired end result for your life and then apply the corresponding actions. Let us spend time in the Word of God and in the presence of God and find out God's specific plans for our lives. Then let us hold fast in faith to the promises of God, agree with God with our words and see God's plans come to pass. Remember, this earth is temporal, God is eternal

so everything we do should have our ultimate eternal destination in mind.

And just in case you may be wondering my political affiliation. It is registered Independent!

© By Dr. Sheila Hayford.

February 2
Hopeful Endurance

2 Peter Chapter 3, verse 9:

The Lord is not slow in keeping his promise, as some understand slowness. Instead he is patient with you, not wanting anyone to perish, but everyone to come to repentance. (NIV)

Prayer: Dear Lord Jesus, help me not to only endure the tests of life, but to be an overcomer by your Word and by your power. May I live life fully and in patient expectation of your soon return. Amen.

My definition of patience is hopeful endurance. Somehow, when we know that the end will be okay it is easier to endure the process that will get us there. And therein lies the hopeful aspect. We do not complain when we are learning to use a new piece of smart technology because we are hopeful that it will make our life easier in the end.

When we look at the promise of the second coming of the Lord Jesus Christ, it may seem like it is taking too long. Why doesn't Jesus come now and end the injustice and pain that make up many of the news headlines? But when we consider eternity, the opportunity of salvation for many before the second coming of Jesus and the rewards that will be ours if we persevere in our Christian living, we have hope and are able to endure the tests of life.

© By Dr. Sheila Hayford.

February 3
Are You Satisfied?

Matthew Chapter 5, verse 6:
Blessed are they which do hunger and thirst after righteousness: for they shall be filled.

Prayer: Dear Holy Spirit; as a child of God my reality is what God says about me, not what my emotions or flesh may try to dictate. Help my regenerated spirit yield to God the Holy Spirit. Enable me to instruct and submit my soul and my flesh to the authority of the Word of God. In Jesus' Name, Amen.

You cannot tempt someone with something for which they have no appetite. I have found that many times the thing that offends or tempts a person indicates their area of weakness. In a sense, that is a good thing because you know in which areas to exercise caution and carefulness. However, just because you are tempted or offended in one area does not mean every one is tempted in the same area. A sleeveless dress may just be a pretty dress that looks good on the wearer. Nothing more. In this passage Jesus is talking about those who want more of God. Jesus promises to satisfy the desire of every heart that yearns for more of God. Are you satisfied with your relationship with God, or do you want more?

© By Dr. Sheila Hayford.

February 4
Preparation Equals Provision

Genesis Chapter 41, verses 48-49:
And he gathered up all the food of the seven years, which were in the land of Egypt, and laid up the food in the cities: the food of the field, which was round about every city, laid he up in the same. And Joseph

gathered corn as the sand of the sea, very much, until he left numbering; for it was without number.

Prayer: Dear Lord God; thank you for the ability to plan and for the provision that you give to us. Joseph is an amazing example of one who persevered when he was mistreated, lied on, hated and who ultimately used the authority he was given to plan and thereby have enough food to feed entire nations that were experiencing famine. Help us to be faithful stewards of what you give us. In Jesus Name. Amen.

Joseph had more than enough food because he was prepared. Yes, God had revealed to Joseph that there would be seven years of plenty followed by seven years of famine. It was up to Joseph to plan and save food during the plentiful years so that there would still be enough food to last during the years of famine. And because Joseph had saved the food, the rest of the world at that time came to him during the famine to buy food. Today, some who have not prepared for unexpected financial situations are forced to borrow high interest loans because they do not have other viable options. God wants us to plan at all times, seeking God first for direction and modification of our plans as needed. Start planning today!

© By Dr. Sheila Hayford.

February 5
You Had Better Thank God...

Matthew Chapter 12, verses 36, 37:
But I say unto you, That every idle word that men shall speak, they shall give account thereof in the day of judgment. For by thy words thou shalt be justified, and by thy words thou shalt be condemned.

Prayer: Dear Lord Jesus, sometimes it seems easier to lash out our feelings in words. Help us to keep our focus on you and the power of the Holy Spirit who resides within us. May our words be pleasing to you. Amen.

There have been times in my life when I have wanted to respond to a "foolish" remark made by someone else. At that time, I am not thinking of my own imperfections, I am ready to give them a piece of what I am thinking in the flesh. Especially when I know I am right! Just then the Holy Spirit will ask me to keep silent and hold my peace. And so I am stopped in my tracks. I think, "Is the person I am about to respond to worth disobeying the Holy Spirit?" My answer is, "Of course not!" And so I say to them in my thoughts, "You had better thank God ... otherwise I would have given you a piece of my thoughts." Words may seem insignificant or a small detail to some, but words are very significant to God. Remember, God began creation with His words. The Lord Jesus says our words will determine justification or condemnation on the day of judgement. When a person receives the Lord Jesus into their heart and life, they must declare their decision with their words. And we must continuously yield to the Holy Spirit in our words and actions.

© By Dr. Sheila Hayford.

February 6
The God of the Ant

Proverbs Chapter 6, verse 6:
Go to the ant, thou sluggard; consider her ways, and be wise:
Prayer: Dear God, when we look at the ant, no human being has any excuse for laziness. So help us to be diligent in work and to take good care of the bodies and resources you have entrusted to us. In Jesus' Name we pray. Amen.

If God can create life in a tiny ant, the size of a pencil tip in some cases, nothing is impossible with God. Not only did God create the ant, God teaches mankind life lessons using the ant. Those hardworking creatures, yes, those ants we could easily step on, go about their tasks dutifully. It is amazing to see huge ant moles created by the diligence, effort and work of these creatures. May God help us use our gifts and our time wisely. Let us not let the ants put man to shame.

© By Dr. Sheila Hayford.

February 7
For Such A Time As This

Exodus Chapter 9, verse 13:

And the Lord said unto Moses, Rise up early in the morning, and stand before Pharaoh, and say unto him, Thus saith the Lord God of the Hebrews, Let my people go, that they may serve me.

Prayer: Our heavenly Father; what a privilege to be used by you! Enable us not to focus on our circumstances but to focus on your plans and bring you glory. In Jesus' Name. Amen

The people of Israel were in bondage to the Egyptians and it seemed there was no relief from their suffering. Behind the scenes, though, God had been preparing an unlikely person, Moses, to be the instrument God would use to deliver the Israelites.

The birth of Moses in itself was a miracle. King Pharaoh told the midwives to kill the Hebrew babies at birth but somehow the life of Moses was spared. Then God miraculously had Moses raised up as an adopted child of King Pharaoh's daughter. Even though it was not apparent to others at the time, Moses sensed the call of God on his life when he committed murder attempting to resolve the injustice towards the Jewish people in his own strength. Moses was now a fugitive, running from the law. Why would God ask Moses, the fugitive, to go back to King Pharaoh and ask that the King release the Israelites from bondage? The answer is found in Exodus Chapter 9, verse 16: "And in very deed for this cause have I raised thee up, for to shew in thee my power; and that my name may be declared throughout all the earth." You too have been raised up by God for such a time as this.

© By Dr. Sheila Hayford.

February 8
God Allowed It

Ecclesiastes Chapter 3, verse 1:
To every thing there is a season, and a time to every purpose under the heaven:
Prayer: Dear heavenly Father, help me to trust you enough to know that you are working all things out for my good. In Jesus' Name, Amen.

God allowed it for a reason and for a season.

© By Dr. Sheila Hayford.

February 9
And The Door Was Shut

Matthew Chapter 25, verses 9, 10:
But the wise answered, saying, Not so; lest there be not enough for us and you: but go ye rather to them that sell, and buy for yourselves. And while they went to buy, the bridegroom came; and they that were ready went in with him to the marriage: and the door was shut.
Prayer: Dear God, we know that is not your will that any should perish but that all mankind would come to salvation through our Lord Jesus Christ. Enable me to do my part to warn those who do not yet know you and be diligent to make my calling and election sure, not wasting time but using the time and resources you give me wisely. In Jesus' Name. Amen.

Wow! What a sobering story! The ten virgins all started out with excitement and anticipation as they waited for the bridegroom. The bridegroom, the Lord Jesus, took longer than they expected because He wanted more people to be a part of his wedding feast. The wise virgins were in it for the long haul. They were prepared; spiritually, physically and emotionally. They were prayerful, spending time studying the Word of God and enjoying quality time with God. They walked in love, refused to hold grudges or walk in unforgiveness and took good care of their physical bodies. The foolish virgins, however, did not have enough oil for their lamps. The wise virgins did not want to risk running out of oil by parting with the spiritual and physical disciplines that were sustaining them by the power of the Holy Spirit. So the foolish virgins went out to buy oil and while they were out the bridegroom, the Lord Jesus Christ, arrived. Immediately the Lord Jesus entered, the door was shut. Whoever was ready at the Lord Jesus' coming was in the presence of Jesus; the rest were eternally shut out. Don't get left behind!

© By Dr. Sheila Hayford.

February 10
The Christian Pyramid

James Chapter 2, verses 17, 18:
Even so faith, if it hath not works, is dead, being alone. Yea, a man may say, Thou hast faith, and I have works: shew me thy faith without thy works, and I will shew thee my faith by my works.

Prayer: Help us, dear Lord God, to demonstrate our faith in our actions. In Jesus' Name, Amen.

You could not get much if you tried to eat uncooked rice. But boil it, season it, check it from time to time to make sure it is properly cooked and the cooked rice is tender and edible. I cannot imagine anyone would want to eat hard raw frozen chicken. However, thaw the chicken, season it, bake, broil or fry it and you have chicken fit for a king. Add the cooked chicken to the cooked rice, add your fruit and vegetables and you have a meal. So, if it is okay to have a food pyramid, why not a Christian pyramid? Faith without works is dead faith. But add some heat (testings in life), some seasoning (prayers in accordance with God's will revealed in the Holy Bible), check your faith from time to time (during fellowship with other believers in Bible study, church services, community events, etc.) and you have active living faith. Add some fruit (love, joy and the other fruit of the Holy Spirit), some vegetables (the wisdom of God), some dessert (the gifts of the Holy Spirit) and you have a well-balanced, healthy Christian. What part of the Christian pyramid are you lacking?

© By Dr. Sheila Hayford.

February 11
The Wall

Revelation Chapter 21, verse 12:

And had a wall great and high, and had twelve gates, and at the gates twelve angels, and names written thereon, which are the names of the twelve tribes of the children of Israel:

Prayer: Dear Holy Spirit: I get excited reading about the New Jerusalem. It will be more beautiful than words can describe. Help me share the good news of salvation in Jesus Christ with many. Amen.

Here in the United States, we had an interesting discussion about walls during the Presidential political campaigns. President-elect Donald Trump during his campaign said he was going to build a tall wall on the border between the United States and Mexico to keep immigrants from crossing the border and entering the United States illegally. Some people were in agreement, others were not. Walls can be a good thing. Walls provide boundaries, they offer protection, they keep people in, and they prevent others from entering in. In the New Jerusalem, the wall is high and has twelve gates. In the New Jerusalem, only those whose names are in the Lamb's Book of Life shall enter in. The Lamb of God is our Lord Jesus Christ and all who receive Him as Lord and Savior have their names written in this Book of Life. Is your name written in His book? If not, it can be today. Heed the invitation of the Lord Jesus in Revelation Chapter 3, verse 20 and invite the Lord Jesus into your heart today.

© By Dr. Sheila Hayford.

February 12
Taste And See

Exodus Chapter 16, verse 31:

And the house of Israel called the name thereof Manna: and it was like coriander seed, white; and the taste of it was like wafers made with honey.

Prayer: Dear Lord God, how sweet it is for mankind to experience your great love. Help us to share your great love with others. In Jesus' Name. Amen.

Growing up I heard a song that expressed the virtues of a particular dish. It ended with a proverb that said that the one who tasted the food was the one who bore witness to the deliciousness of the dish; the one who did not taste the food could not enjoy it and was left hungry. Taste (experience God) and see (realize, acknowledge) that the Lord is good. Be a living witness of God's goodness. Blessed (happy, favored and at peace) is the one who trusts in God.

© By Dr. Sheila Hayford.

February 13
Emergency Blanket

Psalm 86, verses 12, 13:

I will praise thee, O Lord my God, with all my heart: and I will glorify thy name for evermore. For great is thy mercy toward me: and thou hast delivered my soul from the lowest hell.

Prayer: Dear God; forgive me when I have met those who do not know my Savior Jesus Christ and have not offered them the opportunity to receive the Lord Jesus as Lord and Savior. Help me to pray and trust you to lead me to those I need to share Christ with. Let me follow and obey the Holy Spirit as I witness for Christ. In Jesus' Name. Amen.

It was a brisk cold, windy day downtown. I heard a man asking loudly if anyone needed an emergency blanket. There was a man at the street corner that looked like he had his belongings with him. A woman asked what an emergency blanket was. The man replied it was made of aluminum foil that people could wrap around themselves to keep warm. I was horrified! I use aluminum foil to cook and wrap food and I know it has other uses but never imagined that one. As I cooked my hot meal that evening, I recalled that event. There are people dying and going to a real hell every day. For those, hell will be their eternal destiny. The Lord Jesus Christ is the emergency blanket God has provided to rescue humanity from a burning hell. Like the man with the emergency blankets, will we ask those we meet if they would like to receive the Lord Jesus? The man did not force the blankets on anyone; he just gave people the chance to receive them. We should not do less. Offer the Lord Jesus today!

© By Dr. Sheila Hayford.

February 14
Love Won

John Chapter 15, verse 9:
As the Father hath loved me, so have I loved you: continue ye in my love.

Prayer: Dear Lord Jesus, I love you. Help me share my love for you with others. Amen.

Bishop Doreina C. Miles, Pastor at the time, just loves the youth. The youth felt her love, reciprocated it and flocked to church services. Hers was a love with mentoring. At Bishop Miles retirement dinner, it was fitting that her brother shared this humorous true story. A young single lady came to Bishop Miles, unwed but excited. She was pregnant and was excited about her baby. "What are you going to name the baby?" Bishop asked. The lady said a name that sounded like Treyschan so

Bishop Miles asked the lady to spell it. "T, r, a, pause …s, h, c, pause …an", the young lady replied. "Honey!" Bishop Miles responded, "You just spelled trash can." The young lady got the message and changed the baby's name. Love had won! We must note that some have been hurt, intentionally or unintentionally, by those who say they love them. The Lord Jesus Christ is our perfect example of love. Jesus gave himself sacrificially, dying for the sins of a people who did not understand his atoning sacrifice. Moreover, he asks us to love others with God's kind of love; unconditionally! In a sin-filled world, we have to remember that true love cannot hide behind a lack of self-esteem. In other words, a person should not allow another person to abuse them, physically or verbally, and equate that with love. When we love ourselves, we can obey the Lord Jesus' commandment to love your neighbor as yourself. Do you love God? Do you love you? Do you love your neighbor?

© By Dr. Sheila Hayford.

GREAT CARS

CALL 302-378-1402 TODAY!

February 15
With God ...

Matthew Chapter 19, verse 26:

But Jesus beheld them, and said unto them, With men this is impossible; but with God all things are possible.

Prayer: Dear God: I love recounting your marvelous works in my life. Each day is a new adventure with you and I love it! Thank you so much for my Lord Jesus Christ, the one who brings us into the family of God. For it is in His Name that I pray, Amen.

I have faced so many seemingly impossible situations in my life. Looking back, some of them were hilarious, even though it did not seem so at the time.

Several years ago, I gave up one of my jobs to focus on studying for an exam. I was living within my means and able to pay my mortgage but I had company coming for Christmas and could use extra income that would not require working during the Christmas holidays. It so happened that I went to a store and tried on a dress. In the store they had a large pin on the floor which pierced through my shoe and I began to bleed at the injury site. I knew I needed a tetanus vaccine so I decided to go to the nearest doctor's office. As we talked, the physician told me she was about to have surgery and needed someone to cover her office for six weeks. The six weeks would end just before Christmas! I told her I was available and could work for her. The hours there would not conflict with my job. I got the part-time job in her office and thoroughly enjoyed it. Just before Christmas, I received a check for a little under two thousand dollars. I had money enough and to spare for the Christmas holidays and we all enjoyed the company. Who would have thought that God would use a rusty pin to give me the seasonal job that I needed! And yes, I passed the exam!

© By Dr. Sheila Hayford.

February 16
God Turned It Around

Acts Chapter 9, verses 20-22:
At once he began to preach in the synagogues that Jesus is the Son of God. All those who heard him were astonished and asked, "Isn't he the man who raised havoc in Jerusalem among those who call on this name? And hasn't he come here to take them as prisoners to the chief priests?" Yet Saul grew more and more powerful and baffled the Jews living in Damascus by proving that Jesus is the Messiah. (N.I.V.)

Prayer: Dear Lord God; enable us to show others a clear witness of the transforming power of God. In Jesus' Name. Amen.

Saul, whose name was later changed to Paul, was a great persecutor of the Christians. Even when Stephen was martyred for his faith, Saul was consenting to Stephen's death. Satan thought he had Saul in wraps but God turned Saul around and changed his name to Paul. God then used the Apostle Paul for the glory of God, including the writing of several books in the New Testament of the Bible. Something interesting happens when a person known to be a "celebrity" accepts and receives the Lord Jesus as their personal Lord and Savior. Suddenly the platform they had which may not have been used for the glory of God is used as an instrument for the advancement of the purposes of God. Each of us has a platform or sphere of influence. Let us use it for the glory of God.

© By Dr. Sheila Hayford.

February 17
The Sin Problem

Nehemiah Chapter 1, verses 5-7:
And said, I beseech thee, O Lord God of heaven, the great and terrible God, that keepeth covenant and mercy for them that love him and

observe his commandments: Let thine ear now be attentive, and thine eyes open, that thou mayest hear the prayer of thy servant, which I pray before thee now, day and night, for the children of Israel thy servants, and confess the sins of the children of Israel, which we have sinned against thee: both I and my father's house have sinned. We have dealt very corruptly against thee, and have not kept the commandments, nor the statutes, nor the judgments, which thou commandedst thy servant Moses.

Prayer: Dear Lord God, I humble myself before you. Use me as you will, to accomplish your purposes in this generation and generations to come. In Jesus' Name. Amen.

It is easy to confess our own sins. We ask for God's forgiveness and trust the Holy Spirit to empower us to live holy. Nehemiah went a step further. He confessed the sins of his household and the sins of his nation. In 2 Chronicles Chapter 7, verse 14 we read, "If my people, which are called by my name, shall humble themselves, and pray, and seek my face, and turn from their wicked ways; then will I hear from heaven, and will forgive their sin, and will heal their land." We are told by God that if the children of God humble themselves and pray God will heal the land.

So, in effect, the state of any nation reflects the state of the born again believers collectively in that nation. The wicked and the unsaved may not be living for God but it is the responsibility of the born again believers in the nation to humble ourselves before God, seek God diligently, turn from evil in true repentance and ask God for forgiveness and healing.

Criticism of evil without bringing the presence of God to bear on the situation is a futile endeavor.

Will we each do our part for God and our country today?

© By Dr. Sheila Hayford.

"If my people, which are called by my name, shall humble themselves, and pray ..."

February 18
Cheerleading For Jesus

John Chapter 16, verse 33:

These things I have spoken unto you, that in me ye might have peace. In the world ye shall have tribulation: but be of good cheer; I have overcome the world.

Prayer: Dear Holy Spirit; help me to be of good cheer and to rejoice in the victory that is mine. Through Jesus Christ, my Lord. Amen.

I was at a youth church musical program and the young girl looked to be about five or six years old. She seemed the youngest in her group, which comprised of a few teenagers. This girl knew the words of the songs and danced with gusto. She was so filled with joy she refused to be intimidated. I said to myself, "that's Jesus' cheerleader!" The Lord Jesus told us ahead of time that we will have tests and challenges in this world. Nevertheless, he does not want us the tests to weigh us down. Instead, we should be cheerful, trusting God to help us walk in victory. No matter what we go through, we should trust God. And get our dance moves on!

© By Dr. Sheila Hayford.

February 19
Everlasting Love

Psalm 103, verses 17, 18:

But from everlasting to everlasting the Lord's love is with those who fear him, and his righteousness with their children's children - with those who keep his covenant and remember to obey his precepts.

Prayer: Dear Lord God: Thank you for the power of your love and for sending the Lord Jesus to save a lost humanity. We do not take your love lightly and reverence you as our holy God. In Jesus' Name. Amen.

February is a month we focus on love as many in the world celebrate Valentine's Day. Yes, the Lord Jesus is your Valentine. But He is your God first. Reverence Him every day of the year!

© By Dr. Sheila Hayford.

Tap, Ballet, Lyrical, Jazz, Hip-Hop, Acrobatics, Cheer Dance, and More.

Dance Delaware is a family friendly & professional dance studio that provides a positive atmosphere where students of all ages and levels can grow and strive to be the dancer of their dreams. Come join us, and become part of the Dance Delaware Family.

302-998-1222
DanceDelaware Studios
www.dancedelaware.com
2005 Concord Pike, Suite 204 Wilmington Delaware 19803
(located above IHOP)

Instagram: dancedelaware_studios
Facebook: https://www.facebook.com/DanceDelaware/

February 20

God: The Great Astonisher

Romans Chapter 11, verse 33:
O the depth of the riches both of the wisdom and knowledge of God! how unsearchable are his judgments, and his ways past finding out!

Prayer: Dear God; May You never cease to amaze me. In the Name of Jesus. Amen.

Just when you might begin to think that you are familiar with the ways of God, God astonishes you! I have found myself nodding in amazement at all the wonderful, sometimes surprising, acts of kindness of a great God. I was looking to buy a pair of comfortable shoes and ordered one from a store. When I went into the store to pick them up they apologized because one of their employees had spilled soda on the shoes they held for me at the back and they would have to order another pair. I did not want to wait that much longer. Disappointed, I said I would buy a different pair of shoes at another store and headed to the other store. At the other store I still did not find the shoe style I was looking for and left a little ticked off. Well, God had it such that I was given a gift and it was a pair of shoes. And they are so... comfortable! It was made by the Clarks brand. Clarks was the second store I had gone to on that shopping day and it was a brand I was familiar with since childhood. God knew the good surprise He had in store for me all along and I loved it. Great God; the Great Astonisher!

© By Dr. Sheila Hayford.

February 21
So Honored To Be God's Child

Romans Chapter 8, verse 14:
For as many as are led by the Spirit of God, they are the sons of God.
Prayer: Dear God, The angels peer to see how the royal children you have made us are being favored. We are so blessed, so happy and so honored. Let us never take our relationship with you for granted because it was secured by none other than your only begotten Son, our Lord and Savior Jesus Christ. Thank you. Amen.

We see countries with the monarchal system of government and sometimes marvel at the royal treatment their royal families enjoy. Some are fascinated by their favorite celebrity and others by the favorite sports teams. But we sometimes forget that being God's child has special privileges. For you see, being a child of the Most High God, the Almighty, put you at a higher level than the angels of God. It puts you at a higher level than any human monarchy, any celebrity or your favorite sports team. As a child of God, through the Lord Jesus Christ you are entitled to all the privileges and authority given to us in Christ. The promises God has given us assure us that God is a great heavenly Father and will do His part in taking care of us. Our part is to believe what God says and to obey God. The Bible says the angels wonder at the privileges afforded born again believers through Jesus Christ. I am so honored to be God's child because I could never have earned it. Neither could you. We are all recipients of God's love gift to mankind, Jesus Christ. And so we thank you, dear heavenly Father!

© By Dr. Sheila Hayford.

February 22
Personal Responsibility

Matthew Chapter 18, verse 9:
And if thine eye offend thee, pluck it out, and cast it from thee: it is better for thee to enter into life with one eye, rather than having two eyes to be cast into hell fire.

Prayer: Dear Lord Jesus: It is easy to point figures because the sins of others may be glaring. However, no human being is without sin and we all need your love, power and forgiveness. Help us take personal responsibility for the work we do and the way we live. In the Name of Jesus, Amen.

If Reverend Dr. Martin Luther King, Jr. was alive on this earth today I believe he would be championing a different cause and that would be the campaign for Personal Responsibility. And I say it would be: Personal Responsibility whether you are doing Right or have been dealt Wrong.

We see the perfect example of this in the Lord Jesus Christ. The Lord Jesus was sent by God the Father to this earth with a mission. The Lord Jesus was to live a sinless life, destroy the works of the devil, take upon himself the punishment of the sins of mankind by dying on the cross on our behalf, rise from the dead and fulfil his eternal destiny. The Lord Jesus took personal responsibility for his mission. He prayed regularly with God the Father; sometimes alone, other times with others. He went about teaching and doing good.

Not everyone was happy with what the Lord Jesus was doing. Nevertheless, the Lord Jesus continued to fulfil his mission. He was misunderstood, sometimes by the very disciples he spent so much time teaching, but the Lord Jesus never gave up on his mission. Even when he was dealt wrongfully by being given a death sentence in a horrible torturous way on the cross, the Lord Jesus entrusted his God to be the ultimate judge in the matter. The Lord Jesus did not condone evil. Indeed, he spoke out against the double standard practices of the Pharisees. He knew some were plotting to kill him because they hated him and his message but the Lord Jesus refused to live his life blaming others for the wrongs he had experienced.

Are you a parent? You have a personal responsibility to take care of your children. Are you married? You have personal responsibility towards your marriage. Are you an employer? You have a personal responsibility to take good care of your employees. Are you an employee? You have a personal responsibility to do an excellent job. Are you a member of the community? You have personal responsibility to play your role in a safe and orderly manner.

Collectively, we can get the job God has called us to do accomplished. To achieve that will take everyone doing their part. Are you doing your part?

© By Dr. Sheila Hayford.

February 23
Change

Hebrews Chapter 13, verse 8:

Jesus Christ is the same yesterday and today and forever. (NIV)

Prayer: Dear God: We know change can be a good thing because you want us our lives to be transformed so we live more like Jesus Christ. We entrust ourselves to the God who never changes. In Jesus' Name, Amen.

Change in our world is inevitable. We hear people say, "here today, gone tomorrow" to emphasize that point. We visit childhood landmarks and are astonished to see how things have changed. Retailers encourage you to get that sale price today because those prices may be gone tomorrow. Not so with God. The character of God will never change. Jesus Christ is the same yesterday, today and forever. The love of God will never change. The faithfulness of God will never change. The Word of God will never change. Trust your changes to the God who never changes.

© By Dr. Sheila Hayford.

February 24
Let God Encourage You

Romans Chapter 15, verse 13:

May the God of hope fill you with all joy and peace as you trust in him, so that you may overflow with hope by the power of the Holy Spirit.

Prayer: Dear Lord Jesus; thank you for being my example. In the Garden of Gethsemane, you cried out to our heavenly Father and God encouraged you. In our lives, when we cry out to you, you encourage us. Thank you for the Holy Spirit who strengthens us. Amen.

It is comforting when you have someone who has experienced your present circumstances giving you advice or words of encouragement. Perhaps you are apprehensive about starting your own business and then you meet someone who felt the same way but succeeded in his or her business. You figure, if he or she could do it, so can you.

The neat thing about the Lord Jesus Christ is that he lived on this earth and experienced life with all its challenges and temptations without sinning. In everything the Lord Jesus did here on earth, God was glorified. So when we face a challenge, we can talk to Jesus. Jesus promised us that he would send the Holy Spirit to encourage, exhort, comfort and teach us and he is true to his Word. For indeed, the Lord Jesus is the living Word of God.

So, while it is great to have others encourage you, allow God to be your Number One "go to" Encourager.

© By Dr. Sheila Hayford.

February 25
Who Is In Your Midst

Luke Chapter 24, verses 28-35:
They approached the village where they were going. Jesus kept walking as if he were going farther. But they tried hard to keep him from leaving. They said, "Stay with us. It is nearly evening. The day is almost over." So he went in to stay with them. He joined them at the table. Then he took bread and gave thanks. He broke it and began to give it to them. Their eyes were opened, and they recognized him. But then he disappeared from their sight. They said to each other, "He explained to us what the Scriptures meant. Weren't we excited as he talked with us on the road?" They got up and returned at once to Jerusalem. There they found the 11 disciples and those with them. They were all gathered together. They were saying, "It's true! The Lord has risen! He has appeared to Simon!" Then the two of them told what had happened to them on the way. They told how they had recognized Jesus when he broke the bread.

Prayer: Dear Lord Jesus: Help me to live soberly; recognizing the daily opportunities and blessings you afford me. Help me not to act like the Pharisees who would broadcast their good works for the praise of men. Enable me to treat all men with dignity and do my part in lifting up my fellow man. In Jesus' Name, Amen.

I heard one of "The Shark Tank" television show investors, Robert Herjavec, say that during a trying time following his divorce he went to Seattle's Union Gospel Mission House after consulting with his Pastor and stayed there for a short time. This Mission house provides shelter, emergency care and services to the homeless. One of the things he said was that most of the people there did not know who he was. Imagine all the people there who had million dollar ideas and inventions that could lift them out of their present situations. Imagine all the advice he could have given if they had asked. Some of them might even have had their ideas funded through the Shark Tank television program or through other sources. All that may have been required to start the funding for their dream or idea might have been a friendly conversation. However, many were probably so preoccupied with their current circumstances they were oblivious to the fact that someone in their midst could help them.

There are many times God sends people to help us but they do not always show up in a suit and tie. A Pastor told the true story of how his church was going bankrupt because they began reaching out to the homeless in their community and many of the large church donors had left in protest. The Pastor called a meeting with the homeless people they were ministering to and told them that the church's financial problem would impact the church's ability to help them. At that meeting one of the homeless men asked the Pastor how much money was needed and ended up providing the funds that kept that church from going bankrupt.

The Lord Jesus is standing at the door of every human heart. He has the solution to our every need but we have to invite him in.

Who is in your midst?

© By Dr. Sheila Hayford.

February 26:
The God Who Knows Ahead Of Time

Psalm 139, verses 13, 14:

For you created my inmost being; you knit me together in my mother's womb. I praise you because I am fearfully and wonderfully made; your works are wonderful, I know that full well. (NIV)

Prayer: My heavenly Father, you are Awesome! I acknowledge your sovereignty in my life and in the affairs of men. I give you all the glory. In Jesus' Name, Amen.

God knows the days of the life of every human being on this earth. Even more amazing, God has this knowledge before we were born. Some years ago, God had showed me where I would be living, with my car in the driveway. I drove around different neighborhoods looking to see if I saw a place that looked like that area. I did not at the time, stopped looking and forgot about it.

Fast forward some years later. I got a job in an area I had not previously considered and, sure enough, it was the way God had showed it to me. When it was time to buy a new car I went to the car dealership. I wanted to buy a car in the color God had shown me. "We don't have a car in that color." the salesman told me. He then went on to say they were not expecting one in that color any time soon. I told him he would soon get one in that color and that he should call me when he got it. A day later he called me, quite surprised. "You wouldn't believe it!" he said, "The car in the color you want just came into the dealership." I was not surprised. I went in and bought the car. As it stood in my driveway, I reflected on the God who knows ahead of time.

There is no need for us to worry. No need for us to fret. God took care of the challenge before we got there.

Trust God!

© By Dr. Sheila Hayford.

February 27
Awesome!

Exodus Chapter 3, verses 13-15:

And Moses said unto God, Behold, when I come unto the children of Israel, and shall say unto them, The God of your fathers hath sent me unto you; and they shall say to me, What is his name? what shall I say unto them? And God said unto Moses, I Am That I Am: and he said, Thus shalt thou say unto the children of Israel, I Am hath sent me unto you. And God said moreover unto Moses, Thus shalt thou say unto the children of Israel, the Lord God of your fathers, the God of Abraham, the God of Isaac, and the God of Jacob, hath sent me unto you: this is my name for ever, and this is my memorial unto all generations.

Prayer: Dear God, words cannot express our awe and reverence for you for you are truly amazing. You are God, the Creator of the Universe and yet through Jesus Christ, you are everything that we need you to be to us and for us. Thank you. Amen.

Here in the United States of America, we use the word awesome for just about everything. We may use the term after we have experienced a spectacular concert performance. Some may use the term after they have had their favorite morning coffee. Still others may use the term when they behold God's creation.

As inspiring as all of these are, they are no comparison to the awesomeness of our God. Listen to what God is saying. His Name is "I AM ..." In other words, whatever it is that you need God to be for you, He is that to you. Healer? Deliverer? Provider? Protector? Father? God? And so much more! For all generations; for you, your family, those who came before you, those who will come after you. Now, that is Awesome.

What a truly awesome God!

© By Dr. Sheila Hayford.

February 28
Let Jonah Off Your Boat

Jonah Chapter 1, verses 8-16:

So they asked him, "Tell us, who is responsible for making all this trouble for us? What kind of work do you do? Where do you come from? What is your country? From what people are you?" He answered, "I am a Hebrew and I worship the Lord, the God of heaven, who made the sea and the dry land." This terrified them and they asked, "What have you done?" (They knew he was running away from the Lord, because he had already told them so.) The sea was getting rougher and rougher. So they asked him, "What should we do to you to make the sea calm down for us?" "Pick me up and throw me into the sea," he replied, "and it will become calm. I know that it is my fault that this great storm has come upon you." Instead, the men did their best to row back to land. But they could not, for the sea grew even wilder than before. Then they cried out to the Lord, "Please, Lord, do not let us die for taking this man's life. Do not hold us accountable for killing an innocent man, for you, Lord, have done as you pleased." Then they took Jonah and threw him overboard, and the raging sea grew calm. At this the men greatly feared the Lord, and they offered a sacrifice to the Lord and made vows to him. (NIV)

Prayer: Dear God: Sometimes in our attempt to "help" people we tolerate foolishness. Give us the discernment, wisdom and grace to make wise decisions and to spend the time you give us resourcefully. Help us remember that you take idle words seriously and enable us to do right by you. In Jesus' Name we pray. Amen.

We often hear this passage when people talk about Jonah trying to run away from obeying the commands of God. A person may try to run but they cannot hide from God. However, I believe this verse is about more than just the consequences of disobeying God. It is about allowing toxic relationships to get your life off course. Note the sequence of events. The sailors were minding their own business. Jonah was running away from God, or at the least, trying to run away from God. But look at what happened. Jonah did not just ran from the command of God to preach to the people of Nineveh, he paid the sailors to sail in their boat even while he was disobeying God. The sailors thought they were helping Jonah until a strange thing happened. The peaceful boat of the sailors began to toss and turn as the winds became contrary and a storm arose. While the sailors were feverishly trying to right the ship, Jonah, the cause of the problem, was sleeping. Finally, after serious discussion with the sailors, Jonah compelled them to let him off their boat. "Throw me overboard", Jonah was essentially saying but the sailors were hesitant to do that. "Surely they must be some other way", the sailors probably thought and did their best to row back to land. When that failed, they prayerfully threw Jonah off their boat. That was what they should have done earlier when Jonah told them he was running from God. Immediately Jonah was off the boat the raging sea became calm. The men who had seen the hand of God firsthand in their situation feared God and offered sacrifices and made vows to God.

Why would anyone want to be an accomplice for a person who is willfully disobeying God and trying to involve others in his or her mess? Why would anyone allow toxic relationships to throw their life off course, and possibly take them away from their peaceful relationship in right standing with God? God will show you when a relationship is toxic. In this case, the sailors recognized Jonah was "toxic" for them by what Jonah said. If they had continued to let Jonah stay in their boat they might have perished with him. Yes, we are to love everybody. However, if a person willfully chooses to disobey God, you can love them, pray for them and refer them to resources suited to help them deal with their situation without getting involved with their disobedient lifestyle and thereby displeasing God.

Off the boat, Jonah got swallowed by a whale and while in the belly of the whale got his life back on track with God. Letting Jonah off your boat might cause the person to be swallowed up by a large fish or circumstances that seem greater than they can handle. But that may be just what the person needs to get back on track to a right relationship with God. And that may be just what you need to get some peace back in your life and rededicate your life back to God.

© By Dr. Sheila Hayford.

March 1
The Diligent

Proverbs 13, verse 4:
The soul of the sluggard desireth, and hath nothing: but the soul of the diligent shall be made fat.

Prayer; Dear Lord God; all through Scripture we see men and women stepping up to the command you gave Adam and Eve that we work and take care of our assignments. Help us to be diligent so that we will have the privilege of hearing your words, "Well Done!" In Jesus Name we pray. Amen.

Have you heard anyone say they were totally unprepared for what happened? In other words, they had not made any provision that took into account that particular situation. Planning for the future does not show a lack of faith. In fact, it tells God that you are serious about your future and need His help to plan for success. God has provided us with so many planning resources, beginning with the Holy Bible. Financial advisors and planners are also available to take into account our individual life circumstances thereby helping us make well thought out plans.

So what if you experience something out of the ordinary that catches you off guard? Keep calm and remember that your situation did not catch God off guard. God can still work things out for your good. Pray, study what the Bible says concerning your situation, seek godly counsel and, as needed, professional advice. And then follow through, trusting God to be the all sufficient God in your life.

© By Dr. Sheila Hayford.

March 2
Tomorrow, Tomorrow ...

Isaiah Chapter 52, verse 7:
How beautiful upon the mountains are the feet of him that bringeth good tidings, that publisheth peace; that bringeth good tidings of good, that publisheth salvation; that saith unto Zion, Thy God reigneth!

Prayer: Dear Lord God, help me not to procrastinate. I do not want to rob myself of the joy of experiencing my future in its fullness. In the Name of Jesus I pray. Amen.

Do you realize that today is the tomorrow you prayed about yesterday? And that tomorrow will be in your past the day after tomorrow? What is my point here? It is that God has made everything beautiful in its time. There are moments today that you will never again experience and that are for you to enjoy. We hear the expression "once in a lifetime" when we think of concerts, Super Bowl football games, vacations and "special" events but there are literally thousands of "once in a lifetime" moments for us to enjoy each day. So as we perform our daily tasks, and prepare responsibly for the future, let us take the time to enjoy each precious day.

© By Dr. Sheila Hayford.

March 3
Faith = Yes, I Got It!

Mark Chapter 11, verse 24:
Therefore I say unto you, What things soever ye desire, when ye pray, believe that ye receive them, and ye shall have them.

Prayer: Dear Lord Jesus; Our faith dictates the way we pray. If we expect from you, we will receive from you. So help us believe your words and live out God's plans and purposes. Thank you for showing us that it can be done. Amen.

For years I had carried the dream of various projects God has called me to do. And for years it had been just that - a dream. Yes, I had made some plans and drawn the framework but it was just a dream. One morning as I began to pray the Holy Spirit changed the way I began to pray about the project. Suddenly I realized I was praying as if the dream had become a reality. "Yes, I got it!" I exclaimed. By faith I had visualized the reality of my projects. That was when the Holy Spirit gave me this definition of faith; Faith equals Yes, I Got It! Yes, we are in agreement with God's promises. Yes, I have received what God has promised. Hallelujah! Have you received yours?

© By Dr. Sheila Hayford.

March 4
I Gave You The Victory; Use It!

1 John Chapter 5, verse 4:

For whatsoever is born of God overcometh the world: and this is the victory that overcometh the world, even our faith.

Prayer: My heavenly Father, help me not to use prayer as an excuse for inaction. In Jesus' Name, Amen.

I like to get to places on time. And I like to get projects completed on time. The problem is I tend to wait till the last minute to get ready, then rush and arrive ahead of or on time somewhat flustered. I wake up early, but then I do more things around the house. I have extra time in the morning and decide to have a "heavy" breakfast. Then I rush and make it to the event or place ahead of time. After I have rested for about five to ten minutes, I start wondering about the late folk! "That is so disrespectful, not showing up on time" I say about the ones arriving late as I wait "patiently" for the others to arrive. Eventually the event starts late. One day I had had enough of rushing to get things done at the last minute. "Dear Holy Spirit," I prayed, "I need your help!" To which the Holy Spirit lovingly replied, "I gave you the victory, use it!" For you see, there are some things that we do not need to pray about. If God says, love your neighbor as yourself, we do not need to pray to ask God if we should love your neighbor. If you need help loving your neighbor, then of course, it is appropriate to ask God for help. The Holy Spirit in me has given me everything I need to be victorious in life through Jesus Christ. Whatever I face, the Greater One lives in me. I need to use what I have in Christ. So do you!

© By Dr. Sheila Hayford.

March 5
Appointed By God

Ezra Chapter 1, verses 1-6:

Now in the first year of Cyrus king of Persia, that the word of the Lord by the mouth of Jeremiah might be fulfilled, the Lord stirred up the spirit of Cyrus king of Persia, that he made a proclamation throughout all his kingdom, and put it also in writing, saying, Thus saith Cyrus king of Persia, The Lord God of heaven hath given me all the kingdoms of the earth; and he hath charged me to build him an house at Jerusalem, which is in Judah. Who is there among you of all his people? his God be with him, and let him go up to Jerusalem, which is in Judah, and build the house of the Lord God of Israel, (he is the God,) which is in Jerusalem. And whosoever remaineth in any place where he sojourneth, let the men of his place help him with silver, and with gold, and with goods, and with beasts, beside the freewill offering for the house of God that is in Jerusalem. Then rose up the chief of the fathers of Judah and Benjamin, and the priests, and the Levites, with all them whose spirit God had raised, to go up to build the house of the Lord which is in Jerusalem. And all they that were about them strengthened their hands with vessels of silver, with gold, with goods, and with beasts, and with precious things, beside all that was willingly offered.

Prayer: Dear Lord; thank you for the governments you have set up to fulfill your purpose on this earth. Let us not give excuses for or only offer harsh criticism of their actions, but uphold them daily in prayer. Help us to advance in the mission and plan you have for us. We pray in Jesus' Name. Amen.

Appointed by God? A secular government appointed by God? Yes! For no government can exist without God's permission. What the government does with that authority should be influenced by the people of God praying for those in authority. Here Cyrus, king of Persia, was used by God to fulfill God's purpose to build God's temple in Jerusalem. And note the words of King Cyrus, "The Lord God of heaven hath given me all the kingdoms of the earth; and he hath charged me to build him an house at Jerusalem, which is in Judah. Who is there among you of all his people? his God be with him, and let him go up ..." How encouraging! King Cyrus recognized the source of his power and authority, the purpose of his kingship and took steps to comply with God's mission for his life. This is a proclamation of the King of Persia. What are you saying about God's plan and purpose for you? And are you taking the necessary steps with God to fulfill that mission? The Lord, your God, be with you and let us go up!

© By Dr. Sheila Hayford.

March 6
Even Kings Need Counsel

Ester Chapter 1, verse 11-13:
To bring Vashti the queen before the king with the crown royal, to shew the people and the princes her beauty: for she was fair to look on. But the queen Vashti refused to come at the king's commandment by his chamberlains: therefore was the king very wroth, and his anger burned in him. Then the king said to the wise men, which knew the times, (for so was the king's manner toward all that knew law and judgment:

Prayer; Dear Holy Spirit, I give you permission to give me wisdom and wise counsel. Give me spiritual understanding, empower me to be all that God would have me be and enable me to accomplish all that God will have me do. Amen.

King Ahasuerus had given a command requesting that his beautiful queen Vashti come before him, adorned with her royal crown. You would think that Queen Vashti would be happy to oblige, having found favor with the king. However, she refused. Now King Ahasuerus was understandably upset and embarrassed but note what he did next. He did not make a declaration of war against another country in his anger, nor did he immediately send Queen Vashti out of the palace. Instead King Ahasuerus consulted with the wise men, the men who knew about law and judgment. He went to seek counsel from those who were experienced in the area he need advice. By associating and taking counsel from wise men, King Ahasuerus was able to make a wise decision. We note the wise men did not just tell king Ahasuerus what to do, they gave him the basis for their decision. What a wonderful example. We should seek godly advice when we are faced with challenges and when asked, give godly advice based on the Word of God. Yes, in Christ, we are kings and priests in the family of God. And yes, even kings need counsel.

© By Dr. Sheila Hayford.

March 7
The Seven Beatitudes of Revelation

Revelation Chapter 1, verse 3:
Blessed is he that readeth, and they that hear the words of this prophecy, and keep those things which are written therein: for the time is at hand.

Prayer: Dear heavenly Father: Thank you for the Holy Spirit who makes it easy to read and understand your Word. Help me to be obedient to you and to be an example of godly living to those with whom I have influence. In Jesus' Name, Amen.

Beginning today we will be studying the seven beatitudes of the book of Revelation. This verse starts with: Blessed is he that readeth. It is somewhat disturbing to me when I hear people say that they do not read. Every day I am thankful for parents who encouraged me and gave me the opportunity to love reading, writing and literature. God is calling those who read this prophetic book of Revelation blessed. Why? It is because we are afforded the opportunity to read on the pages of the book visions that God gave the Apostle John of coming events. But the blessing is conditional. Not only are we to read the book of Revelation, we are to hear and understand this book by the power of the Holy Spirit and then do what God instructs us to do. We are informed, favored and fortunate to have this book of Revelation. It is not a book to be feared, it is not a book that defies understanding. It is a loving God giving us glimpses of the future. And why are we blessed? It is because the time is at hand. As we look at current events we see parts of the book of Revelation being fulfilled. It is a book designed to get us ready for the soon return of our Lord Jesus Christ. Be prepared!

© By Dr. Sheila Hayford.

March 8
Forever Blessed

Revelation Chapter 14, verse 13:
And I heard a voice from heaven saying unto me, Write, **Blessed** are the dead which die in the Lord from henceforth: Yea, saith the Spirit, that they may rest from their labours; and their works do follow them.

Prayer: Dear Lord God: There is a time to work and a time to rest and help us not to confuse the two. Help us so to work that at the end of our journey on this earth we will have fully spent ourselves on earth for the glory of God, ready to enjoy all you have for us. Amen.

Many times we associate blessings with life on this earth but this verse calls the dead who die in the Lord blessed. Wow! So blessings are not necessarily limited to life on this earth. So how can those who die in the Lord be happy, favored or fortunate? It is because they have transitioned from this life to a better place, eternal life in the presence of our Lord Jesus Christ. In contrast, those who die without accepting the salvation offered through our Lord Jesus Christ are forever separated from God. That is a hard truth. It has been suggested that would be a reason for God to wipe the tears from the eyes of those in God's heaven. We are favored or blessed by God to know what happens after life on this earth ahead of time so that it will guide our decision making on this earth. So have hope; those who have gone on ahead in faith are safe in Christ in God. And their works do follow them. Eternal blessings. Eternal rewards. Hallelujah!

© By Dr. Sheila Hayford.

March 9
The Marriage Supper of the Lamb

Revelation Chapter 10, verse 9:

And he saith unto me, Write, **Blessed** are they which are called unto the marriage supper of the Lamb. And he saith unto me, These are the true sayings of God.

Prayer: My, my, oh my! Dear Lord God: I am so excited thinking about that day; the wedding celebration of the Lord Jesus Christ, when he is united with us, the body of Christ. What a great God! What a precious Savior! Hallelujah! Glory to God!

Have you ever been invited to a wedding? It was an honor to receive the invitation in the first place. Then you read the name of the future bride and bridegroom and you are filled with joy in anticipation of the wedding. You begin to think about what dress you are going to wear. What gift are you going to give the couple? You wonder where they are going to go for their honeymoon. Where do they plan to live after the wedding? All these emotions and thoughts from a single invitation! This

Marriage Supper in Revelation is the Ultimate of Weddings. It is a Big Deal! The Lord Jesus Christ is our Bridegroom and we are the beloved bride of Christ. Our robes are white and purchased through the blood of our Savior Jesus Christ. We give our bridegroom the gift of ourselves for Jesus gave Himself for us. We are going to enjoy great feasting and we get to spend eternity with our Lord Jesus Christ. Hallelujah! To God be all glory!

© By Dr. Sheila Hayford.

March 10
The First Resurrection

Revelation Chapter 20, verse 6:
Blessed and holy is he that hath part in the first resurrection: on such the second death hath no power, but they shall be priests of God and of Christ, and shall reign with him a thousand years.

Prayer: Dear Lord Jesus; we anticipate and look forward to your second coming with joy. Pray for us, that by the power of the Holy Spirit we will be ready. Amen.

The book of Revelation is a fascinating book! What is the first resurrection the book of Revelation describes? The Lord Jesus is coming back to earth again. This is good news! And we read in 1 Thessalonians Chapter 4 that when the Lord Jesus comes back to earth those who have died after receiving Jesus as their Lord and Savior on this earth will rise up from the dead to be with Jesus. Then those who are alive at the time of the appearing of the Lord Jesus will be caught up to be with the Lord Jesus. When this happens those individuals left on earth will experience unrestrained evil to a large extent. This is because those Christians who were holding back the powers of darkness by prayer and the power of the Holy Spirit will have been ruptured. It will still be possible for those left on earth at that time to receive the Lord Jesus Christ as Lord and Savior, but it will be more difficult as those who do so will be killed. Those who die as martyrs in this era will be resurrected to reign with Jesus for a thousand years. This is the first resurrection described in Revelation Chapter 20.

Okay, so what is the second death? There is going to be a great Judgement day. After this judgement, those whose names are not in the book of life will be cast into the lake of fire. The Lake of Fire is the second death. However, happy and favored are we whose names are in the book of life for we will be with the Lord Jesus and will never experience the second death. Glory to God!

© By Dr. Sheila Hayford.

March 11
Behold I Come Quickly

Revelation Chapter 22, verses 7, 12:
Behold, I come quickly: **blessed** is he that keepeth the sayings of the prophecy of this book. And, behold, I come quickly; and my reward is with me, to give every man according as his work shall be.

Prayer: Dear God; it is sobering to think that what we do on this earth will determine our eternal rewards. Stephen, your faithful disciple preached to his accusers who were ready to stone him even as the Lord Jesus stood up to welcome him into your heaven. Help me to be about my heavenly Father's business. In Jesus' Name, Amen.

Faithfulness is very attractive. There is something honorable about a person with what appears to be a legitimate reason to abandon their faith, who is willing to die as a martyr for Christ. A valued employee, who can be depended on to do his or her job well whether the boss is present or on vacation, is commended for their faithfulness. A dog who refuses to leave his hurting master's side is described as a faithful friend. The Lord Jesus is telling us here that He is coming soon and that He has rewards for those on this earth who have faithfully kept and lived by the words of God.

May we be found favored to be in that company!

© By Dr. Sheila Hayford.

March 12
Obedience Has Its Privileges

Revelations Chapter 22, verse 14:

Blessed are they that do his commandments, that they may have right to the tree of life, and may enter in through the gates into the city.

Prayer: Dear Lord God; it is amazing to read the many promises you have for those who obey you, on this earth and in eternity. We so look forward to spending eternity with you. Amen.

The definitions of privilege are varied: a special advantage, immunity, permission, right, or benefit granted to or enjoyed by an individual or group; such an advantage, immunity, or right is held as a prerogative of status and exercised to the exclusion or detriment of others. In this chapter, we learn that obedience to the commandments of God gives us access and the right to enjoy the fruit and leaves of the tree of life and the privilege to enter through the gates to the holy city, the New Jerusalem where Jesus Christ dwells. Hallelujah!

© By Dr. Sheila Hayford.

March 13
Forgiveness; An Act Of Your Will

Mark Chapter 11, verse 25-26:

And when ye stand praying, forgive, if ye have ought against any: that your Father also which is in heaven may forgive you your trespasses. But if ye do not forgive, neither will your Father which is in heaven forgive your trespasses.

Prayer: Dear Holy Spirit, I choose to forgive by an act of my will. Enable me to manifest the reality of my decision to forgive by your power. Through Jesus Christ my Lord. Amen.

Forgiveness is not a feeling. It is an act of your will. In other words, you cannot judge whether you have or have not forgiven a person by your emotions. The Bible instructs us to forgive those who wrong us, so forgiveness is an act of obedience to God. Moreover, obedience always involves a conscious decision to take action. When I decide to forgive a person I say, "I forgive … by an act of my will and the power of the Holy Spirit." Then I consider it done. The Holy Spirit is the one who enables me to apply the love and forgiveness of God to another person and when I am willing and obedient, God always comes through for me. I do not care whether I feel like forgiving or not at the time. The devil would love you to walk in condemnation because your emotions have not yet caught up with your decision to forgive. Remember, your emotions are subject to your will and your will is subject to the Word of God and the power of the Holy Spirit. So go ahead; Forgive!

© By Dr. Sheila Hayford.

Brandywine Dance Shoppe

3417 Silverside Road, Talleyville Shopping Center
Tel: (302) 476-4403
For Your Praise and Worship Teams, Ballet and Dance Shop Needs!

SHOP TRAVEL DEALS.US

- ✓ Do you love to travel? Vacation? Business? Group Tours?
- ✓ Would you like to know about special travel package deals?
- ✓ Would you like to earn free travel when you travel and use your rewards for more than just travel?
- ✓ Isn't it time you had your share of fun in the sun?

We may have just what you are looking for.

VISIT:

www.shoptraveldeals.us

IT'S TIME FOR YOUR SHARE OF FUN IN THE SUN!

March 14
Basking In The Goodness Of God

Psalm 27, verse 13:

I remain confident of this: I will see the goodness of the Lord in the land of the living. (NIV)

Prayer: Dear Lord God, we acknowledge and thank you for your many blessings. Help us never to take you for granted or despise your grace, goodness and mercy to us. In Jesus' Name. Amen.

We have had some cold weather, recent snow and ice and basking on the beautiful beaches under sunny skies seems like a great idea. However, that usually involves money, time and travel. How blessed we are that we do not have to travel nor purchase with cash the goodness of God in the land of the living. Every day we live is another day to bask in God's goodness. We get to breathe God's free air, admire God's beautiful creation and enjoy the favor of God that is ours through the Lord Jesus Christ. No sunglasses are required to bask in God's goodness, just a capacity to receive all that God has and desires for you. Get your Word of God "lotion" on and bask in the goodness of the Son!

© By Dr. Sheila Hayford.

March 15
Zeal

Numbers Chapter 25, verses 10 to 13:

The Lord said to Moses, "Phinehas son of Eleazar, the son of Aaron, the priest, has turned my anger away from the Israelites. Since he was as zealous for my honor among them as I am, I did not put an end to them in my zeal. Therefore tell him I am making my covenant of peace with him. He and his descendants will have a covenant of a lasting priesthood, because he was zealous for the honor of his God and made atonement for the Israelites.

Prayer: My heavenly Father, I am deeply moved by your grace and tender mercies, revealed to me through my Savior Jesus Christ. Thank you so much. In Jesus' Name. Amen.

I was approaching the end of the time schedule given to me by the Holy Spirit to complete this book. I should have had it done but between holidays, distractions and procrastinations I now had five days left. As much as I had written, I was not sure I would have it complete by then. So sheepishly, I asked the Holy Spirit if I would have it completed by then. The Lord God replied that it would not be by that date but it would be close. "Oh dear!" I was thinking because I did not want to think about the consequences if you miss God's schedule. The Lord continued, "But that's alright. I have given you a grace period." (Paraphrased). I was taken aback. He continued, "You know how when you have a due date to pay a bill they give you a grace period." I understood. The Lord told me that He loved what I am doing and it was about my zeal. The verse that came to me then was John Chapter 2, verse 17 where it talks about zeal for God's house consuming the Lord Jesus after Jesus overturned the tables of the money changers in the temple. By this time, I was deeply moved. I was and still am so grateful, eternally grateful. Thank you God.

© By Dr. Sheila Hayford.

March 16
Love Is A Beautiful Thing

Jude Chapter1, verses 1, 2:
Jude, the servant of Jesus Christ, and brother of James, to them that are sanctified by God the Father, and preserved in Jesus Christ, and called: Mercy unto you, and peace, and love, be multiplied.

Prayer: Dear Lord Jesus: I know I am a sinner. I am thankful that you paid the price for my sins by dying for me on the cross of Calvary. I am sorry for my sins and ask you to forgive me and cleanse me of every sin. I invite you into my heart and my life now to be my Lord and Savior. Fill me with your Holy Spirit and help me live for you. Thank you that I am now part of God's family. Amen.

Love is a beautiful thing. And love multiplied with God's mercy and peace is priceless. So how do we get to experience all three? Simple. Have a relationship with the God of love, mercy and peace through the Lord Jesus Christ. So how do you begin this relationship? First, agree with God that you are a sinner. And that you have sinned against God and your fellow man. Accept God's word that the price for your sin is death and that Jesus Christ paid the price for your sin when he died on the cross for you. Invite the Lord Jesus into your heart and life and ask him to forgive you, cleanse you from all sin, fill you with the Holy Spirit and help you live for him. After you pray this prayer, you are born again into to the family of God. Read your Bible every day, starting with the gospel of John. Share your faith in Jesus with family and friends. Attend a church fellowship where the Word of God is preached regularly. Enjoy God's love, God's mercy and peace, multiplied!

© By Dr. Sheila Hayford.

March 17
Hold Tight, It's Coming Up!

Jeremiah Chapter 29, verse 11:
For I know the thoughts that I think toward you, saith the LORD, thoughts of peace, and not of evil, to give you an expected end.
Prayer: Dear God, I am excited about what you have coming up in my life for you know what is best for me. Thank you. I would not have it any other way! In Jesus' Name. Amen.

Have you been to a restaurant and ordered a dish that took longer than usual to prepare? Maybe you ordered a well-done steak and like me specified, "No red when you cut it." As you waited, you would see others being served their food. From time to time your server would remind you to wait just a little bit longer and that your meal would be coming up. Even though you were hungry, you knew your well cooked and well prepared dish would be worth the wait. Sometimes when we ask God for great things we forgot that we have to patient with God. It may be that the person God is going to have work with us on a particular project is at another job and has to move in order for your project to start. It may be that you or someone else has to go through a specific training or experience for God to answer your prayer. Whatever the reason, God is working behind the scenes to answer your prayer, as long as it is a prayer in accordance with God's will and purpose. So what if the answers to your promise from God are taking longer than expected. If God said it, God will bring it to pass. Hold tight, your answer from God is coming up. And it will be worth the wait!

© By Dr. Sheila Hayford.

March 18
God Is A God Of His Word

Numbers Chapter 23, verse 19:
God is not a man, that he should lie; neither the son of man, that he should repent: hath he said, and shall he not do it? or hath he spoken, and shall he not make it good?

Prayer: Our heavenly Father, we are so grateful that you are God, without the fallibles of man. We trust ourselves to you and to your Word. In the name of Jesus we pray. Amen.

What promises has God made to you? What conditions were attached? Are you willing to see those promises fulfilled? Are you obeying God's instructions? Are you forgiving towards others and walking in love? If so, trust God to be a God who keeps His Word.

© By Dr. Sheila Hayford.

March 19
A Higher Level of Praise

Psalm 65, verses 11-13:
You crown the year with your bounty, and your carts overflow with abundance. The grasslands of the wilderness overflow; the hills are clothed with gladness. The meadows are covered with flocks and the valleys are mantled with grain; they shout for joy and sing. (NIV)

Prayer: Dear God; what a joy to join nature in singing the praises of our great God, the Creator of heaven and earth! Thank you for all the people and good things you have blessed us with. And thank you most of all for the gift of your Son, our Lord Jesus Christ. Amen.

It is easy to praise and thank God for answered prayer. It is easy to praise God in worship with fellow believers at a church service. Thank God for the Lord Jesus Christ, through whom we enjoy salvation. How about praising God for the many things we sometimes take for granted? How about praising God for the rain he provides, the food he allows us to grow and harvest, the flocks he has created that we have for food, even the free air that we breathe? The challenge is a higher level of praise to our God. Let us join the hills, the meadows and creation in songs of praise to our God!

© By Dr. Sheila Hayford.

March 20
Ornaments

Revelations Chapter 3, verse 12:
Him that overcometh will I make a pillar in the temple of my God, and he shall go no more out: and I will write upon him the name of my God, and the name of the city of my God, which is new Jerusalem, which cometh down out of heaven from my God: and I will write upon him my new name.

Prayer: Dear God; help me to display the beautiful ornaments the Holy Spirit has adorned me; in meekness, with joy and the radiance of your love. In Jesus' Name. Amen.

I gave a friend a card and enclosed an ornament with the word "JOY". She was elated and shared with me that she had chosen Joy as the theme for her home for the holidays and the coming year. After that, I was shopping for Christmas gifts for two friends and the Holy Spirit led me to two beautiful ornaments. Then I went to buy a box of Christmas cards and, you probably guessed, it included designs of different ornaments! It dawned on me that the Holy Spirit was trying to tell me something. An ornament is usually a thing of beauty. It is not meant to be hidden; it is meant to be displayed. We admire the beauty and sometimes the intricacy of the ornament. We admire the talent of the creator of the ornament. And we enjoy displaying the ornament so others can also experience the joy of its beauty. As the bride of Christ we are to be adorned with the beautiful ornaments the Holy Spirit gives to us, love, joy, peace and the fruit of the Holy Spirit. Our ornaments are meant to be displayed, to be shared, and to give glory to our creator. What do your ornaments say about you? And what do your ornaments tell others about your Creator? In the New Jerusalem the foundations of the walls of the city will be garnished with all manner of precious stones, beautifully decorated. The presence of God will dwell in that holy city. Will you be there?

© By Dr. Sheila Hayford.

March 21
Pay Your Vows

Deuteronomy Chapter 23, verse 21:
When thou shalt vow a vow unto the LORD thy God, thou shalt not slack to pay it: for the LORD thy God will surely require it of thee; and it would be sin in thee.

Prayer: Dear Lord God; help me fulfill my vows for you have no pleasure in foolish, impulsive vows. In the name of Jesus. Amen.

At the beginning of a New Year, many people make New Year Resolutions. Think of the resolutions you made for this year. How many of those have you kept? Resolutions, somehow, are by definition flexible. If you want, you can change them. If you do not keep them, you generally are not penalized. Not so with vows. When you make a vow to your spouse, you are committing yourself to keep them. And when you make a vow to God, God is holding you accountable to keep it. If a person breaks their marriage vows there are usually unpleasant consequences. If a person breaks their vows to God, the same is generally true. Indeed, it is better not to make a vow to God than to make one and not keep it. So what should we do if we make a vow to God and do not keep it? Are we to live under condemnation? No! The Lord Jesus came that we who believe on him will not be condemned. If we fail to keep a vow to God, the first thing we must do is acknowledge that sin against God and ask God for forgiveness through our Lord Jesus Christ. The Holy Spirit is available to help us fulfil our vows to God but we have our part to play. God is not interested in rash vows, made without careful consideration. We must also make realistic vows, or sometimes conditional vows, that we intend to keep. We must only make or enter into vows that are pleasing to God. When Queen Jezebel vowed to kill the prophet Elijah, she in effect cursed herself and her body was torn up by dogs in the end. The reward of a vow made to God and kept is priceless!

© By Dr. Sheila Hayford.

March 22
Do It For The Sake Of Peace

Romans Chapter 12, verse 18:
If it be possible, as much as lieth in you, live peaceably with all men.

Prayer: Dear God: Help me to pursue peace, first with you and then with my fellow man. Help me remember my allegiance is to you first, so I will not compromise my walk or participate in evil in a misguided attempt to keep the peace at all costs. In the Name of Jesus, I pray. Amen.

The lady had a particular idiosyncrasy; it was not harmful, nor sinful, it was just inconvenient and most of the time unnecessary. I remember the time I did not feel like accommodating her. "Do it anyway!" the Holy Spirit said to me. "Why?" I asked. "For the sake of peace." was the Holy Spirit's reply. I did, and gained favor; favor with God and man. Hallelujah!

© By Dr. Sheila Hayford.

March 23
Good Soil: The Soil Of Obedience

Matthew Chapter 13, verse 23:
But the seed falling on good soil refers to someone who hears the word and understands it. This is the one who produces a crop, yielding a hundred, sixty or thirty times what was sown." (N.I.V.)

Prayer: Dear God, may I always be good seed into which the word of God is sown. May the harvest of my obedience to you be a bountiful one, one that is so abundant it has to be shared. And may we give you all the glory. In Jesus Name, Amen.

In this verse, the seed falling on good soil refers to the one who does something with what he hears and understands. This person responds to what God says with action and that action is in obedience to God. As a result, their works yield good fruit. The Bible tells us in the book of Matthew Chapter 7 that we will be known by the fruit we produce.

What fruit are we yielding?

© By Dr. Sheila Hayford.

March 24
Break Free

Genesis Chapter 24, verses 55-58:

And her brother and her mother said, Let the damsel abide with us a few days, at the least ten; after that she shall go. And he said unto them, Hinder me not, seeing the Lord hath prospered my way; send me away that I may go to my master. And they said, We will call the damsel, and enquire at her mouth. And they called Rebekah, and said unto her, Wilt thou go with this man? And she said, I will go.

Prayer: Dear Lord God, help me not to allow myself to be hindered by unnecessary weights or by the words and actions of others. I declare that I break free into my future with great rejoicing. Amen.

- Break loose from your past
- Break free from bondage, hindrances and oppression
- Break free into your future
- Break out in Song!

© By Dr. Sheila Hayford.

March 25
The Power To Build And The Power To Tear Down

Jeremiah Chapter 1, verses 8-10:

Then the Lord put forth his hand, and touched my mouth. And the Lord said unto me, Behold, I have put my words in thy mouth. See, I have this day set thee over the nations and over the kingdoms, to root out, and to pull down, and to destroy, and to throw down, to build, and to plant.

Prayer: My heavenly Father, over the years I have been astounded at the power of my words, words that were spoken in the power of God.

Help me to remain faithful to you and to your call. In the Name of Jesus I pray. Amen.

How powerful are your words? Very powerful! What a profound revelation! In these verses God promises to give Jeremiah the words to speak. And note the effects or the results that will accompany the words that Jeremiah speaks. His words will have effect over nations and kingdoms, the power to root out, pull down, destroy, throw down, build and to plant. What is true of Jeremiah's words is still true of our words today. Since this is true, why don't many use their words to effect positive change? Part of the reason may be that they do not realize how powerful their words are. Words are an essential tool of communication and satan knows that. Words can hurt and words can destroy. However, words can also heal, build and plant. In verse 12 of the same chapter, we see that God is watching over God's words to bring them to pass. On the other side, the devil is listening to your words to see whether he can find an opening to wreak havoc in your life. So whose words will you agree to speak, God's or satan's? The power of God is in your words because every word has to bow to words spoken in the authority of our Lord and Savior Jesus Christ. Speak God's powerful words!

© By Dr. Sheila Hayford.

March 26
Thankfulness ... And The List Goes On ...

Psalm 92, verse 1:
It is a good thing to give thanks unto the Lord, and to sing praises unto thy name, O Most High:
Prayer: Dear Lord God: Thank you for the opportunity to say thanks for all your manifold blessings. We could not find enough words to express our gratitude for we do not know all the things you do for us behind the scenes. We bless you, we magnify your holy name, we give

you glory and we say with all our being, Thank you! In Jesus' Name. Amen.

Thankfulness to God and to our fellow man, thankful for who we are and for what God has blessed us with. There are just so many reasons to be thankful. List some of the reasons you are thankful. And the list goes on and on and on …

© By Dr. Sheila Hayford.

March 27
Too Large To Fit

Isaiah Chapter 57, verse 15:
For thus saith the high and lofty One that inhabiteth eternity, whose name is Holy; I dwell in the high and holy place, with him also that is of a contrite and humble spirit, to revive the spirit of the humble, and to revive the heart of the contrite ones.

Prayer: Dear Lord Jesus, thank you for the gift of the Holy Spirit. Help us to remember that the Holy Spirit inside us is limitless and he will enable us to live large in Christ in God. Amen.

When the National Museum of African American History and Culture was being built in Washington, D.C., there were some items that needed to be in there that would not fit through the regular size doors for passage. The solution? Put that item in place and then build around it. The same is true of every born again believer. The Holy Spirit that lives inside of us is too large to fit into our finite minds. So the Holy Spirit works through our spirit to reveal the plans, purpose and will of God for us and for mankind. Then our spirit understands what our mind may not have fully grasped about God. As we renew our way of thinking and living with the Word of God, God's building in us becomes evident. The National History of African American History and Culture is very inspiring, not because everything in it is right or perfect but because it brings to light the sacrifices and the struggles of a people seeking to live out their true identity. As we live for God we will experience challenges, and for some sacrifices. The process is not flawless; it is a testament to the transforming power of God to bring us a mighty long way.

© By Dr. Sheila Hayford.

March 28
Permeate With Joy

1 Kings Chapter 8, verse 66:
On the eighth day he sent the people away: and they blessed the king, and went unto their tents joyful and glad of heart for all the goodness that the Lord had done for David his servant, and for Israel his people.

Prayer: Dear Holy Spirit, joy is such a beautiful thing and we need more of it in the world. Help us so live that we will permeate our environment with the fragrance of your joy. Amen.

When you permeate an area with something, you saturate the area in such a way that its fragrance is obvious. When you saturate your circumstances with the joy of the Lord, you saturate your circumstances with a fragrance that is pleasing to God. And you allow the presence of God to encourage, strengthen and uplift you. For as Nehemiah Chapter 8, verse 10 reminds us, the joy of the Lord is our strength. Do not let the pressures of life wear you down; let the joy of the Lord lift you up!

© By Dr. Sheila Hayford.

March 29
Transparent Words

Psalm 139, verse 4:
Before a word is on my tongue you, Lord, know it completely. (NIV)

Prayer: What an awesome God you are! You know me thoroughly, human imperfections and all, and yet you still chose me before the foundation of the world.

Thank you for sending Jesus Christ to die for the sins of mankind. Help us to always be transparent with you. Amen.

Growing up, we were taught to think about what we were going to say before we spoke. The idea was you could not go back and as it were "eat your words." That was a great lesson in self-control and that adage would still do much good if applied today.

Now imagine this. God, all-knowing, knows what you are planning to say completely, whether you actually say the words or not. In other words, God knows completely what we are thinking. God also knows the motives behind our words and thoughts. What God desires from us is transparency before Him. In our relationship with God, God desires an honest expression of who we are, where we are, what we are thinking and feeling and what we want to be and do when we come to him. Being truthful with God and each other opens the door for authentic relationships. Speak the truth in love, not out of a desire to hurt or damage a person's self-esteem.

Let us allow the Holy Spirit to speak to us, speak in us as we pray, and to speak through us as we reach out to others.

© By Dr. Sheila Hayford.

March 30
It Is What God Says It Is

Numbers Chapter 23, verse 19:

God is not a man, that he should lie; neither the son of man, that he should repent: hath he said, and shall he not do it? or hath he spoken, and shall he not make it good?

Prayer: Dear Lord God, we do not have all the answers but you do. That is why it is so reassuring to hear you affirm your infallibility. Keep us by your keeping power. In Jesus' name. Amen.

You may have heard some say, "it is what it is" to describe a situation over which they feel they have no control. I personally do not use that expression. I say, "It is what God says it is." Why? The former implies that there is nothing you can do to change or fix the situation. I say, God's Word is always the final word in any situation. What if one is experiencing something that is not in conformity to God's will? I can and should always pray about the situation and ask God for direction on how to proceed. It may be that God wants me to stay put and use me as a vehicle of change. It may be that God, who knows the end from the beginning, wants me to move out of that situation because God has other plans for me. Either way, I live my life knowing that it is what God says it is.

© By Dr. Sheila Hayford.

March 31
Don't Fret

Isaiah Chapter 29, verse 24-26:
Can plunder be taken from warriors, or captives be rescued from the fierce? But this is what the Lord says: "Yes, captives will be taken from warriors, and plunder retrieved from the fierce; I will contend with those who contend with you, and your children I will save. (NIV)
Prayer: Dear Lord God, I make the decision to trust you and not to worry. I believe in you and I believe your Word. And that is more than enough for me. Amen.

Most of us have been treated unfairly at one time or another. In the past I would pray, fret and seek some godly counsel but I did not experience the peace of God. That was until God revealed the depth of this verse to me. God is contending with those who contend with me. What! There is just no way anyone can fight against God and win. I have this all powerful God contending on a present continual basis on my behalf! I can rest thoroughly assured that God knows exactly what He is doing and how to accomplish His end result. Now, I allow God to do His work and I focus on what God has called me to do. I love working with God and consider my adversary an indication of my greater success with God. You know, God had been doing this all along. However, because the victory manifestation sometimes took years it looked in the beginning like evil won. Until God was finished. Then God's victory was apparent. We serve a God who is interested in our personal wellbeing. Fret not! We are all on God's time!

© By Dr. Sheila Hayford.

April 1
Minister Out Of Your Healing

Luke Chapter 8, verse 18:
Take heed therefore how ye hear: for whosoever hath, to him shall be given; and whosoever hath not, from him shall be taken even that which he seemeth to have.

Prayer: Dear Lord God, we love to share your goodness with others. Help us to depend on you for the right words, the right attitude and the right timing. In the Name of Jesus we pray, Amen.

Minister to others out of your healing, not out of your hurt. I have heard people say that sometimes you go through an experience so that you can help someone who may be going through the same or a similar experience. While that is true, you have to be careful who you allow to speak into your life. If someone has just come through a bitter divorce and cannot talk about their ex-spouse without spluttering a curse word, it would not be wise to seek marriage counsel from that person. But if that person has allowed God to heal them, has reevaluated their life and can clearly see some of the pitfalls that if prevented could have saved their marriage, their counsel to a young bride may be extremely helpful and possibly invaluable. The moral of this example? Allow people to earn the right to speak into your life and take heed what and how you hear.

© By Dr. Sheila Hayford.

April 2
Justice Delayed

Psalms 9, verses 7, 8:
But the Lord shall endure for ever: he hath prepared his throne for judgment. And he shall judge the world in righteousness, he shall minister judgment to the people in uprightness.

Prayer: Dear God, with you there is no such thing as justice denied. Thankfully we live in a day of God's justice tempered with God's grace and God's mercy. Help us not to squander your goodness for a day is coming where those who reject God and persist in sin will face their day of reckoning with you. Help us do our part to lead others to your grace and mercy. Amen.

With God justice delayed is not denied. Sometimes you hear expressions such as "they got away with ..." In other words, they did not get the just punishment or reprimand for their actions. Not so with God. There is a day coming when the Lord will judge every person righteously. Is that supposed to be a day of terror? It depends on whose side you are on. We are living in a day of God's grace and mercy, grace and mercy intended to give mankind the opportunity to repent of sin and turn to the Lord Jesus for salvation.

Hebrews Chapter 10 tells us: For we know him that hath said, Vengeance belongeth unto me, I will recompense, saith the Lord. Let God do God's thing in God's time.

© By Dr. Sheila Hayford.

April 3
No Parties In Hell

Luke Chapter 16, verses 23-29:

And in hell he lift up his eyes, being in torments, and seeth Abraham afar off, and Lazarus in his bosom. And he cried and said, Father Abraham, have mercy on me, and send Lazarus, that he may dip the tip of his finger in water, and cool my tongue; for I am tormented in this flame. But Abraham said, Son, remember that thou in thy lifetime receivedst thy good things, and likewise Lazarus evil things: but now he is comforted, and thou art tormented. And beside all this, between us and you there is a great gulf fixed: so that they which would pass from hence to you cannot; neither can they pass to us, that would come from thence. Then he said, I pray thee therefore, father, that thou wouldest send him to my father's house: For I have five brethren; that he may testify unto them, lest they also come into this place of torment. Abraham saith unto him, They have Moses and the prophets; let them hear them.

Prayer: Dear Lord Jesus; we are eternally grateful to you for our salvation. Hell is not a fun place and we have no part of hell because of you. Help us to do our part to warn others of the deceitful lies of satan. Amen.

In my teenage years, when we would share our faith with others some would say in jest that they would be partying in hell and then they would name some people that they thought they would be partying with in hell. Hell is too serious a subject to take lightly. The Bible says hell is a real place where the fire burns forever but the flesh of those in hell is not consumed. There is only torment in hell, no partying. The man in this story wanted someone to warn those on earth about the torment in hell so they would not come to hell. God reminded him that those on earth have the words of the prophets, written for us in the Bible. Take heed and take action. The Lord Jesus does not want you in hell; the Lord Jesus wants you to spend eternity with him. He died on the cross for the sins of all humanity so we will not have to spend eternity in hell. Repent of your sins, ask the Lord Jesus for forgiveness and invite the Lord Jesus Christ into your heart as your Lord and Savior. You will be welcomed with open arms into the family of God. Then tell satan you are having no part in hell!

© By Dr. Sheila Hayford.

April 4
Who Baked The Cake?

Isaiah Chapter 44, verses 2, 3: Thus saith the Lord that made thee, and formed thee from the womb, which will help thee; Fear not, O Jacob, my servant; and thou, Jesurun, whom I have chosen. For I will pour water upon him that is thirsty, and floods upon the dry ground: I will pour my spirit upon thy seed, and my blessing upon thine offspring:

Prayer: Dear God; you have made your creation so beautiful and your will in creation known. We adore you! In Jesus' Name. Amen.

Imagine you walked into a beautiful, pristine clean kitchen. And there in the center of the kitchen table is a beautiful baked cake. While you are looking at the kitchen and the cake someone tells you the cake just appeared there. "What do you mean the cake just appeared? Someone had to have baked it and put it there." is your reply.

When we look at creation, we read the Biblical account of God creating the heavens and the earth. We see nature, the trees, the flowers, the rivers. We look at the beautiful newborn baby wrapped in blankets shortly after birth. As you look at your newborn "cake" someone gives you a theory about how your newborn baby just came to be. You contrast that with what the Bible says. And then you make up your mind for yourself.

© By Dr. Sheila Hayford.

April 5
Afraid To Share Jesus

Ezekiel Chapter 3, verses 18, 19: When I say unto the wicked, Thou shalt surely die; and thou givest him not warning, nor speakest to warn the wicked from his wicked way, to save his life; the same wicked man shall die in his iniquity; but his blood will I require at thine hand. Yet if thou warn the wicked, and he turn not from his wickedness, nor from his wicked way, he shall die in his iniquity; but thou hast delivered thy soul.

Prayer: Dear Lord Jesus, help me not to be a selfish Christian. I repent for withholding the goodness of your salvation in the busyness of daily life. Enable me to be sensitive to the promptings of the Holy Spirit and do my part in sharing you with others. Amen.

I was in transit when this woman came up to me. She was so excited. She turned to me and said Jesus had done something wonderful for her. And so I said, "What did Jesus do for you?" Suddenly her demeanor changed. "You see that lady over there, she can tell you what happened. I looked and that lady was further down so I said to her, "Since you are right here, why don't you tell me what happened?" I did not tell her I was a Christian. She replied, "I'd rather not." And then she walked away.

The warning in Ezekiel is clear. "Yet if thou warn the wicked, and he turn not from his wickedness, nor from his wicked way, he shall die in his iniquity; but thou hast delivered thy soul." May we each do our part in sharing Jesus.

© By Dr. Sheila Hayford.

April 6
Humility

Hebrews Chapter 10, verses 9-10:

Then said he, Lo, I come to do thy will, O God. He taketh away the first, that he may establish the second. By the which will we are sanctified through the offering of the body of Jesus Christ once for all.

Prayer: Dear Lord Jesus: Your humility amazes me. Thank you for submitting to the will of God in the salvation of humanity. Enable us to willingly and joyfully submit to God's will for our lives. Amen.

Here we see the Lord Jesus, referred to in Scripture as the second Adam, willingly submitting to the will of God even though it was not always pretty and in his death downright degrading. The Son of God was asked by God the Father to come to earth, live as a man and die for the sins of humanity. Sin came about because of the disobedience of Adam and Eve, the forefathers of the human race, towards God. The salvation of humanity comes as a result of the obedience of the Lord Jesus to God.

What do you do when God asks you to do something that is not of your liking or seemingly inconvenient? You obey God anyway by humbly submitting to the will of God. The Lord Jesus rose from the dead and God our heavenly Father rewarded the Lord Jesus with a Name that is above every name and with a bride comprised of the church from all tribes and nations of the world. Was it worth it? Definitely! You and I are now part of the family of God.

© By Dr. Sheila Hayford.

April 7
Promoted By God

Philippians Chapter 2, verses 5-9:

Let this mind be in you, which was also in Christ Jesus: Who, being in the form of God, thought it not robbery to be equal with God: But made himself of no reputation, and took upon him the form of a servant, and was made in the likeness of men: And being found in fashion as a man, he humbled himself, and became obedient unto death, even the death of the cross. Wherefore God also hath highly exalted him, and given him a name which is above every name:

Prayer: Dear Lord God, sometimes satan tries to make obedience to God seem restricting, unpleasant or undesirable. Help us reject satan's lies and look forward with joy to the eternal rewards you have planned for us as we live in obedience to you. In Jesus' Name. Amen.

Growing up, I was taught in class to memorize Chapter 2 of the book of Philippians. This chapter has been and will always be very special to me. Here we see the Lord Jesus humble himself in obedience to the will and ways of God.

Remember the Lord Jesus was with God the Father and God the Holy Spirit in Creation. However, the Lord Jesus did not say it was too low for him to come and live among men and then die on the cross for our sins. Obedience to God's will is never the end of the story because God rewards obedience. Jesus' obedience to God set him up for promotion by God. What promotion is God setting you up for? You will have to obey God to find out.

© By Dr. Sheila Hayford.

April 8
By Chance Or By Choice

Genesis Chapter 1, verse 8:
And the child grew, and was weaned: and Abraham made a great feast the same day that Isaac was weaned.

Prayer: Dear God; when we look at our life events we see your hand at work. We see the good you intended and the good you worked out of what satan hoped would be evil. Like Joseph in the book of Genesis, we know it is for the saving of many. For unto you belongs all the glory! Amen.

It was a Baby Dedication ceremony and the baby girl looked so beautiful. The baby girl had on a gorgeous outfit, smiled and did not cry all throughout the baby dedication. Her parents were young and looked to be in their twenties. Even though they were not married, they both wanted their daughter dedicated during the church service. The two godmothers at their side looked to be in their twenties also. I silently prayed that God would provide older members who could also help mentor the young parents. The Pastor was very gracious. He was very respectful of the two godmothers and the baby dedication went on without a glitch. The rest of the service continued. The presence of the Holy Spirit was obvious. At the end of the service the Pastor gave the invitation for those who would like to accept the Lord Jesus as Lord and Savior. He asked those who wished to invite the Lord Jesus into their heart to come forward to the altar. One of the godmothers came down and affirmed her decision to invite the Lord Jesus into her heart as Lord and Savior. She prayed the prayer of salvation and was thus born again, this time into the family of God. I do not know who was the happier; the godmother who had just received Christ, the Pastor, the congregation, the angels rejoicing in heaven, the baby girl or her parents! For sure, our Lord Jesus was super happy!

As I reflected on the events of the day I said to myself, "We had two baby dedications, one born naturally and the other born supernaturally." The young parents and their baby girl had sown a wonderful seed into the kingdom of God, the baby's godmother. And God would certainly bless them. No wonder the baby girl was smiling all throughout the dedication! And then I thought, with God nothing happens by chance, only by choice. Wouldn't you agree?

© By Dr. Sheila Hayford.

April 9
God Cannot ...

1 Corinthians Chapter 15, verse 57:

But thanks be to God, which giveth us the victory through our Lord Jesus Christ.

Prayer: Dear God, you have already given me the victory through Jesus Christ! I choose to align myself with your mission and your purpose, knowing that as God, you will never fail. Hallelujah! Thank you, Jesus! Amen.

- God cannot change
- God cannot fail
- God cannot gloss over sin
- God cannot lie
- God cannot lose

And so, beloved in Christ, through our Lord Jesus Christ we win!

© By Dr. Sheila Hayford.

April 10
Double Standards

Matthew Chapter 23, verse 23:

Woe unto you, scribes and Pharisees, hypocrites! for ye pay tithe of mint and anise and cummin, and have omitted the weightier matters of the law, judgment, mercy, and faith: these ought ye to have done, and not to leave the other undone.

Prayer: Dear Lord Jesus, you hate hypocrisy or "phony" for our heavenly Father is just. Help me do my part for the betterment of society. Amen.

Double standards abound in society. You cannot take someone else's money by "crooked" means and then when caught expect the consumer you wronged to bail you out. That is, unless you are a bank that is deemed "too big to fail" and the very consumers are the ones who are made to bail you out. You cannot have true justice when the results are determined by whether a person is rich or poor, black or white, educated or uneducated, in or out of uniform, informed or uninformed.

So what does the Lord God have to say about this? Plenty! You see, it is one thing to acknowledge that the problem exists but when you hold others to a standard and fail to hold yourself to that standard, there is a disconnect and God would rather have you be "all in" or "all out."

© By Dr. Sheila Hayford.

April 11
Coming With Everything Pure

Ephesians Chapter 4, verse 18:

Till we all come in the unity of the faith, and of the knowledge of the Son of God, unto a perfect man, unto the measure of the stature of the fulness of Christ:

Prayer: My heavenly Father, what joy and privilege to spend time with you, even while the angels are doing your bidding. I love you and I bless you. In Jesus' Name, Amen.

It was past my chosen time for prayer and meditation with God and I had already hit the snooze button a couple of times. I went downstairs, prepared a quick breakfast and came back upstairs. The Holy Spirit gently nudged me, reminding me that God was waiting for my time with Him. That got me thinking. Who was happier about our meeting? Was it me; because I love to hear God speak? On the other hand, was it God?

Then I had this revelation. God is coming to meet me with <u>Everything Pure.</u> Pure Motives. Pure Agenda. Pure Love. Pure Truth. Pure Jesus. Pure everything! Through the righteousness of our Lord Jesus Christ, human beings have an audience with this Pure God. There is no matching that!

© By Dr. Sheila Hayford.

SALON RISPOLI

Tel: (302) 731-9202

- Hair Styling. Waxing. Traditional and Fashion Color Services.
- Hair Texture Services. Keratin Treatments ... and More!

Gift certificates available!

◆ ◆ ◆ ◆

AVON – Skin Care, Fragrance, Apparel and Much more....

Kate and Emmy- Your Avon Representatives
701 N. Broad Street, Middletown Farmers Market
Call or come in for catalogs, orders,
FREE Avon samples, plus we deliver
Let Us Wow you with our Season specials!

302-995-2447 (Sun to Wed)
302-354-3565 (Thurs to Sat)

You may also order online at:
www.youravon.com/kateandemmy

Come in for your FREE Lipstick samples

* * * PAMPER YOURSELF * * *

April 12
Serving God

Job Chapter 1, verse 9, 10:

Then Satan answered the Lord, and said, Doth Job fear God for nought? Hast not thou made an hedge about him, and about his house, and about all that he hath on every side? thou hast blessed the work of his hands, and his substance is increased in the land.

Prayer; Dear God, we come to you, not primarily for the gifts but first because of who you are; God. We acknowledge and appreciate you and thank you for all your gifts. In Jesus' Name we pray. Amen.

Serving God has its benefits. Satan knows that. Even satan acknowledged these benefits of Job's service to God; God's protection on Job and all that Job had, the blessing of Job's work and wealth. As the accuser of the brethren, satan tried to ascribe to Job an ulterior motive for serving God by implying that Job was only serving God for what he could get from God.

If satan acknowledged that God our heavenly Father is giving good things to his children, why do some have a hard time acknowledging the fact that God is a good God? God, who knew Job's heart, knew that was not Job's motive and allowed Job to prove that to satan. Listen to Job's Words in Job Chapter 13, "Though he slay me, yet will I trust in him: but I will maintain mine own ways before him." Wow!

Can God count on you, with God's power, to put satan's words about you to naught? If you asked Job if his challenges were worthwhile in the end, he would say "Yes!" And God? God gave Job twice as much as he had before; double blessings for all Job's troubles!

© By Dr. Sheila Hayford.

April 13
Put Your Mouth To Work!

Matthew Chapter 17, verse 20:
He replied, "Because you have so little faith. Truly I tell you, if you have faith as small as a mustard seed, you can say to this mountain, 'Move from here to there,' and it will move. Nothing will be impossible for you."

Prayer: Dear Lord Jesus, sometimes the obstacles and challenges in life may look intimidating. However, everything is subject to the authority of your Name, the Name of Jesus. May we follow your example and speak in faith to our mountains daily in your Name, for then nothing will be impossible for us. Amen.

The Lord Jesus says it so well in this verse. When we have a mountain in our life we should not just look passively at the mountain, complain or gossip about the mountain. We need to speak to the mountain and tell the mountain what we want it to do by faith, using the authority of the Name of Jesus. With Jesus authority, speaking the will of God for your life in faith will bring about the desired result because Jesus said nothing will be impossible for you. Do you believe this? If so, put your mouth to work for you!

© By Dr. Sheila Hayford.

April 14
Stereotyping Breeds Resentment

Deuteronomy Chapter 27, verse 19:
"Cursed is anyone who withholds justice from the foreigner, the fatherless or the widow." Then all the people shall say, "Amen!"
Prayer: My heavenly Father, thank you for the diversity you created in mankind. The devil is the author of division and discord and tries to sow discord among the brethren and in this world. Enable us to walk in wisdom for we know that there are wolves who try to devour the innocent. We are not intimidated by fear for God's perfect love casts out all fear. And so we choose to walk in God's love and to extend God's love towards others. In Jesus' Name. Amen.

Is racial profiling Biblical? Is it fair to say, "All blacks are…", all whites are…", "all Hispanics are…", "all Muslims are …", all Buddhists are…", or to use terms such as "angry white men" or "angry black women" and the like. I would hear people say things like, "all the young people these days are…" and then use negative words to describe them. When I would ask them if their kids were like that they would reply in horror: "No!" And then I would say, "So all young people are not like that." In America, many organizations and businesses ask clients to fill out forms that ask for their race. And we generally do not think twice about that. Well, one day there was a parent who came into the office and on the form where it asked for the race of her child, she put the word, "human." It seemed funny at the time but in all seriousness, she "got it!" Every human being is a part of humanity, the human race. And every human being is entitled to dignity and respect. The devil is a master mind when it comes to planting division and strife and he gives many the opportunity to pick their mode of division; Democrat or Republican, black or white, rich or poor, educated or un-educated, male or female, Roman Catholic or Protestant, Native American or immigrant. In truth, the main thing that unites all humanity is our need for a Savior, and that need is independent of race, gender, socio-economic or educational status. It is our response to the Lord Jesus that will determine where and how we spend eternity. Eternity is a long time and heaven and hell are real places. Life on this earth is temporal. Wouldn't it be more productive to share the love of God and the good news of salvation with others?

© By Dr. Sheila Hayford.

April 15
The Manna Principal – Sufficient For The Journey

Exodus Chapter 16, verse 35:
The Israelites ate manna forty years, until they came to a land that was settled; they ate manna until they reached the border of Canaan.

Prayer: Dear God, you are the perfect Father and we will always receive your care, nourishment and protection as we live in obedience to you. You are more than enough for our journey, on this earth and throughout eternity. Amen.

God gave the Israelites the food described as manna with specific instructions. They were to gather what they would eat for the day, except for the sixth day when they would gather enough for the sixth and seventh days. If manna was left over till the following day, it would breed worms and stink. God gave us what I refer to as The Manna Principle.

There are times in life when we do not need to be cumbered by what worked in the past. The manna provided nourishment at a specific time in the journey of the Israelites after they left Egypt as they headed for the land of Canaan. God provided the manna they needed for each day in the wilderness. When they got to Canaan and could work and plant their own food, the miraculous manna provision by God stopped. What is sufficient for your journey today may not get you where you want to be tomorrow. What provided nourishment for you yesterday may not necessarily nourish you today. It might even "stink" if you tried to eat it today. What you brought into this year is not necessarily meant for you to take into next year. It takes God's wisdom and direction to discern what we need to have and when we need to have it.

Let us look to God for His guidance and wisdom today.

© By Dr. Sheila Hayford.

April 16
Always Learning

Proverbs Chapter 1, verse 5:
A wise man will hear, and will increase learning; and a man of understanding shall attain unto wise counsels:
Prayer: Dear Holy Spirit, help me to appreciate and value wisdom with understanding and enable me to be submissive to your teaching and your correction. Through Jesus Christ the Lord, Amen.

We can always learn something. A wise person will have a humble attitude because you can always learn something, even from a little child.

When a person stops learning, they stunt their growth and stop growing. That is why it is possible for a person to be older in age but not necessarily wiser. This verse takes learning a step further. A wise person will also seek wise counsel. In other words, a wise person will hang around those who can give him good counsel. Psalm 111 says that the fear (or reverence) of the Lord is the beginning of wisdom. Are you seeking God's wisdom? Are you applying God's wisdom? Are you learning from God's wisdom?

© By Dr. Sheila Hayford.

April 17
Come And Talk With Me

Isaiah Chapter 1, verse 18:
Come now, and let us reason together, saith the Lord: though your sins be as scarlet, they shall be as white as snow; though they be red like crimson, they shall be as wool.

Prayer: Dear God, I receive your invitation to talk with you and so I come to you now in humility. Let's talk! In Jesus' Name. Amen.

The Lord God gives us the invitation to come and talk with him. "But you don't understand" you might say, "I know I should have done such and such (whatever that such and such may be) but I did not." To which God replies, "Come and talk to me about it."

There is no need to come up with excuses to have a conversation with God. No need to wait till you are worthy of God. God wants to talk with us about our issues, cleanse us of all sin and empower us to live victoriously.

That's an invitation I cannot refuse!

© By Dr. Sheila Hayford.

April 18
God's Witnesses

Isaiah Chapter 43, verses 10, 11:

Ye are my witnesses, saith the Lord, and my servant whom I have chosen: that ye may know and believe me, and understand that I am he: before me there was no God formed, neither shall there be after me. I, even I, am the Lord; and beside me there is no saviour.

Prayer: What an honor to share who God is in my life and what God does for me. Lead my steps, dear God. In Jesus' Name I pray. Amen.

A witness for God? How can that be? Remember, God is and was before we were conceived. So what is God saying here? A witness is one who can testify about something. It really has nothing to do with age. Did you see it? Did you experience it? You would ask these questions of a witness. As we interact with others, God wants us to share our love for and experience with God with them. We do not have to know everything about God but we do know what God has done for us through the Lord Jesus Christ. If an angel told you the good news about what God will do for you, you would probably be elated. If your fellow man shared with you what God did in their lives, you would probably say, "If God did that for them, God can do this for me." That way, you get to experience God for yourself. You now become God's witness. And the God gift sharing continues. Hallelujah!

© By Dr. Sheila Hayford.

April 19
God's Love Has Purpose

John Chapter 3, verses 16, 17:

For God so loved the world, that he gave his only begotten Son, that whosoever believeth in him should not perish, but have everlasting life.

For God sent not his Son into the world to condemn the world; but that the world through him might be saved.

Prayer: Dear God, help me share your tremendous love for mankind with others. In Jesus' Name, Amen.

There are many aspects of love; one of the most important is purpose. Remember, we are talking here of true, agape, unconditional love. Does such a love have purpose? Sure, it does. God saw the plight of sinful mankind. Adam and Eve had fallen for satan's words and were now reaping the just consequences of their sin. With their disobedience came separation of man from God. God is full and complete in His divinity and was under no obligation to redeem man. Nevertheless, God is a God of love and God's love has purpose. In God's love, God provided a way of redemption for mankind to have a restored relationship with God. He sent His only begotten Son, the Lord Jesus Christ, to take on the punishment for our sins.

That is good news. Share it!

© By Dr. Sheila Hayford.

April 20
Forgiveness Begins with You

Matthew Chapter 6, verse 14:

For if ye forgive men their trespasses, your heavenly Father will also forgive you

Prayer; Dear God, I have received forgiveness from you and so I extend forgiveness to others. In the power of God the Holy Spirit. Amen.

I thought forgiveness starts with God. It does, just as love starts with God. We love because God first loved us. We give because God first gave to us. And so we forgive because God first forgave us. Why then do I write forgiveness begins with you? It is because God gives us the choice to forgive or walk in unforgiveness? And since the Lord Jesus instructs us to forgive those who offend us, unforgiveness is disobedience to the commands of God. Therefore, if a person forgives their fellow man or woman, they are walking in obedience to God and their prayers are not hindered. When that person asks God for forgiveness, they get the answer to prayer. If a person disobeys God and walks in unforgiveness, that person's prayers are hindered by disobedience to God's word. To get answers to prayer, the person has to repent of unforgiveness and walk in forgiveness and love.

You forgive, your heavenly Father forgives you; it is that simple in the eyes of God.

© By Dr. Sheila Hayford.

April 21
Respect

Daniel Chapter 6, verses 10-11: Now when Daniel knew that the writing was signed, he went into his house; and his windows being open in his chamber toward Jerusalem, he kneeled upon his knees three times a day, and prayed, and gave thanks before his God, as he did aforetime. Then these men assembled, and found Daniel praying and making supplication before his God.

Prayer: Dear God; enable me to extend respect and honor to those to whom it is due. I respect and honor who I am in Christ. Thank you for your transforming power. In Jesus' Name I pray. Amen.

I have always admired and respected Christians who are willing to stand up for their faith, especially when it involves personal sacrifice on their part. Daniel's wicked peers were jealous of his knowledge, wisdom, good works and excellent spirit and lured King Darius into signing a law that would require anyone who made a petition to their God, other than going to the king, to be thrown into the den of lions. Daniel regularly prayed three times a day by an open window so his foes thought for sure they had him. But Daniel was fearless. After the king signed the decree,

Daniel went by his window and prayed as he did before. As a result, Daniel was thrown into the den of lions. When King Darius realized the law was a plot to kill Daniel, his trusted advisor, King Darius spent the night fasting and hoping that the God of Daniel would save Daniel.

And so, early in the morning King Darius went to the den of lions asking a very pertinent question "O Daniel, servant of the living God, is thy God, whom thou servest continually, able to deliver thee from the lions?" And to the King's amazement, Daniel answered him back. God had sent his angel to shut the mouth of the hungry lions and Daniel was safe.

King Darius had Daniel released from the den of lions. But God was not done. As a result of Daniel's boldness, a new decree went out; in every dominion of King Darius, people were to reverence the God of Daniel who had rescued Daniel so miraculously.

And what happened to Daniel's accusers? They were thrown into the den of lions where the lions devoured them.

What changes are awaiting your bold and fearless Christian stance?

© By Dr. Sheila Hayford.

April 22
Second Hand Offerings

Leviticus Chapter 1, verse 3: If his offering be a burnt sacrifice of the herd, let him offer a male without blemish: he shall offer it of his own voluntary will at the door of the tabernacle of the congregation before the Lord.

Prayer: Dear God, help me not dishonor you by bringing you less than my best. I know it is not so much the amount of the offering that matters, as much as the intent and motives of the heart that offers it. The widow's mite is a perfect example. So let me not judge others for what they bring to you, but rather focus on what and how I give to you. In Jesus' Name. Amen.

It is sad but true; many people give God their second hand offerings. They allow their taxes, their Social Security, maybe even their 401K Retirement fund contribution to be taken out of their paycheck before they receive it and then out of what is left they give God a "tip" offering. Some look among their clothes and household items and see old clothes that they would not wear if they were to receive them and send them to their local Goodwill or thrift store as a "donation."

In this verse the Lord God told Moses to tell the congregation not to bring God a blemished offering, nor to bring God an offering under compulsion. It is our rightful duty to offer God our best in love and appreciation for all He has done for us in Jesus Christ, and for all that God continues to do and will do in our lives. When we make vows to God let us keep them and not make excuses.

Give God your best. For God deserves nothing less.

© By Dr. Sheila Hayford.

April 23
Lavish Appreciation

Psalm 27, verse 6:
That I may publish with the voice of thanksgiving, and tell of all thy wondrous works.

Prayer: Dear Lord God, what a joy to live a life of lavish appreciation! Thank you for all you do and all that you do through others. Help me make each day a Lavish Appreciation day, first to you and then to my fellow men and women. Amen.

One of my friends is lavish in her sincere appreciations and it is so refreshing. I gave her a calendar and she told me the calendar was so beautiful it looked like it needed to be framed! In a world with much negativity, how does she maintain such thoughtful lavish appreciation? It is because she is secure in Christ; comfortable and appreciative of the gifting and call of the Holy Spirit in and on her life. And so her lavish appreciation comes effortlessly.

What if spouses decided to have a Lavish Appreciation Day? What if children had a Lavish Appreciation Day for their parents? What if businesses had a Lavish Appreciation Month for their employees?

What if each of us made every day a genuine Lavish Appreciation Day?

© By Dr. Sheila Hayford.

Recommended Child Reads:

Miya: Caring and Sharing
Alisha – The Dog Rescuer

Available for purchase online at www. amazon.com

April 24
No Second Thoughts

Genesis Chapter 21, verse 2:

For Sarah conceived, and bare Abraham a son in his old age, at the set time of which God had spoken to him

Prayer: Dear Lord God; we know that you always have a good plan for us. Help us to trust you as we take the first steps to obey you, knowing that your timing is perfect. You will perform what you promised. Thank you. In Jesus' Name. Amen.

Why is it that God does not always show us the process when he asks us to take that first step of faith? It is because God does not want us to have second thoughts about taking that first step. God's plans for your life are that important to God!

© By Dr. Sheila Hayford.

April 25
Obey or Disobey?

Jeremiah Chapter 38, verses 17-21:

Then said Jeremiah unto Zedekiah, Thus saith the Lord, the God of hosts, the God of Israel; If thou wilt assuredly go forth unto the king of Babylon's princes, then thy soul shall live, and this city shall not be burned with fire; and thou shalt live, and thine house: But if thou wilt not go forth to the king of Babylon's princes, then shall this city be given into the hand of the Chaldeans, and they shall burn it with fire, and thou shalt not escape out of their hand. And Zedekiah the king said unto Jeremiah, I am afraid of the Jews that are fallen to the Chaldeans, lest they deliver me into their hand, and they mock me. But Jeremiah said, They shall not deliver thee. Obey, I beseech thee, the voice of the Lord, which I speak unto thee: so it shall be well unto thee, and thy soul shall live. But if thou refuse to go forth, this is the word that the Lord hath shewed me:

Prayer: Dear God; help us place our love and reverence for God and the Word of God as our first priority in life. When you speak, help us make the right choice and that is to always obey you, no matter what. In the Name of Jesus, I pray. Amen.

To obey or disobey God? It is your choice! The prophet gave King Zedekiah specific instructions from God. If obeyed, King Zedekiah and his household and the city of Jerusalem would be spared. If disobeyed, God's judgement and destruction of the city of Jerusalem would follow. So why would God warn King Zedekiah? It was because of God's love for King Zedekiah. And why would King Zedekiah disregard the instructions of God? It was because King Zedekiah had more fear for the Jews that had been captured by the Chaldeans than he had for God.

Just as God forewarned, King Nebuchadnezzar besieged and attacked Jerusalem, killing King Zedekiah's sons right in front of King Zedekiah. After that king Zedekiah's eyes were put out, he was bound in chains and carried captive.

The city of Jerusalem had to go through all that suffering because of one man's selfish disobedience to God. That is why prayer and engagement at the local and national levels are important. If the leader goes wrong, the country is pulled in the wrong direction. If the leader does right, the country is led right.

You are the leader in your family with a God given opportunity to lead your family according to God's principles. And you have the choice; to obey or disobey God? It is your call!

© By Dr. Sheila Hayford.

God's Soundbites
2016 Edition

Available at
www.amazon.com

April 26
Accountability

Proverbs Chapter 27, verses 23-27:

Be thou diligent to know the state of thy flocks, and look well to thy herds. For riches are not for ever: and doth the crown endure to every generation? The hay appeareth, and the tender grass sheweth itself, and herbs of the mountains are gathered. The lambs are for thy clothing, and the goats are the price of the field. And thou shalt have goats' milk enough for thy food, for the food of thy household, and for the maintenance for thy maidens.

Prayer: Dear God; you have entrusted us with so much. Help us, by the power of the Holy Spirit, to be good stewards and do well by you and by those you have placed in our care and under our authority. Amen.

How can you be accountable if you do not know what you have? In other words, you must take stock of what you have. As a steward of

God's resources you must ask yourself: What are your assets? What is the state of your assets? If your 401K retirement plan has age restrictions, all your money may not be available to you. After you take inventory of your assets, take inventory of your liabilities. The house you so enjoy may be costing you a million dollars by the time you finish paying all that interest. Then make changes and plans accordingly.

In my young adult life, I would buy clothes on sale, clearance and also at full price. I would wear them for a short time and then pack them in bags and give them away. It dawned on me that I needed a "budget" to limit my clothes spending so I cut it down to buying one new dress a month. Then I did even better. It was a process. If I had saved that clothes money back then it would have gained some interest!

So what are the rewards of your faithfulness and accountability to God and to others? You will have enough for yourself, your family and those to whom you have been assigned on earth and you will hear God's blessed words, "Well Done! Thou good and faithful servant!" as you are ushered in to enjoy the rewards God has planned for you eternally.

© By Dr. Sheila Hayford.

April 27
Finite Or Infinite?

Isaiah Chapter 57, verse 15:
For thus saith the high and lofty One that inhabiteth eternity, whose name is Holy; I dwell in the high and holy place, with him also that is of

a contrite and humble spirit, to revive the spirit of the humble, and to revive the heart of the contrite ones.

Prayer: Dear God, my heavenly Father; I come to you in humility. Thank you for my Savior, the Lord Jesus Christ. Thank you for the gift of the Holy Spirit who lives in me. You are always with me and I thank you for your everlasting presence. Amen.

We are all on God's time, that is, the finite time God has given us to live on this earth. And it is important that we make the most of and excel in the use of our time. So how do we do that? By setting the right priorities and focusing on the right things. That is, as we live out the finite portion of our life on this earth in Christ in God. And we can trust the infinite eternal God, our heavenly Father, who has this universe timed just right.

© By Dr. Sheila Hayford.

April 28
Strength Of Humor

Psalm 126, verses 2-3:
Then was our mouth filled with laughter, and our tongue with singing: then said they among the heathen, The Lord hath done great things for them. The Lord hath done great things for us; whereof we are glad.

Prayer: Dear Lord God; thank you for all you do for us, great and small. We continue to share the good news of your blessings, deliverance and favor in your power. May our witness draw many into the right relationship with you. In the name of Jesus we pray. Amen.

Many times we unwittingly equate God with man when we say that God has a sense of humor. The truth is that God has strength of humor. We may laugh because something is genuinely funny, something is so not funny or at the satire of the situation. However, our laughter is usually from a finite perspective. When God laughs, God laughs with eternity in mind. God, who knows the end from the beginning and everything in between, laughs at the wicked because he knows that wickedness will not continue forever. When God mocks the proud it is because God knows He has set a time when every knee will bow to the Name of Jesus Christ. So have God's strength of humor laughing with you, not at you.

© By Dr. Sheila Hayford.

April 29
Give Me Some Children!

Acts Chapter 2, verse 39:
For the promise is unto you, and to your children, and to all that are afar off, even as many as the Lord our God shall call.

Matthew Chapter 19, verse 14: Jesus said, "Let the little children come to me, and do not hinder them, for the kingdom of heaven belongs to such as these." (NIV)

Prayer: Dear God; words cannot express my appreciation for your wonderful newborn babies. I am amazed as I see their little fingers and toes and admire your glorious handiwork. Help us treat these little ones with the care and respect they deserve. In Jesus' Name. Amen.

I so appreciate God's amazing newborn babies. My colleagues in other specialties would ask me whether caring for the kids was work or play and I would say "work" with a big smile. Others would ask, "How can you stand to hear children crying?" and I would ask "what crying?" What I heard was a child expressing their discomfort or pain or their need for attention, whether it be feeding or a diaper change. What I really love about kids is that they are always happy to let you know when they feel better, whether by a look of gratitude, a smile or their exuberant youthful conversation. And yes, they grow up so fast!

So we love them, take care of them, protect them, demonstrate secure relationships they can emulate, teach them and correct them in the fear of the Lord God. God wants all of us to come to Him in childlike faith and trust. The Lord Jesus said it well when he said asked his disciples to allow the children to come to him, "Let the little children come to me, and do not hinder them, for the kingdom of heaven belongs to such as these."

© By Dr. Sheila Hayford.

April 30
After Its Kind

Genesis Chapter 1, verse 12:
And the earth brought forth grass, and herb yielding seed after his kind, and the tree yielding fruit, whose seed was in itself, after his kind: and God saw that it was good.

Prayer: Dear God, help me realize the awesome responsibility of training and mentoring a child. Help me be a godly example they may emulate. In the name of Jesus, I pray. Amen.

It is just not right the kind of bad rap many of the youth are getting these days. Is everything peachy, peachy? No! Do some youth act in ways they should not? Yes, you only have to read some of the news headlines. The more important issue should be; who raised them? In this verse, God shows us the principle of reproduction after its kind. An apple tree will naturally produce apples. If you train up a child in the right way, the natural result is for the child to live responsibly.

Is it sometimes possible for a tree to bear fruit that is different from its kind? Yes, you can graft a branch from the original tree into a different tree and obtain a fruit that is different from the original fruit. So is it possible that a child who has been acting out can be redeemed? Yes! When the child or youth is grafted with the appropriate resources that will make it possible for them to yield the right fruit.

The first grafting that has to take place is grafting into the family of God. That grafting takes place when a person receives the Lord Jesus into their heart as their Lord and Savior. So parents, do not despair if for some reason your child got grafted with the wrong crowd. God can take him or her and graft that child into greatness, greatness achieved by the power of the Holy Spirit.

Introduce children and the youth to the Lord Jesus. And then, let the Lord Jesus give them a good rap!

© By Dr. Sheila Hayford.

May 1
Obnoxious? No!

Colossians Chapter 2, verse 16:
Let no man therefore judge you in meat, or in drink, or in respect of an holyday, or of the new moon, or of the sabbath days:

James Chapter 3, verse 17: But the wisdom that is from above is first pure, then peaceable, gentle, and easy to be intreated, full of mercy and good fruits, without partiality, and without hypocrisy.

Prayer: Dear Lord God; help me to represent you well wherever I go. In the Name of Jesus, Amen.

I was at a book event, seated at my book table. It was a Saturday and I had collaborated with a local company to autograph some of my published books with each book purchase. An African-American man stopped at the table. As he looked at the Christian books on the table, he became very angry and said to me, "How can you call yourself a Christian and sell books on the sabbath?" I knew some denominations have rules for Saturdays and so I asked him to which denomination he belonged. He angrily told me he was one of the twelve tribes of Israel and asked which one of the twelve tribes of Israel I belonged to. As he continued to speak, it was obvious to me he was not of Jewish descent and that he was not talking of spiritual Israel. I could see the futility of any further discussions with him so I politely ended the conversation.

Does the Holy Spirit speak the truth in love? Yes. Is the Holy Spirit convicting? Yes. Is the Holy Spirit a wise counsellor? Yes. Is the Holy Spirit obnoxious? No!

Let our words be words the Holy Spirit would approve.

© By Dr. Sheila Hayford.

May 2
Suddenly: The Power of Unity

Acts Chapter 2, verses 1, 2:
And when the day of Pentecost was fully come, they were all with one accord in one place. And suddenly there came a sound from heaven as of a rushing mighty wind, and it filled all the house where they were sitting.

Prayer: My goodness, dear Holy Spirit, this world would be a better place if born again believers would unite and work in unity. Forgive us where we have allowed denominations, political affiliations, race and socio-economic class to cause tension and strife, instead of focusing on the core message of salvation through Jesus Christ for humanity. Enable us to see this world through God's eyes of compassion. In Jesus' Name we pray. Amen.

The Lord Jesus Christ had asked his disciples to wait in Jerusalem until they received power. And so it was that they were in Jerusalem praying. It was when they were all with one accord that the power of the Holy Spirit suddenly came.

The Lord Jesus in the garden of Gethsemane prayed for the unity of all believers. Consider how many prayers would be answered suddenly if believers were of one accord instead of the "I belong to Paul" or "I belong to this denomination" strife. The Lord Jesus said in Matthew Chapter 24, verse 14: And this gospel of the kingdom shall be preached in all the world for a witness unto all nations; and then shall the end come. So you see, God is depending on our obedience in his plan of events. This great commission is for all believers. How many suddenlys has God lined up for us?

© By Dr. Sheila Hayford.

May 3
Do You Love You?

Psalm 139, verse 14:

I will praise thee; for I am fearfully and wonderfully made: marvellous are thy works; and that my soul knoweth right well.

Prayer: Dear God; thank you for the miraculous wonder of each life. Help me not to take life for granted, but serve you lovingly with my body, mind and soul. In the name of Jesus I pray. Amen.

I find that a child reared in a loving secure home is usually loving, trusting and caring. Why? It is because the environment plays an important part in how we think about ourselves and how we relate to others. While the physical environment is important, the spiritual and soul environment is more important. Whose spiritual voice are you listening to? God or satan's? Whose thoughts are shaping your thoughts? What God says or what secular society says? And whose company do you allow in your life? Do you love the "you" God so wonderfully made? If so, show God your appreciation in praise and thanksgiving.

© By Dr. Sheila Hayford.

May 4
Build God A House

Haggai Chapter 1, verse 9:

Ye looked for much, and, lo it came to little; and when ye brought it home, I did blow upon it. Why? saith the LORD of hosts. Because of mine house that is waste, and ye run every man unto his own house

2 Corinthians Chapter 6, verse 16:

And what agreement hath the temple of God with idols? for ye are the temple of the living God; as God hath said, I will dwell in them, and walk in them; and I will be their God, and they shall be my people.

Prayer: Dear God; help us always to put you and your interests first in everything we do. In the Name of Jesus we pray. Amen.

At the beginning of the book of Haggai, God had a gripe with the Governor and people of Judah. They were saying it was not time to build God's house or temple which lay physically in ruins, even while they went about building their own houses. Think of this. If a parent provided everything for their children, wouldn't it be nice if the children did something special for the parent instead of always tending to their own needs? If that parent felt ignored or neglected by their children, would you blame that parent if they cut off their provisions for the children?

As God's creation, God has every right to demand something from us. The truth is that God has the right to demand accountability for everything he has given us. In Chapter 6 of the book of 2nd Corinthians we are reminded that the Holy Spirit lives inside every born again believer. As such, we are living temples or houses for the Holy Spirit intended to be used for the glory of God. We must, therefore, take care how we use our bodies and all God has given us.

The people of Judah experienced famine and lack when they failed to build God's house. The good news is that they heeded the word of God. The Governor and the people of Judah came together to rebuild God's temple and God promised that the glory of that temple would be greater than the former. So you see, when we repent, God has the ability to restore us and add even more blessings. And that is good news. If you want God to take care of your house, take care of God's house first!

© By Dr. Sheila Hayford.

May 5
It Looks A Mess Right Now!

Ephesians Chapter 2, verse 10:

For we are his workmanship, created in Christ Jesus unto good works, which God hath before ordained that we should walk in them.

Prayer: Dear Lord God, help me to be patient with you and the work you are doing in my life. Enable me, by the power of the Holy Spirit, to walk in sync with you. Thank you for the good works you have planned for me. In the Name of Jesus I pray. Amen

Have you seen a commercial building under construction? In the beginning, especially when the foundation is being dug, everything looks a mess. There are high tall cranes swirling around, there may be some rocks, some clay, some water, tired looking construction workers depending on the time of day and construction signs affecting the free flow of traffic. Everything looks a mess! But take a look at the architect's picture of the finished product, give it some time and lo and behold, a construction marvel! High rise expensive condominiums now up for sale! The investor knew the rewards were coming, maybe before most people did. He or she did something with their faith and the finished product proves the point. As believers in Christ, we are God's workmanship, under construction. Sometimes the process does not look pretty. Sometimes the process is uncomfortable. But God already has the finished product view in mind and knows it is just a matter of giving the process time to work. And then voila! Here we are in glory, clothed in Christ glorious righteousness, shining for the universe to behold!

© By Dr. Sheila Hayford.

May 6
The Anointing

Isaiah Chapter 61, verse 1:

The Spirit of the Lord God is upon me; because the Lord hath anointed me to preach good tidings unto the meek; he hath sent me to bind up the brokenhearted, to proclaim liberty to the captives, and the opening of the prison to them that are bound;

Prayer: Dear Holy Spirit; we are thankful and grateful for your presence in us and your anointing in and through us. Enable us to willingly submit to you as we look to you for answers, direction, and wisdom for living. In Jesus' Name. Amen.

One of the words we hear a lot in Christian circles is the word "anointing." Sometimes it is jokingly used to justify a preference in the choice of clothes, accessories or food. However, the Anointing of God is a very serious matter. So what does it mean? The Holy Bible tells us that every born again believer in the Lord Jesus has the gift of God the Holy Spirit residing in them. The Holy Spirit is our seal or confirmation that we are a part of the family of God. The anointing of God implies a person has been set apart by God. And the anointing of God means a person has been gifted or graced by God to perform a particular task or live a particular lifestyle according to the will of God.

The anointing of God is not weird. If a person cannot stand the sound of children screaming and crying in pain it would be hard to believe that person is anointed to be a pediatric nurse. On the other hand, if you cannot stand to see people mistreated you may be anointed by God for service in an area that will help alleviate suffering and mistreatment. That was the life of Reverend Dr. Martin Luther King, Jr.

So check your likes and dislikes. They may give you a clue as to your anointing. Above all, seek God directly in prayer and let Him reveal His anointings in you.

© By Dr. Sheila Hayford.

May 7
A Friend

Proverbs Chapter 27, verse 9:
Ointment and perfume rejoice the heart: so doth the sweetness of a man's friend by hearty counsel.

Prayer; Dear God; we thank you for the gift of faithful friends, and for our best friend, Jesus Christ, our Lord and Savior, Amen.

You know when you have a true friend. A friend who has earned the right to give you wise counsel. A friend with whom you can share the good times and the challenging times. Priceless moments! I was working on a project and one of the participants was not doing well physically. He needed help with his writing. Why not visit him and help him put his words in writing? Two of us decided to do just that. Some months later I heard that he had transitioned into God's eternal presence. I was so glad I had contributed in some part to his written legacy. Treasure your friendship moments. You may never fully know the impact.

© By Dr. Sheila Hayford.

May 8
Who Gave It To You?

1 Chronicles Chapter 29, verses 10-14:
Wherefore David blessed the Lord before all the congregation: and David said, Blessed be thou, Lord God of Israel our father, for ever and ever. Thine, O Lord is the greatness, and the power, and the glory, and the victory, and the majesty: for all that is in the heaven and in the earth is thine; thine is the kingdom, O Lord, and thou art exalted as head above all. Both riches and honour come of thee, and thou reignest over all; and in thine hand is power and might; and in thine hand it is to make great, and to give strength unto all. Now therefore, our God, we thank thee, and praise thy glorious name. But who am I, and what is my people, that we should be able to offer so willingly after this sort? for all things come of thee, and of thine own have we given thee.

Prayer: Dear God; we are so grateful for all that you give us, for you go above and beyond what we deserve. Through the Lord Jesus Christ, you have elevated us to be your sons and daughters with all the benefits and privileges therein. Enable us to be humble before you for you are our

God. We bless you, praise and magnify your holy Name, and thank you for the gift of the Lord Jesus Christ, in whose Name we pray. Amen.

I love the humility of King David. King David never forgot the God who elevated him. King David magnified the Lord God in public and in private and these verses are a beautiful illustration of that. All that we have comes from God; our lives, our health, our talents, our gifts, everything! Do you acknowledge that to God? Do you acknowledge that to yourself? Do you acknowledge that to others?

© By Dr. Sheila Hayford.

May 9
Youthful Days

Ecclesiastes Chapter 12, verses 1, 14:
Remember now thy Creator in the days of thy youth, while the evil days come not, nor the years draw nigh, when thou shalt say, I have no pleasure in them; For God shall bring every work into judgment, with every secret thing, whether it be good, or whether it be evil.

Dear God: As I look back over my life I am in sheer gratitude. Thank you for saving me in my youth and granting me the privilege of enjoying my youth. Help me to be a source of inspiration for the upcoming youth and to use the gifts you have given me to advance your kingdom. In Jesus' Name I pray. Amen.

I remember those youthful days. We had almost no responsibility, except to obey our parents, study and play. I will always be thankful that the Holy Spirit drew me into a personal relationship with my Lord Jesus during my teenage years. I had a lot of positive peer pressure. It was great! We studied the Bible individually and together, prayed together, shared our faith and our testimony with others and were as bold as lions!

Sure, challenges came as we grew older, but God kept us, still keeps us and bless God the Almighty, we are still pressing on in Christ. Do not wait until the pressures of life get you down. Invite the Lord Jesus into your life today!

© By Dr. Sheila Hayford.

May 10
The Lord Is There

Ezekiel Chapter 48, verse 35:
It was round about eighteen thousand measures: and the name of the city from that day shall be, The Lord is there.

Prayer: Dear God; we are so thankful for your presence in us. Help us to share our faith and be salt in this earth, wherever we may be. May others declare after being in our presence, "Surely, the Lord is there!"

The Lord is there! What a lovely name for a city! Is that how others describe your city? Is that how others describe your home, your community or your nation? How do you describe your home, your city, your nation? May it be: The Lord is here!

© By Dr. Sheila Hayford.

May 11
Take The Time

Luke Chapter 17, verse 17:
And Jesus answering said, Were there not ten cleansed? but where are the nine?

1 Thessalonians Chapter 5, verse 18: In every thing give thanks: for this is the will of God in Christ Jesus concerning you.

Prayer: Dear God; help us always to be grateful and appreciative of you and all you do for us. Help us not take our family, friends and co-workers for granted, but show them our appreciation, our love and our thanks. In the name of Jesus we pray. Amen.

Take The Time:

- To Pray ▪ To Fast ▪ To Eat
- To Laugh ▪ To Love ▪ To Rest
- To Heal ▪ To Give Thanks.

Do not be like the nine who failed to thank the Lord Jesus for their healing. Always be thankful! God is working everything out for your good!

© By Dr. Sheila Hayford.

May 12
Length Of Days

Exodus Chapter 20, verse 12:

Honour thy father and thy mother: that thy days may be long upon the land which the Lord thy God giveth thee.

Prayer: Dear God: The older I get, the more I appreciate my parents. Thank you for the genius of fatherhood and motherhood. Help us to love our parents and obey your commandment to honor our fathers and our mothers. In Jesus' name we pray. Amen.

In the Ten Commandments, this is the only commandment with a promise of long life on this earth. Note it reads, honor your father and your mother, not one or the other. In other words, respect and appreciate both parents who were equally necessary in ensuring your birth.

For many, this commandment comes easily. Their parents are "worthy" of honor. Their parents take good care of their children, provide for their needs and provide exemplary role models. For others, adhering to this commandment may be a challenge. Maybe you had an absentee father, a stressed out single mother or grew up in an abusive home. Whatever the scenario, honor your parents, no matter what.

As an adult, I am more appreciative of my parents and am eternally grateful to God for the privilege of being their daughter. Remember, there are no perfect human parents and there is no perfect you on this side of eternity. But there is a perfect God, our heavenly Father, who deserves our admiration, appreciation, honor and respect.

Honor God! Honor your parents!

© By Dr. Sheila Hayford.

May 13
Don't Get Too Close To The Edge

Proverbs Chapter 8, verses 12-14:

I, wisdom, dwell together with prudence; I possess knowledge and discretion. To fear the Lord is to hate evil; I hate pride and arrogance, evil behavior and perverse speech. Counsel and sound judgment are mine; I have insight, I have power. (NIV)

Prayer: Dear Holy Spirit; grant us wisdom in our everyday living. Enable us to make wise choices. In Jesus' name we pray. Amen.

Figuratively speaking, some people walk all the way to the edge of the cliff, tip over and then dare God not to let them fall. Why take a chance with sin?

Some will defile their bodies and then pray they do not fall sick. Others willfully hang around those whose actions mock God, not sharing Jesus Christ with them, just enjoying their sinful conversations and company. And then they hope and pray they will not be influenced by those negative actions.

Still others tempt God by trying to use their God given gifts and talents to advance their selfish agenda, thereby hurting others in the process.

Sin will usually take a person further than they intended to go. Don't get too close to the edge! Ask God for godly wisdom and then apply it.

© By Dr. Sheila Hayford.

May 14
Pride

Proverbs Chapter 16, verse 18:
Pride goeth before destruction, and an haughty spirit before a fall.
Prayer: Dear God; you hate pride and so should we. Help us to always humble ourselves before you for you are our God, the Almighty God. In Jesus' Name we pray. Amen.

When we use the word "pride" we are usually describing the attitude of a person who is overconfident in their abilities, or who forgets the people and the good breaks that got them to their present position. But what about the person in a bad place who is too prideful to ask for help or refuses help because of pride? As an example, it is freezing cold outside and a homeless person refuses to accept a blanket or a warm shelter. What about a failing student who refuses to accept free tutoring?

What does God say about pride at any level? As hard as it may seem, God destroys the proud in the imagination of their hearts. A person who refuses to acknowledge the source of their being and all God has blessed them with is in a precarious place. God says humanity was destined to hell because of Adam and Eve's sin and that Jesus Christ died on the cross to pay the price for mankind's sin. Whoever humbles themselves before God and surrenders their life and heart to the Lord Jesus by inviting Jesus into their heart as Lord and Savior will be saved.

As long as we have life, there is hope of redemption; and that is by repenting, aligning our thoughts to God's way of thinking and living the way God wants us to live. Those who are too proud to humble themselves before Almighty God, the Holy Bible says, will be condemned to eternal separation from God.

Do not let pride get in your way?

© By Dr. Sheila Hayford.

May 15
Adversaries

Nehemiah Chapter 4, verses 6, 7:

So built we the wall; and all the wall was joined together unto the half thereof: for the people had a mind to work. But it came to pass, that when Sanballat, and Tobiah, and the Arabians, and the Ammonites, and the Ashdodites, heard that the walls of Jerusalem were made up, and that the breaches began to be stopped, then they were very wroth,

Prayer: Dear God; help us not fall for the distractions of satan or others. In Jesus' Name. Amen.

Your adversary is sent by satan to be a distraction to you.

Look at Nehemiah, our example in these verses. Nehemiah had the resources he needed, the letters of authority and the right people willing and able to work with him. Yet Nehemiah's adversaries tried to use taunts, indignation, and intimidation to stop the work of God from going forward.

Nehemiah did not give in to their distractions. Nehemiah was prepared, prayed and finished the work in record time. In other words, Nehemiah's adversaries propelled Nehemiah to get the job done.

One of the worst things you can let your enemy do to you is to allow them to poison your soul. Let them propel you to do what God wants you to do. And yes, let them see you happy and fulfilled in God.

You will be thanking them later!

© By Dr. Sheila Hayford.

Delicious Eats! The GRUB Restaurant

Concord Pike Mall, Wilmington, Delaware

*** Love Their Burgers!***

May 16
Grater Works

John Chapter 14, verse 12:

Verily, verily, I say unto you, He that believeth on me, the works that I do shall he do also; and greater works than these shall he do; because I go unto my Father.

Prayer: Dear Lord Jesus; we believe your words that we will do greater works because you sent the Holy Spirit to live in us. May we not quench the Holy Spirit but do the greater works God has destined for us, with you being our perfect example. Amen.

That is a bold statement. When we think of the ministry of the Lord Jesus, it is pretty amazing all that the Lord Jesus was able to accomplish during his time here on earth. He fed thousands at a time, healed multitudes, cast out demons, taught others and much more.

So why does the Lord Jesus say that those who believe on him will do greater works? It is because the Lord Jesus went back to God, our heavenly Father. When he did, the Lord Jesus sent the Holy Spirit to live in us and to empower us to do the greater works.

We can share the good news of salvation in unprecedented ways; radio, television, print, film, social media, etc. The Holy Spirit enables us to pray the will of God in every situation in life. And with the Word of God we are emboldened to pursue the greater works. You need not fail. So go ahead and make God's day!

© By Dr. Sheila Hayford.

May 17
Crucified With Christ

Galatians Chapter 2 verse 20:

I have been crucified with Christ and I no longer live, but Christ lives in me. The life I now live in the body, I live by faith in the Son of God, who loved me and gave himself for me.

Prayer: Dear Lord Jesus, thank you for dying on the cross for my sins and rising up with all power. It is a joy to live for you. Amen.

Crucified with Christ? That does not sound very hip! That sounds uncomfortable! Isn't the Christian life supposed to make you feel good? Aren't you supposed to have joy? Yes!

So what is all this crucified with Christ stuff? It is the stuff the Lord Jesus talked about when he asks every disciple of the Lord Jesus Christ to consider the cost and pick up their cross. For the Lord Jesus says no one who starts the Christian race and looks back is worthy of the kingdom of God. Sin is a drain on the flesh, but it comes easy to the carnal mind.

When you are born again, your mind has to be renewed with the Word of God and the wisdom of God. You have to flee the lusts of the flesh, the lusts of the eyes and the pride that thinks that man has all the answers. It takes humility, it takes patience, and it takes a dying to sinful desires daily. We were buried into the Lord Jesus's death when we received the Lord Jesus as Savior, and are raised with the Lord Jesus in his resurrection.

So though it sounds a bit "trying" it really isn't that hard. The Holy Spirit gives us the power to follow our Lord Jesus joyfully. It will be one of your most delightful decisions and at the same time one of your most challenging decisions.

Enjoy the journey!

© By Dr. Sheila Hayford.

May 18
Buy It Now!

Luke Chapter 12, verse 15:

And he said unto them, Take heed, and beware of covetousness: for a man's life consisteth not in the abundance of the things which he possesseth.

Prayer: Dear God, help me not to yield to the bombardment of advertisers touting impulsive buying habits. In the Name of Jesus. Amen.

"Buy It Now!" has probably made a lot more stores richer than they would care to admit and left others poorer than they would probably care to admit. Why? It is because "buy it now" is generally impulse buying. After you get home, you might realize you do not really like the item. Sorry, you already bought it! The advertiser knew that if you did not buy it then, you might never buy it.

Of course, there can be the God ordained "buy it now" event where the item you need and prayed for is unexpectedly on sale at a "buy it now" price! However, the Lord Jesus reminds us that the value of a life is not the sum total of a person's material possessions.

So evaluate your life, and your priorities. And just maybe, buy it later or not at all!

© By Dr. Sheila Hayford.

May 19
Misjudged

1 Samuel Chapter 1, verses 13-17:

Now Hannah, she spake in her heart; only her lips moved, but her voice was not heard: therefore Eli thought she had been drunken. And Eli said unto her, How long wilt thou be drunken? put away thy wine from thee. And Hannah answered and said, No, my lord, I am a woman of a sorrowful spirit: I have drunk neither wine nor strong drink, but have poured out my soul before the Lord. Count not thine handmaid for a daughter of Belial: for out of the abundance of my complaint and grief have I spoken hitherto. Then Eli answered and said, Go in peace: and the God of Israel grant thee thy petition that thou hast asked of him**.**

Prayer: Dear God; you alone know the hearts of all men. Help us not to be rash in judging others. Instead, let us soberly consider our lives and seek forgiveness from you for our sins and imperfections. In Jesus' Name. Amen.

Too many people make quick and rash judgements about others just based on what they see. Even Eli, a priest in God's temple was guilty of that. Hannah was so distraught with the treatment she was receiving from Penninah that, as Hannah prayed, only her lips moved. The priest, Eli, looking at Hannah assumed that she was drunk and was almost rude to her.

How many people have been so mistreated inside and outside the church? Eli had the opportunity to repent and to agree with Hannah in prayer. Others may never have that opportunity. So before you are quick to misjudge, take time to know the person and agree with God for what is best for them.

© By Dr. Sheila Hayford.

May 20
Staying Power

Philippians Chapter 1, verse 6:
Being confident of this very thing, that he which hath begun a good work in you will perform it until the day of Jesus Christ:

Prayer: Dear God; I am so glad I can trust you with my life. I would not have it any other way. In Jesus' Name. Amen.

When we first give our heart and life to our Lord and Savior Jesus Christ we will face challenges. We are in a new relationship with God and are learning how to live out our faith. You may sometimes wonder if you will make it. I can assure you, based on God's word in this verse, that God has the staying power to keep you connected in Jesus Christ in God. Your part is to trust God, do what God asks you to do and to obtain grace, forgiveness and mercy from God when you sin.

Forgive yourself when you fall short and be patient with yourself. The Christian race is for the long haul. And it gets better. So share what God is doing in your life. You will be amazed at all the growth. And God gets the glory!

© By Dr. Sheila Hayford.

May 21
Show Honor

1 Peter Chapter 2, verse 17:

Honour all men. Love the brotherhood. Fear God. Honour the king.

Prayer: Dear God; respect and honor for our fellow man seems to be disappearing in society. But that does not change your desire that we respect and honor the dignity of man. So help us honor and reverence you, and honor and respect our fellow man. In Jesus' Name. Amen.

Honor is a lot like love. You cannot show a person honor without doing something. If you honor a person, you will respect them in words and action. You will be kind to them. You will obey them and you will appreciate them. The list given us here is a first start. Honor all men. Love the brethren. Fear God. Honor the King/President. If you are able to master these, you can talk to God about the next step.

© By Dr. Sheila Hayford.

May 22
From My Youth

Matthew Chapter 19, verses 16-21:

And, behold, one came and said unto him, Good Master, what good thing shall I do, that I may have eternal life? And he said unto him, Why callest thou me good? there is none good but one, that is, God: but if thou wilt enter into life, keep the commandments. He saith unto him, Which? Jesus said, Thou shalt do no murder, Thou shalt not commit adultery, Thou shalt not steal, Thou shalt not bear false witness, Honour thy father and thy mother: and, Thou shalt love thy neighbour as thyself. The young man saith unto him, All these things have I kept from my youth up: what lack I yet? Jesus said unto him, If thou wilt be perfect, go and sell that thou hast, and give to the poor, and thou shalt have treasure in heaven: and come and follow me.

Prayer: Dear God; thank you for sharing the story of this young man with us. This young man came to Jesus and wanted to know what he needed to do to obtain eternal life. Coming to the Lord Jesus with his genuine question and concern is a commendable act for young and old alike. And so the Lord Jesus did not upbraid him, but instead gave the young man his next step. Help us to always come to you in sincerity and truth. In the Name of Jesus we pray. Amen.

It would seem the young man was brash. This young man was telling the Lord Jesus that he had honored his parents and loved his neighbor as himself from his youth. "What more do I lack?" he asked. The Lord Jesus did not upbraid him. Instead, the Lord Jesus directed him towards maturity. For maturity is learning to submit and surrender to God, God's will, God's pleasure and God's authority. What is your next step?

© By Dr. Sheila Hayford.

May 23
Minding Your Business

John Chapter 21, verse 20-22:
Then Peter, turning about, seeth the disciple whom Jesus loved following; which also leaned on his breast at supper, and said, Lord, which is he that betrayeth thee? Peter seeing him saith to Jesus, Lord,

and what shall this man do? Jesus saith unto him, If I will that he tarry till I come, what is that to thee? follow thou me.

Prayer: Dear Holy Spirit; help each of us remember that we have so much growth and accomplishments ahead of us that we cannot afford to be busybodies. Help us, by the power of the Holy Spirit, to live lives that are pleasing to God. In Jesus' Name. Amen.

The admonition to mind your own business has been around for a long time. The Lord Jesus had just given Peter instructions on what he wanted Peter to do and he told Peter what was going to happen to Peter in the future. Not satisfied with that, Peter wanted to know what was going to happen to John, his fellow disciple. Why should that concern Peter? When we realize what <u>we</u> need to do to fulfil the call of God on our lives, there is no time to be a busybody.

Work on the assignment God has given you and mind your business!"

© By Dr. Sheila Hayford.

May 24
God Is Always Good

1 John Chapter 1, verse 4-6:
And these things write we unto you, that your joy may be full. This then is the message which we have heard of him, and declare unto you, that God is light, and in him is no darkness at all. If we say that we have fellowship with him, and walk in darkness, we lie, and do not the truth:

Prayer: Dear God; you are always good. Let us believe that deep in our spirit and recognize that you always want what is best for us. In the Name of Jesus we pray. Amen.

How many times has God gotten an unfair rap? The television program features an earthquake with destroyed homes and some ask why God would do that. God is all good. The devil is the originator of evil, so why do some try to blame God for the evil they see? It may be due to ignorance, it may be because they have a personal issue with God or they may be honestly seeking answers. Whatever the issue, God is always part of the solution. Moreover, God welcomes the dialogue. So go ahead and ask God your questions. Then be willing to accept the truth of God's Word and willingly yield your life to the care of a good God.

© By Dr. Sheila Hayford.

May 25
Satan Tried But God Triumphed

Psalm 92, verse 4:

For thou, Lord, hast made me glad through thy work: I will triumph in the works of thy hands.

Prayer: Oh God; I rejoice in you! You have blessed me with life through Jesus Christ and I marvel at your goodness and your awesome works. Thank you. In Jesus' Name. Amen.

It was going to be a wonderful event. One of my favorite singers was going to perform what was described at the time as her "last" tour and I was determined to attend. This was before the mobile, internet boom so I waited patiently for the tickets to go on sale. On the first day the tickets were available, I called and was told the tickets were all sold out. I was so disappointed! It looked hopeless. However, I did not give up. I prayed. I called shortly afterwards and was told they had just added four front rows of seats. I got one of those front row tickets and enjoyed one of the best events of my life! Satan had tried to sow hopelessness but God triumphed. Give your hopeless situation to God and be ready!

© By Dr. Sheila Hayford.

May 26
The Firstborn

Colossians Chapter 1, verse 18:

And he is the head of the body, the church: who is the beginning, the firstborn from the dead; that in all things he might have the preeminence.

Prayer: Dear Lord Jesus, the firstborn of God's family. We love you and are honored to be part of your family. Amen.

Of whom does this verse speak? It speaks of the Lord Jesus Christ, the head of the church, resurrected from the dead and seated at the right hand of God the Father in glory. God wants us to live in hope. The Lord Jesus Christ is our elder brother, the one who goes before us to prepare us a place with him forever. The Lord Jesus Christ rose from the dead so we will rise from the dead. The Lord Jesus reigns in His glorified body and so we will reign with him in our glorified bodies. So encourage yourself and encourage each other when the going seems rough. For you are living with your eternal destination in mind!

© By Dr. Sheila Hayford.

May 27
Who Is Doing The Laughing?

Psalm 52, verses 6-8:

The righteous also shall see, and fear, and shall laugh at him: Lo, this is the man that made not God his strength; but trusted in the abundance of his riches, and strengthened himself in his wickedness. But I am like a green olive tree in the house of God: I trust in the mercy of God for ever and ever.

Prayer: Dear Lord Jesus, help me not make satan laugh. Amen.

There are times when laughter is expected. At a wedding, a graduation, times of celebration and wholesome laughter. But there are times when it seems the laughter is misguided or misplaced. People are hurt because of an evil act and you see others cheering and laughing.

In the Psalm above, the righteous observe the end of a wicked person who trusted in the abundant wealth he had instead of trusting in God. In the beginning it seemed like satan was doing the laughing but that was not so at the end. The righteous man, however, entrusted himself to God's mercy and is in awe of God's righteous judgment against the wicked.

In the end, God always does the laughing.

© By Dr. Sheila Hayford.

May 28
Godly Family Traditions

1 Chronicles Chapter 1, verse 1:
Adam, Seth, Enosh
Genesis Chapter 4, verses 25-26:
And Adam knew his wife again; and she bare a son, and called his name Seth: For God, said she, hath appointed me another seed instead of Abel, whom Cain slew. And to Seth, to him also there was born a son; and he called his name Enos: then began men to call upon the name of the Lord.

Prayer: Dear God; thank you for the blessings of a godly family. In Jesus' name. Amen.

It is interesting that verse 1 of the first Chapter of the book of 1 Chronicles starts with Adam, the first human being God created and then lists two of the children of Adam. When we read the book of Genesis Chapter 4, we get some more insight. Abel, Adam's son had been killed by his brother Cain before the birth of Seth. Seth had a son named Enos and the sentence after that tells us that **then** people began to call on the name of the Lord. How beautiful! Seth and Enos were the beginning of a godly tradition, after their earlier ancestors had messed things up.

Thank God for the Lord Jesus! Humanity through Adam was messed up by sin but our Lord and Savior, Jesus Christ, started a godly family tradition. Whoever invites the Lord Jesus Christ into their heart and life as their Lord and Savior and declares their salvation becomes part of the family of God, a family that calls on the name of the Lord Jesus.

How cool is that!

© By Dr. Sheila Hayford.

May 29
Godly Wisdom

2 Chronicles Chapter 1, verses 8-12:

And Solomon said unto God, Thou hast shewed great mercy unto David my father, and hast made me to reign in his stead. Now, O Lord God, let thy promise unto David my father be established: for thou hast made me king over a people like the dust of the earth in multitude. Give me now wisdom and knowledge, that I may go out and come in before this people: for who can judge this thy people, that is so great? And God said to Solomon, Because this was in thine heart, and thou hast not asked riches, wealth, or honour, nor the life of thine enemies, neither yet hast asked long life; but hast asked wisdom and knowledge for thyself, that thou mayest judge my people, over whom I have made thee king: Wisdom and knowledge is granted unto thee; and I will give thee riches, and wealth, and honour, such as none of the kings have had that have been before thee, neither shall there any after thee have the like.

Prayer: Dear Holy Spirit, we need your wisdom and direction daily. Enable us to hear you clearly and to obey you fully. For we ask this in the name of Jesus. Amen.

King David must have taught His son, King Solomon, the importance of applying God's wisdom. When God gave King Solomon the opportunity in verse 7 to ask God for **anything,** King Solomon asked for wisdom. God was so impressed with King Solomon's answer, God added material wealth and riches. The principle here? When you have God's wisdom you have everything. God's wisdom will reveal God's plan of salvation and enable one to make decisions that please God. When we please God we have favor with God. Can you imagine ALL the good things God has in store for us? So do not despise the wisdom of God. Seek God's wisdom, and respect God enough to apply the wisdom God gives you. Then experience the benefits of a life pleasing to God.

© By Dr. Sheila Hayford.

1450 S. DuPont Highway, Dover, DE 19901

1-800-323-0828

www.townsendchevy.com

New and Used Cars at Great Deals!
COME SEE US TODAY!

May 30
Walk In The Light

2 John Chapter 1, verse 5: And now I beseech thee, lady, not as though I wrote a new commandment unto thee, but that which we had from the beginning, that we love one another.

Prayer: Dear God, help us to love you with all our being, and to love others with your love. In Jesus' name. Amen.

If you hate your Christian brother or sister because they belong to a different political party, race or class you are still walking in darkness or carnality. Walk in God's light, by God's Holy Spirit, and you will not fulfill the lusts of the flesh.

© By Dr. Sheila Hayford.

May 31
Faith First

Isaiah Chapter 53, verse 11:

He shall see of the travail of his soul, and shall be satisfied: by his knowledge shall my righteous servant justify many; for he shall bear their iniquities.

Prayer: Dear God; we remember the martyrs of the faith who sacrificed their very lives for the sake of the gospel of Jesus Christ. As we honor the men and women who lost their lives in the service of this country, help us to remember that there is a cost to freedom. For our freedom cost the Lord Jesus the brutal death on the cross as he bled and died for the sins of humanity. May we respond in love and appreciation and in wholehearted service to you. In the name of Jesus we pray. Amen.

As we celebrate Memorial Day in the United States, we remember the brave men and women who paid the ultimate price. These warriors had faith in the cause; even though they did not live to enjoy the freedoms many now take for granted.

Faith is a biblical principle. We all believe something, and whom we believe and what we believe determines how we live. The Lord Jesus believed in the cause to save sinful humanity and he believed in the God who was able to raise him up from the dead. As a result, believers worldwide are recipients of all the benefits of salvation.

So we thank God for that Memorial Day at Calvary and honor our Lord Jesus Christ. Each day the Lord Jesus is saying to us: "Have faith in God and the rest will follow."

© By Dr. Sheila Hayford.

June 1
Limiting Situations Are Only Temporary

Philippians Chapter 4, verse 19:

But my God shall supply all your need according to his riches in glory by Christ Jesus.

Prayer: Dear God, I am a grateful recipient of your daily provision. Thank you for the air I breathe, the beauty of your creation, your goodness and your pleasant surprises. Help me trust you, whatever the challenge. In Jesus' Name. Amen.

As long as we are on this earth, we will face challenges that try to limit or confine us. While you may have many grand plans, you might start out with limited resources. What do you do? It is always important to find out what God's word says about a particular situation. God is a limitless God. This earth that we live in is temporary. To put one's trust in temporary things instead of in God is futile. Trusting in a limitless God to bring you the resources you need to accomplish His will in your life is a rewarding adventure. Go for it!

© By Dr. Sheila Hayford.

June 2
I Am Praying For You

Romans Chapter 8, verses 33, 34:

Who shall lay any thing to the charge of God's elect? It is God that justifieth. Who is he that condemneth? It is Christ that died, yea rather, that is risen again, who is even at the right hand of God, who also maketh intercession for us.

Prayer: Dear Lord Jesus, thank you for interceding for us. Amen.

Sometimes the phrase "I will pray for you" is almost a cliché. While prayer is one of the most powerful things you can do for a person, merely saying those words without any real intention of praying for that person is wrong. When the living Lord Jesus, seated at the right hand of God our Father, says, "I am praying for you" He really means it. And that should make your heart glad.

© By Dr. Sheila Hayford.

June 3
Blessed Is The Man

Psalm 1, verse 1:

Blessed is the man who does not walk in the counsel of the wicked or stand in the way of sinners or sit in the seat of mockers.

Prayer: Dear God: Please forgive us when we have passed judgment on the glaring sins of others and have not taken the time to study, meditate on your Word and examine ourselves in the light of your Word. Thank you for Jesus Christ and for the gift of your Holy Spirit. Let us so live that we are blessed, happy and at peace with you. In Jesus' Name. Amen.

Many times we stress the fact that the Christian life is not just about living by a set of "Thou shalt not" rules. However, this verse not only tells us three things we should not do but starts by calling us blessed, or as I would say, favored and at peace with God. When we think of the word "counsel" we usually think of the giving of good advice. We might think of a school counselor giving advice to students or a lawyer providing legal counsel, but here the Psalmist is talking about the advice or counsel of the wicked. So who is a wicked person? It is the one whose thoughts, words and actions are contrary to the laws and principles of God. In the book of Matthew Chapter 25, verse 26 Jesus calls the person who buried his God given talent and refused to share and multiply what he had been given "wicked." So let us break what Jesus is saying into today's examples. A person has been happily married for twenty-five years to a wonderful Christian spouse. That person attends a local church fellowship with a lot of young, unwed teenage mothers struggling to raise their kids as single parents. He or she has a wealth of knowledge to share by mentoring, babysitting when possible and modeling godly behavior. But when asked how he or she made it for twenty-five years in a strong marriage she replies: "I just got lucky!" Really? Is that all the advice to give a young unwed mother? Maybe the unwed mother did not grow up in a Christian home. What would Jesus say?

Suppose your coworker says to you, "I would call in sick if I were you and take Friday off to head to the beach. That way you will beat the rush hour traffic headed that way for the weekend." No discussion about robbing your employer who would be unknowingly paying for your time at the beach, thinking you were using an employee sick day benefit truthfully. Do you take that advice? I believe it is generally respectful to listen to advice that is sincerely given, even if that person is not necessarily right. However, acting on advice that is clearly at odds with God's command is sinful.

We are being challenged to move higher in our walk with God. When we do what God asks us to do, not what a secular society says we should do if that goes against or mocks God's laws, sin becomes less attractive. So how do we do that? The answer is found in verse 2 of this Psalm which completes the sentence began in verse 1.

When we delight ourselves in God and God's law, and spend time meditating, studying and applying God's principles, sin becomes less attractive. The Holy Spirit who lives in every born again child of God will empower us to live right. Do we fail God at times? Of course, and that is because of our humanity. Do born again believers enjoy sinning against God? No! When we confess our sins in true repentance, God will forgive our sins, past, present and future and walk hand in hand with us until we make it to our glorious eternal destination.

© By Dr. Sheila Hayford.

June 4
God's Anointed

2 Samuel Chapter 1, verses 14-16:

And David said unto him, How wast thou not afraid to stretch forth thine hand to destroy the Lord's anointed? And David called one of the young men, and said, Go near, and fall upon him. And he smote him that he died. And David said unto him, Thy blood be upon thy head; for thy mouth hath testified against thee, saying, I have slain the Lord's anointed.

Prayer: Dear God; give us the discernment to recognize those you have appointed to your service. In Jesus' Name. Amen.

King David askes a very important question. "How wast thou not afraid to stretch forth thine hand to destroy the Lord's anointed?" Many people have done so many harmful things in the name of God. The young man thought he was doing King David a favor by killing Saul, especially since Saul had tried to kill David in the past.

God has a way of dealing with His disobedient children. God will speak to them directly, through Scripture, through others or through their circumstances. If they repent, God will decide how to handle the situation. If they refuse to repent, God knows how to deal with them also.

The discernment and direction of the Holy Spirit should guide every decision we make, especially in relationship to our Christian brethren. No one should want to be fighting against God.

© By Dr. Sheila Hayford.

June 5
Prepare The Way Of The Lord

Mark Chapter 1, verse 3:
The voice of one crying in the wilderness, Prepare ye the way of the Lord, make his paths straight.

Prayer: Dear God, each one of your children has been commissioned by the Lord Jesus to share the good news of salvation with others. Help me to do my part. In Jesus' Name I pray. Amen.

How do we prepare the way of the Lord? John the Baptist was literally in the wilderness, warning people to repent and pointing people to the coming Messiah. Today, we have several ways to prepare the way of the Lord.

The first would be to be in right relationship with God. For how can you effectively lead people to God if you do not have a relationship with God?

The second way is to pray and ask God to show you your assignment. God had an assignment for John the Baptist before John the Baptist was conceived. And God has an assignment for each one of us.

Then ask God to equip you and lead you as you perform that assignment. There are so many tools available to lead people to Christ; one on one face meetings, seminars, crusades, radio, television, film, social media and many more online and media tools.

The message, however, is the same and that message is that the Jesus still saves lives. Keep that message simple. Keep that message clear.

Prepare the Way of the Lord!

© By Dr. Sheila Hayford.

June 6
Fast Forward

Isaiah Chapter 46, verse 10:
I make known the end from the beginning, from ancient times, what is still to come. I say, 'My purpose will stand, and I will do all that I please.' (NIV)

Prayer: What an awesome God we serve! Thank you, dear heavenly Father, that you know us perfectly. We entrust our lives to you. In the Name of Jesus. Amen.

Isn't it interesting how true some of the science-fiction books and movies turned out? Two hundred years ago, there were no automobiles. If you had to travel you walked, used an animal or travelled by sea. If you had told those alive at that time that it would be possible to speak on the telephone to someone you could not see they would have laughed you to scorn. Today, cars and telephones are commonplace and social media is the new buzz. What changed? The answer depends on where on the spectrum of earth's civilization you start. God's perspective is eternal. He does not need the latest tweet to get the update on what is going on in this earth. God wants us to live on this earth with an eternal perspective in mind, unhindered by finite limitations. And so, how do we do that? By living a possibilities filled life. For with God all things are possible.

© By Dr. Sheila Hayford.

June 7
Power Or Powerful?

John Chapter 14, verse 14:

If ye shall ask any thing in my name, I will do it.

Prayer: Thank you, dear Lord Jesus, that whatever we ask our heavenly Father in your name, you will do it. We believe you. Amen.

Power or powerful? Many people crave power. They want authority and control in the company, charity, or in the government. They want the power to make decisions and rules that will affect not only themselves, but also all who are under their jurisdiction.

However, I have found that it is not so much about who has the earthly power but who is powerful in prayer and in their relationship with God. How so? This is because it is God who has ultimate power. God promotes one and God brings another down. God invites us to bring Him on the scene in every aspect of life. I have prayed and seen wonderful results that could only be explained as the hand of God.

As a true believer in the Lord Jesus Christ you have power designated to you by the Lord Jesus Christ and you are powerful in prayer. Use both wisely.

© By Dr. Sheila Hayford.

June 8
Don't Back Down

Matthew Chapter 14, verse 28-31:
And Peter answered him and said, Lord, if it be thou, bid me come unto thee on the water. And he said, Come. And when Peter was come down out of the ship, he walked on the water, to go to Jesus. But when he saw the wind boisterous, he was afraid; and beginning to sink, he cried, saying, Lord, save me. And immediately Jesus stretched forth his hand, and caught him, and said unto him, O thou of little faith, wherefore didst thou doubt?

Prayer: Dear God, help us not back down from all you have called us to. In Jesus' Name. Amen.

I had placed two exquisitely decorated pillows on hold. I happened to be paying for some other items in the store when one of the cashiers came and told another cashier that those pillows were now marked down to 75% off during the sale. I looked at the pillows and they showed me the printed details of the pillows. "Could you put these pillows on hold for me?" I asked. "Sure!" was the reply. And so I gave them my name and number and the pillows were placed on hold.

After I got home, I wondered if I was being extravagant. I liked both pillows, but thought that maybe I should have just held one of them. That was when the Holy Spirit said to me, "Don't back down!"

How often do you back down from your expectations? You wanted "this", but "this" seemed to take a long time in coming so you just settled for "that". It may be that you are praying and trusting God for something big, but it seems extravagant to you to ask that from God. It is not sinful, it is not contrary to God's will; you just do not think you deserve "all that" from God. If God says you can have it, don't back down!

© By Dr. Sheila Hayford.

June 9
Do Not Begrudge God

Matthew Chapter 18, verses 32-33:

Then his lord, after that he had called him, said unto him, O thou wicked servant, I forgave thee all that debt, because thou desiredst me: Shouldest not thou also have had compassion on thy fellowservant, even as I had pity on thee?

Prayer: Dear God, thank you for showing me mercy and grace. Help me not to begrudge your grace and mercy towards others. In Jesus' Name. Amen.

Never begrudge God for showing mercy to someone else. The man in this parable was forgiven so much debt you would think that would cause him to be merciful to one who owed him a fraction of what he had been forgiven. But no, he dealt so horribly with the one who owed him money that his master was told of his attitude. Immediately his master threw him in jail and demanded he pay all that he owe!

The Lord Jesus is talking to each one of us. All of us owe God a debt we could never pay. The Lord Jesus paid that debt on our behalf and expects us to, in turn, be gracious to our fellow man. Do not say, "I can never forgive … for …!" No sin is too great for God to forgive and so no offense should be too great for you to forgive. Does forgiveness always come easily? No! I would always say I would not begrudge God's mercy on anyone and then one day I read about Rahab the harlot listed in the book of Hebrews with the great men and women of faith. Why would God include a prostitute? I thought. I had to repent for "grading" Rahab's sin.

Forgiving a person for doing the wrong thing to you does not mean you approve of the situation. Forgiveness means you are making a decision not to allow bitterness to take hold of your soul and life because of a real or perceived wrong, while trusting God to work on your behalf. God knows how to mete justice, and God know how to temper justice with mercy. We are all recipients of God's mercy, even though there are some who continually remind others of their failures and mistakes. Do not allow others to begrudge God's mercy towards you. God, in turn, gives us opportunities to be merciful to others. And don't begrudge God's mercy towards others.

© By Dr. Sheila Hayford.

June 10
Patience Of Hope

I Thessalonians Chapter 1, verse 3:
Remembering without ceasing your work of faith, and labour of love, and patience of hope in our Lord Jesus Christ, in the sight of God and our Father;

Prayer: Dear God, patience does not always come easily but it is one of the fruit of the Holy Spirit, so as we mature in Christ, our ability to endure hopefully and patiently grows. Help us to submit to the Holy Spirit in everything. In Jesus' Name. Amen.

What wonderful attributes are described in this verse?
- Remembering the work of faith.
- Laboring in love, for yes, even love can feel weighty.
- Patience of hope. This can be a tough one. You mean I have to wait? And for how long? What if God's reply to this question is, "It depends on you!" It depends on how fast you learn, how long it takes you to get ready, etc. We understand when employers set standards for promotions. So why not God?

- In the sight of God. For ultimately our life is to be lived in the sight of and for the pleasure of God.

© By Dr. Sheila Hayford.

June 11
Disengagement Equals Irrelevance

Acts Chapter 4, verse 13:

When they saw the courage of Peter and John and realized that they were unschooled, ordinary men, they were astonished and they took note that these men had been with Jesus. (NIV)

Prayer: Dear Lord God, help us be part of the conversation in our homes, with our fellow brethren and with society. Let us be the salt that flavors and preserves for your glory. In Jesus' Name. Amen.

If you disengage from the conversation, you become irrelevant in society.

When it comes to voting and other civil matters, Christian apathy equals irrelevance, which in turn infers a lack of influence. In the book of Revelation Chapter 3, we see that God would rather you stand for something; whether it be good or bad, hot or cold, than not stand for anything. When you stand for something, your passion shows and others are more likely to listen to what you have to say. If your cause is wrong, God can turn things around in your life and use your passion for a good cause.

Are you a part of the conversation?

© By Dr. Sheila Hayford.

June 12
Do You Want To Be Well?

John Chapter 5, verses 6, 8-9:

When Jesus saw him lying there and learned that he had been in this condition for a long time, he asked him, "Do you want to get well?" Then Jesus said to him, "Get up! Pick up your mat and walk." At once the man was cured; he picked up his mat and walked. (NIV)

Prayer: Dear Lord Jesus: it was important for the man you healed to first make up his mind that he wanted to be healed. After he did that, you healed him. Help us to personally examine our desires and motives in the light of your Word and to agree with God. Amen.

A person who is always repenting about the same sin has a real problem; it may be due to a weight, a hindrance, a lack of self-control, rebellion or some other reason. The question then becomes, 'Do you want to be set free?" Truly, and in all seriousness, do you want to be set free? If that is so, get up and do what it takes!

© By Dr. Sheila Hayford.

June 13
Are You A Christian First?

Luke Chapter 6, verse 46:
Why do you call me, 'Lord, Lord,' and do not do what I say? NIV)
Prayer: Dear Lord Jesus, help us to show by our obedience that you are our Lord. In Jesus' Name. Amen.

Over the years, I have met people from all walks of life. During the small talk, I find it very interesting how people relate to others. Most will ask where you are from, and what it is that you do. That in turn usually determines how they will relate to you. Some wrongly assume that because I am an intellectual I lack faith. Others assume that because I am a person of faith I throw away reason and common sense. However, what I find most hilarious are those who use Scripture and spiritual words when it suits them. "Pray for those in authority", they say, "God instituted government." And when they do not like those in authority, they insult them like a dog!

Are you a Christian first? If so, your words should be consistent with what you believe. Why call God Lord if you will not do what he says?

© By Dr. Sheila Hayford.

June 14
Allegiance: To Live True To God

Leviticus Chapter 20, verses 6-7:
And the soul that turneth after such as have familiar spirits, and after wizards, to go a whoring after them, I will even set my face against that soul, and will cut him off from among his people. Sanctify yourselves therefore, and be ye holy: for I am the Lord your God.

Prayer: Dear God, you hate witchcraft and so do I. Help us to always stand for you, by the power of the Holy Spirit. In Jesus' Name. Amen.

Some people have to go for others to come into the kingdom of God. Some people have to come into the kingdom of God for others to come into God's kingdom. When King Saul went after familiar spirits, prostituting himself by seeking evil spirits instead of seeking after God, God removed Saul from being King and King David became king in King Saul's place. And through the lineage of King David the Lord Jesus chose to enter humanity.

Why does God cut off from the kingdom of God those who go after demonic worship? It is because God is a holy God and cannot tolerate or gloss over sin. So what should a person do if they have strayed from the commands of God? As long as they are here on earth there is hope. Repent, ask God for forgiveness and invite the Lord Jesus Christ into your life as your Lord and Savior. The Holy Spirit, God's gift to all who invite the Lord Jesus into their heart as Lord and Savior will enable you to live for God and the power of the Name of Jesus will deliver you.

© By Dr. Sheila Hayford.

June 15
Who Is Keeping You?

Jude Chapter 1, verses 24-25:

Now unto him that is able to keep you from falling, and to present you faultless before the presence of his glory with exceeding joy, to the only wise God our Saviour, be glory and majesty, dominion and power, both now and ever. Amen.

Prayer: Dear God, I trust your keeping power. Thank you. In Jesus' Name. Amen.

Who is keeping you? God or man?

© By Dr. Sheila Hayford.

June 16
Why Ask?

John Chapter 16, verse 24:

Hitherto have ye asked nothing in my name: ask, and ye shall receive, that your joy may be full.

Prayer: Dear God, you enjoy giving us everything we need in Christ. Help us not be bashful in asking you for wisdom, for direction, for provision to meet our needs and for our godly desires. You have all the resources we could ever need at your disposal. Thank you. In Jesus' name we pray. Amen.

Why ask? Because you need clarification? Because you are in need? How about, so that your joy may be full? Some in Christian circles make others feel guilty about asking God for things that would bring them joy. "Oh, no!" they say, sounding so spiritual. "I don't want to ask for that; that would be selfish." Perhaps they have a problem with sharing because the more you have the more you are able to give. Jesus is admonishing those who fail to ask God for what they desire. In the Name of Jesus, we can boldly come to the throne of God, ask and receive our godly desires and requests. Do you desire fullness of joy? Ask!

© By Dr. Sheila Hayford.

June 17
God Is Always Good

Psalm 5, verse 4:

For thou art not a God that hath pleasure in wickedness: neither shall evil dwell with thee.

Romans Chapter 8, verses 19-21:

For the creation waits in eager expectation for the children of God to be revealed. For the creation was subjected to frustration, not by its own choice, but by the will of the one who subjected it, in hope that the creation itself will be liberated from its bondage to decay and brought into the freedom and glory of the children of God. (NIV)

Prayer: Dear God; You are always good! I am so grateful for your goodness, shown to us through your Son, the Lord Jesus Christ, in whose Name I pray. Amen.

"How can God do that?" is a question you hear some ask when they read of a natural disaster. Why blame God? Satan is the originator of sin in this earth. Adam and Eve chose to listen and act on what satan told them, disobeying God in the process and leading to the curse as a consequence of their sin. God is <u>equally love, equally good, equally just</u>. As a result, God will allow humanity to experience the wages of sin. However, there is a spiritual remedy through our Lord Jesus Christ. When we receive the Lord Jesus as our Lord and Savior, we are restored to fellowship with God and rightful standing with God and on this earth. And with that we get a chance to influence natural affairs. Yes, we can do our part in filling this physical earth with God's goodness. God's creation is waiting on you!

© By Dr. Sheila Hayford.

June 18
Distractions

Nehemiah Chapter 6, verse 1-3:

Now it came to pass when Sanballat, and Tobiah, and Geshem the Arabian, and the rest of our enemies, heard that I had builded the wall, and that there was no breach left therein; (though at that time I had not set up the doors upon the gates;) That Sanballat and Geshem sent unto me, saying, Come, let us meet together in some one of the villages in the plain of Ono. But they thought to do me mischief.

And I sent messengers unto them, saying, I am doing a great work, so that I cannot come down: why should the work cease, whilst I leave it, and come down to you?

Prayer: Dear God, thank you for the example of Nehemiah. Help me not focus on distractions. Instead help me keep my focus on you and the assignments you have given me, trusting you to enable me to start, continue and finish my assigned jobs. In the Name of Jesus I pray. Amen.

Thank God for the times Nehemiah spent in prayer. Nehemiah prayed, wept, fasted and took his building project to God first. God gave Nehemiah favor with the king, the people and the resources to do the work. You would think satan would have given up. No, satan sent distractions to try to throw Nehemiah off course for satan is a master of distractions.

If satan can get you off focus, he will try to get you off course. So follow the example of Nehemiah. Do your advance praying and your advance planning. Then do the work and do not be distracted.

God will help you finish the job!

© By Dr. Sheila Hayford.

June 19
A Soft Answer

Proverbs Chapter 15, verse 1-3:

A soft answer turneth away wrath: but grievous words stir up anger. The tongue of the wise useth knowledge aright: but the mouth of fools poureth out foolishness. The eyes of the Lord are in every place, beholding the evil and the good.

Prayer: Dear God, help me be quick to discern and wise in speaking. In the Name of Jesus I pray. Amen.

Soft words are like soothing balm. They calm the spirit. Most people do not like to see a child in pain and sometimes parents would come into the office frustrated because a spouse did not respond to their child's pain quickly enough, or so it seemed to them. As a result, they would start the conversation flustered. As I listened, God would enable me to respond with a few calm words and the whole atmosphere would change. We shared the common goal of helping the child get better. Calm words were shared. The child was examined and treated. Everything goes well. Afterwards, the front clerk looks at me and smiles. All is well!

© By Dr. Sheila Hayford.

June 20
Good Shepherd Versus Hireling

John Chapter 10, verses 11-13:

I am the good shepherd: the good shepherd giveth his life for the sheep. But he that is an hireling, and not the shepherd, whose own the sheep are not, seeth the wolf coming, and leaveth the sheep, and fleeth: and the wolf catcheth them, and scattereth the sheep. The hireling fleeth, because he is an hireling, and careth not for the sheep.

Prayer: Dear Lord Jesus, how grateful we are that you are our Good Shepherd. We yield our lives to you. Amen.

The Lord Jesus makes a bold statement. He is the Good Shepherd who cares for his flock enough to sacrifice his life and die for the sins of all mankind. The Lord Jesus saw mankind lost in sin and destined for hell and willingly accepted God's plan to rescue mankind. Thus, the Lord Jesus is well qualified to give us his litmus test of a leader.

A good leader looks out for the welfare of those assigned to them. A hireling can be bought, for the hireling is for hire. Give the hireling the right price and they will abandon the welfare of those under their care.

We all have areas of responsibility and people we are assigned to serve.

Are you a shepherd or a hireling?

© By Dr. Sheila Hayford

June 21
God. Science.

1 Timothy Chapter 6, verse 20:

O Timothy, keep that which is committed to thy trust, avoiding profane and vain babblings, and oppositions of science falsely so called:

Daniel Chapter 1, verse 4:

Children in whom was no blemish, but well favoured, and skilful in all wisdom, and cunning in knowledge, and understanding science, and such as had ability in them to stand in the king's palace, and whom they might teach the learning and the tongue of the Chaldeans.

Prayer: Dear God, we love and trust you knowing you are the source of all knowledge. Thank you for the life and example of Daniel. Help us to be excellent students of the Holy Spirit, in our studies and vocations and to be wise stewards as we live for you on this earth. In Jesus' Name. Amen.

Science is studying what was, what is and what is to come. God is, God was and God is to come. Forever God! So who is chasing who?

© By Dr. Sheila Hayford.

June 22
History In The Unfolding

Romans Chapter 15, verse 4:

For whatsoever things were written aforetime were written for our learning, that we through patience and comfort of the scriptures might have hope.

Prayer: Dear God, thank you for the wonderful memories we are creating each day. Enable us to be patient as you work all things for our good, always holding on to your Word and your promises. In the Name of Jesus I pray. Amen.

Most people remember special events, some of which are indelibly edged in their memory. They can tell you exactly where they were on the day of the event and exactly what they were doing.

Do you realize that each day is history in the unfolding? What memories are you creating? What will be the story of your life's book?

© By Dr. Sheila Hayford.

June 23
People Watchers

Proverbs Chapter 22, verse 6:

Train up a child in the way he should go: and when he is old, he will not depart from it.

Prayer: Dear God, you are the greatest parent. Teach us and help us to be the parents you would have us be, loving and training our children in accordance with your will. In Jesus' Name. Amen.

I love to watch people and I find that the mall is one of the best places to do that. I see families bustling along, sales and many conversations. Invariably, a child will start to misbehave. The child may be tired, hungry or angry. I do not have a problem with that. For the most part, the parent will respond appropriately, even if it means leaving the mall until the child gets their behavior right. I do not have a problem with that. However, sometimes I see a child having a temper tantrum and the parent or adults are just laughing. "That's so cute!" or "That's so funny!" they say. And I say to myself: "in a few years when they are grown adults, those temper tantrums will not be funny." Hindsight is usually perfect and it is easier to criticize a person's actions when you are not directly involved. However, the Bible is right. And so I say, train up a child in the way he or she should <u>grow</u>.

© By Dr. Sheila Hayford

June 24
From Life To Life

1 Chronicles Chapter 4, verse 10:
And Jabez called on the God of Israel, saying, Oh that thou wouldest bless me indeed, and enlarge my coast, and that thine hand might be with me, and that thou wouldest keep me from evil, that it may not grieve me! And God granted him that which he requested.

Prayer: Dear God, thank you for showing us in this prayer of Jabez that you want us to prosper. Enlarge our capacity to receive from you. Keep us from evil, harm and danger and enable us to have our priorities right, for we worship you the giver, not the gifts. In Jesus' Name. Amen.

God wants us to grow from faith to faith, from glory to glory and from life to the life more abundant. The life we live on this earth is not just preparation for death, as the pessimists would suggest, it is preparation for life with the Lord Jesus in a glorified realm. Are you ready?

© By Dr. Sheila Hayford.

June 25
On God's Mission

1 Thessalonians Chapter 2, verse 4:

But as we were allowed of God to be put in trust with the gospel, even so we speak; not as pleasing men, but God, which trieth our hearts.

Prayer: Dear God, let us take the good news of salvation through the Lord Jesus seriously. Enable us not to water down this good news of salvation nor play down the consequences of sin. In Jesus' Name. Amen.

The Apostle Paul knew he was on God's mission, entrusted with sharing the good news of salvation. Even so has our Lord Jesus commissioned each of us to share the good news of salvation. Some born again Christians are intimidated by others and do not publicly acknowledge Christ. Some will not emphasize holy living because they seek the praises of men. When we share the good news of salvation, we must leave the results to God. So what if they do not respond to God's gift of salvation through the Lord Jesus Christ? But, what if they do?

© By Dr. Sheila Hayford.

June 26
What Is In A Name?

Exodus Chapter 1, verse 1:

Now these are the names of the children of Israel, which came into Egypt; every man and his household came with Jacob.

Prayer: Dear God, I am thankful for your character revealed to humanity in your names. I receive the names you have given me. In Jesus' Name. Amen.

Names must be important to God since God took the time to list all the names of Israel in this chapter. Why is a name important? What does a name signify? Is it possible to have more than one name? Yes! You can have a first name, middle names, a surname, a nickname, and so on. God wants to have a relationship with us and He tells us His Names. A name provides a way of identifying a person. We are social beings in relationship with others and respond to our name. Many names have meaning and imply something about the hopes and aspirations of the one who did the naming. God, our heavenly Father, gave the Lord Jesus Christ the Name that is above every name and has given to each of us the names God wants us to be identified with. What is your name? What does your name signify? Are you living up to your God given name?

© By Dr. Sheila Hayford.

June 27
On Point

Colossians Chapter 2, verse 6-8:

As ye have therefore received Christ Jesus the Lord, so walk ye in him: Rooted and built up in him, and stablished in the faith, as ye have been taught, abounding therein with thanksgiving. Beware lest any man spoil you through philosophy and vain deceit, after the tradition of men, after the rudiments of the world, and not after Christ.

Prayer: Dear Lord Jesus, you are the way, the whole truth and the firm anchor of our faith. Grant us discernment, by the power of the Holy Spirit, and keep us in your right way. Amen.

The Apostle Paul is right on point. When a person receives the Lord Jesus as Lord and Savior that is not the end of their faith journey, it is just the beginning. We are to maintain fellowship with God with thanksgiving, read the Bible, pray, learn from the wisdom of the Holy Spirit and live according to God's principles, will and purpose.

Do not let anyone deceive you with nice sounding words or men's traditions if what they say and practice is contrary to the words and will of God. Allow the Holy Spirit to anchor your life in Christ and you will be established.

© By Dr. Sheila Hayford.

June 28
The Last Word

2 Timothy Chapter 3, verses 16, 17:

All scripture is given by inspiration of God, and is profitable for doctrine, for reproof, for correction, for instruction in righteousness: That the man of God may be perfect, thoroughly furnished unto all good works.

Prayer: Dear God, thank you for the infallibility of Scripture, inspired by you to help us live right here on earth. In Jesus' Name. Amen.

Many of us have met people who always feel they must have the last word. They may be right or wrong. However, when it comes to our Christian faith, the Word of God is always the last word.

On any issue, any challenge, on anything, God's word can be fully relied on for teaching, correction, training, approval, and instruction. God's plan for us is to grow and mature, reaching perfection in Christ by the power of the Holy Spirit.

© By Dr. Sheila Hayford.

June 29
Well Doing

1 Peter Chapter 2, verses 15-17:

For so is the will of God, that with well doing ye may put to silence the ignorance of foolish men: As free, and not using your liberty for a cloke of maliciousness, but as the servants of God. Honour all men. Love the brotherhood. Fear God. Honour the king.

Prayer: Dear God, help us to be men and women of excellence; excellence in spirit, soul, body and vocation. In Jesus' Name. Amen.

God does not have a problem with excellence. In fact, God wants us to do all thing well. Our excellent work, whether on or off the job will put the words of the naysayers to naught and bring glory to God. We are not only responsible for doing an excellent job, God also expects us to have an excellent attitude, permeated with love and respect for our fellow man. May we not be found wanting!

© By Dr. Sheila Hayford.

June 30
Love And Order

1 John Chapter 2, verses 4-5:

He that saith, I know him, and keepeth not his commandments, is a liar, and the truth is not in him. But whoso keepeth his word, in him verily is the love of God perfected: hereby know we that we are in him.

Prayer: Dear God, if we love you, we will obey you. Help us show you that we love you by our obedience. In the power of the Holy Spirit. In Jesus' Name we pray. Amen.

As believers, if we truly want to experience God fully, we will study what God says in his word. As we study God's word, our faith matures. If we love God, we will do what God commands us to do. As we obey God, our love for God grows. <u>Therefore, with God, love and order go together.</u>

If a person claims to be spiritual and their lifestyle is totally contrary to God's word, they are not operating in God's truth. So be careful whose counsel you seek and who you choose to follow.

© By Dr. Sheila Hayford.

July 1
Daily Treats

Lamentations Chapter 3, verse 22-23:

It is of the Lord's mercies that we are not consumed, because his compassions fail not. They are new every morning: great is thy faithfulness.

Prayer: Dear God: thank you so much for all the good treats you give to us daily; new mercies, compassion, grace, hope, nature and the breath of life. The list of your good treats goes on for we know you protect us and care for us in ways we may not know. We praise and worship you and we bless you. For it is in Jesus' Name that we pray. Amen.

Enjoy God's daily treats; mercy, compassion, grace, hope, forgiveness, nature, the breath of life, and more!

So what should you do if you did not mail that greeting card you were supposed to send yesterday? Ask God for forgiveness and receive God's "compassion" treat of forgiveness. You are stuck in traffic and the sun is shining so brightly you lower your car shades. Do not complain. Enjoy God's daily treat of sunshine. Life on this earth could not function without the sun. Your child forgot to hand in the homework he or she worked so hard on. Extend God's "compassion" treat to the child.

We get the message, Lord!

© By Dr. Sheila Hayford.

July 2
Strengthened by God

Luke Chapter 22, verse 32:

But I have prayed for thee, that thy faith fail not: and when thou art converted, strengthen thy brethren.

Prayer: Dear Lord Jesus; thank you for praying for us. Strengthen us by the power of God the Holy Spirit. Amen.

You have to be strengthened so you can strengthen someone else. In other words, you cannot give what you do not have.

What do you have to give?

Who do you have to give it to?

© By Dr. Sheila Hayford.

July 3
Joy Loves Company

1 Timothy Chapter 6, verse 17:

Charge them that are rich in this world, that they be not highminded, nor trust in uncertain riches, but in the living God, who giveth us richly all things to enjoy;

Prayer: Dear God, we are grateful for all that you freely give us for we could not earn any of it. Thank you for the ultimate gift of your Son, our Lord and Savior Jesus Christ. Enable us, by the Holy Spirit, to always put our trust in you and not in material possessions, power or position. In Jesus' Name. Amen.

Joy loves company. When you smile at a person, they usually smile back. When you do something nice for someone, it usually prompts them to be kind to someone else.

One of the reasons the Christmas season is so popular is because it is a season of joy. Joy because we celebrate God's gift to mankind. People are generally happier, desire to do good, give to others and promote the peace of God. However, joy should not be limited to the Christmas season for God is always with us. Let us live a life of joy and share our joy with others. Your joyful lifestyle may inspire others to do the same.

And let us always remember to thank God, who gives us so freely all the good things we enjoy.

© By Dr. Sheila Hayford.

July 4
For Freedom's Sake

Galatians Chapter 5, verse 1:

Stand fast therefore in the liberty wherewith Christ hath made us free, and be not entangled again with the yoke of bondage.

Prayer: Dear God; you have made us free in Christ. Help us never to go back into manmade traditions that lead to bondage. In Jesus' Name. Amen.

Freedom is an interesting word. Some use the word loosely as in "freedom" to sin. No! Sin is bondage and not freedom. Others have used the word to describe the different rights they enjoy, such as the freedom of religious worship, the freedom to vote, the freedom to attend the school of your choice.

The thing about freedom is that it usually costs something, or in some cases human lives, for you to enjoy that freedom or benefit. Therefore, while salvation through our Lord Jesus Christ is a gift that is freely given to us, it was very costly. It cost God the death of His only begotten Son for the sins of humanity. It cost the Lord Jesus an agonizing crucifixion on the cross in a manner of death reserved for those who had done wrong or for those who were cursed, even though the Lord Jesus had done nothing wrong and whose life without sin was pleasing to God.

As we enjoy our barbecue cookouts on this Independence Day, let us remember the sacrifice of those who made this celebration possible. And as we celebrate our salvation in Christ in God, let us make every effort to share this good news with others.

Such good news cannot and must not be kept to ourselves.

© By Dr. Sheila Hayford.

July 5
Holy Living

Ephesians Chapter 1, verse 4:

According as he hath chosen us in him before the foundation of the world, that we should be holy and without blame before him in love:

Prayer: Dear Holy Spirit, we are thankful that you reside in us as born again believers in the family of God. Enable us to live holy lives that are pleasing and acceptable to God. In Jesus' Name. Amen.

What is holiness in practical Christian living and why does holiness in Christian living matter? The Bible clearly states what God's standards are in every area of life. If you are married, abstain from adultery. If you are single, abstain from fornication. If your employees work hard, pay them decently. If you see injustice, uphold God's moral standards. The second coming of the Lord Jesus will happen and happen soon. When the Lord Jesus Christ comes, righteous living will be rewarded. Unholy living will be punished. Society is influenced by many cultures and it is important that those of us who say we are Christians demonstrate that we live by what we say. Hopefully, our witness for Christ will lead others to the Lord Jesus Christ. Holiness matters because God says we should live that way. And that is the most important reason of all!

© By Dr. Sheila Hayford.

July 6
Obedience

Numbers Chapter 1, verse 54:

The Israelites did all this just as the Lord commanded Moses. (NIV)

Prayer: Dear God, obedience to you is always attractive to you. It amazes me to see the blessings that we receive on the other side of obedience to you. As we enjoy your blessings on this earth, let us remember that you also have blessings reserved for us in the hereafter. We love you and we bless you. In Jesus' Name. Amen.

Obedience just does! It does not need a lot of explaining, it does not need a lot of talking. It just does.

If you ask your children to clean their room, that is what you expect them to do. Clean their room! If your child starts arguing about the assignment, you might explain to him or her why you want them to perform that specific action but you will probably end by reminding them to do what you told them to do in the first place. In this verse, the Israelites did exactly what God told them to do. What has God instructed you to do? Go ahead and do it!

© By Dr. Sheila Hayford.

July 7
Dry, Clean - Hydrated, Clean

Psalm 24, verses 3-5:

Who shall ascend into the hill of the Lord? or who shall stand in his holy place? He that hath clean hands, and a pure heart; who hath not lifted up his soul unto vanity, nor sworn deceitfully. He shall receive the blessing from the Lord, and righteousness from the God of his salvation.

Prayer: Dear God, we want to be in your presence, so keep us holy for we know you hate sin. In Jesus' Name. Amen.

When you wash your hands with soap and dry them, your hands are clean, but dry. When you apply lotion to your clean hands, your hands are hydrated clean. I thought of the gift of salvation. When a person receives the Lord Jesus into their heart, the blood of Jesus washes away their sin. They are clean newborn babies in Christ. However, they need the hydration of the Word of God, the application of prayer and the fellowship of believers to grow. Dry skin cracks easily and cracks make it easier for germs to enter. A new believer who does not exercise the disciplines of reading the Word of God, prayer and fellowship with other believers, will find it is easier to fall back into sin and thus give satan a way to cause havoc in their lives. The one who exercises these disciplines will grow in Christ and will be used by God to advance the kingdom of God. Are you dry or hydrated clean?

© By Dr. Sheila Hayford.

July 8
Holy People

Deuteronomy Chapter 7, verse 6:
For thou art an holy people unto the Lord thy God: the Lord thy God hath chosen thee to be a special people unto himself, above all people that are upon the face of the earth.

Prayer: Dear God, holiness always matters to you. Help us not to be deceived by those who say or practice otherwise. In Jesus' Name. Amen.

Holiness still matters to God. Worldly standards may change with time, but God's standards and God's words of truth endure forever.

© By Dr. Sheila Hayford.

July 9
Gentleness Is Attractive

2 Timothy Chapter 2, verses 23-25:
But foolish and unlearned questions avoid, knowing that they do gender strifes. And the servant of the Lord must not strive; but be gentle unto all men, apt to teach, patient, In meekness instructing those that oppose themselves; if God peradventure will give them repentance to the acknowledging of the truth;

Prayer: Dear God, sometimes society causes many to project a macho, strong attitude even when they are hurting inside. You know the hearts and desires of all men and you want us to come to you in humility.

Help us to live out the fruit of the Holy Spirit for that includes gentleness. In Jesus' Name. Amen.

Gentleness is an attractive quality. It is very inspiring to see sports athletes taking the time to stoop down to have a conversation with a child. That child will tell "the whole world" that he or she got such special attention. Since gentleness is attractive, why does it seem to be in short supply? There is so much "roughness" out there. You hear the lyrics of some songs are you wonder if they are really referring to women with such horrible words or promoting such hatred and violence.

Gentleness is a part of the character of the Holy Spirit who lives within us. God knows the world has a short supply of gentleness and he expects us, as God's children, to meet that demand. So do your part. Be gentle to yourself and to your fellow man.

I do not foresee a glut of gentleness in this world until our Lord Jesus returns!

© By Dr. Sheila Hayford.

July 10
How Do You Give?

2 Corinthians Chapter 8, verses 2-5:

In the midst of a very severe trial, their overflowing joy and their extreme poverty welled up in rich generosity. For I testify that they gave as much as they were able, and even beyond their ability. Entirely on their own, they urgently pleaded with us for the privilege of sharing in this service to the Lord's people. And they exceeded our expectations: They gave themselves first of all to the Lord, and then by the will of God also to us. (NIV)

Prayer: Dear God, help us always to willingly give to you first. Then enable us as we to give to others. In Jesus' Name. Amen.

How do we give? We give our heart and our very being to God first. Then we give God what we have, willingly and joyfully, sometimes sacrificially. Then, with God's sanctification, we give our resources, time and talents in the service of others as a part of our service to God.

© By Dr. Sheila Hayford.

July 11
Meekness Is Not Weakness

Galatians Chapter 6, verse 1:
Brethren, if a man be overtaken in a fault, ye which are spiritual, restore such an one in the spirit of meekness; considering thyself, lest thou also be tempted.

Prayer: Dear God, it is sometimes so easy to see the faults of others and rush to help. However, you warn us not to be arrogant in correcting or admonishing others, for we are also human beings in need of your strength and keeping power. We thank you that satan can never snatch us out of your hand and so we willingly submit ourselves to you. In Jesus' Name. Amen.

Meekness is one of the manifestations of the fruit of the Holy Spirit so every believer must walk in meekness. However, if meekness is not weakness, what is it? To find the answer we must look to the Lord Jesus Christ. The Lord Jesus was very meek. He was gentle, kind, submissive to his parents and did not take advantage of anybody. He had compassion on the sick and healed them. Nevertheless, he was not weak. When the moneychangers defiled God's temple, the Lord Jesus overturned their tables and put them out. When the Pharisees asked the Lord Jesus questions designed to trick him, the Lord Jesus exposed their hypocrisy. So then, meekness is strength with humility. The Lord Jesus, the Son of God, did not flaunt his divinity. He willingly submitted to our father God by coming to live in a sinful world in order to die for the sins of lost humanity and he did it with love and humility. Let us be meek but not weak as we love and live in the power and strength of the Almighty God.

© By Dr. Sheila Hayford.

July 12
Profanity? Beware!

Leviticus Chapter 19, verse 12:

And ye shall not swear by my name falsely, neither shalt thou profane the name of thy God: I am the Lord.

Prayer: Dear Holy Spirit, help us to speak rightly so that our words will not grieve you. In Jesus' Name. Amen.

God, in his mercy, saved me in my youth so I am thankful that I did not learn to use profanity or curse words. You might not be surprised if someone who did not profess to know the Lord Jesus used profanity or curse words. Saul, who later became the Apostle Paul, was breathing out threats and maybe a few curse words as he entered the houses of men and women persecuting the Christians, until he met the Lord Jesus and became a Christian himself. However, it is unbecoming when a born again believer uses profanity or curse words, and even worse if the use of such profanity involves mentioning the name of God. God has given us the command not to profane his Name. He is our Lord, God the Almighty, so let us take His commands seriously.

© By Dr. Sheila Hayford.

July 13
Good Fruit

Galatians Chapter 5, verse 22-25:

But the fruit of the Spirit is love, joy, peace, longsuffering, gentleness, goodness, faith, Meekness, temperance: against such there is no law. And they that are Christ's have crucified the flesh with the affections and lusts. If we live in the Spirit, let us also walk in the Spirit.

Prayer: Dear Holy Spirit, we are depending on you. Manifest your good fruit in and through us. In the Name of Jesus, we pray. Amen.

If the Holy Spirit lives within you, as He does in every born again believer, the fruit of the Holy Spirit should be manifest. The interesting thing about fruit is that it does not appear right away. An apple tree has the potential to produce apples but it has to grow and as it matures, it produces apples and then more apples over time. Those apples in turn have the potential of producing more apples. When we receive the Lord Jesus Christ in our lives we receive the Holy Spirit, in a sense in seed form. As we grow and mature in faith, and as the anointing of God the Holy Spirit increases in our life, we are to bring forth the fruit of the Spirit. Something is wrong if a person cannot be identified by their fruit. With time the believer's fruit manifested as love, joy, longsuffering, and the like should produce even more fruit as we impact the lives of many. Let us live our lives consistent with whom we know lives within us.

© By Dr. Sheila Hayford.

July 14
Lying Vanities

Jonah Chapter 2, verses 8, 9:
They that observe lying vanities forsake their own mercy. But I will sacrifice unto thee with the voice of thanksgiving; I will pay that that I have vowed. Salvation is of the LORD.

Prayer: Dear Lord Jesus, we thank you for your gift of salvation to us. It is a gift humanity could never earn and therefore we have no reason to boast in ourselves. Help us always come to you in faith and humility. Amen.

We usually associate the word "vanity" with the word "vain". A vain person is someone who is puffed up with excessive pride because of their looks, qualifications, possessions, etc. So why do these verses talk about lying vanities? It is because a person may be deceived to think that the qualities they have, or their possessions are a result of their own power, forgetting that these are all gifts bestowed upon them by the grace and mercy of God. Those who put their trust in vanities forsake God's mercy because they fail to come to God in humility, asking for mercy for their imperfections and forgiveness from sin. Give God what is due God, acknowledge God's grace, God's mercy and thank God for his manifold gifts.

© By Dr. Sheila Hayford.

July 15
The Proper Order

James Chapter 4, verse 7:
Submit yourselves therefore to God. Resist the devil, and he will flee from you.

Prayer: Dear Holy Spirit, enable me to live according to God's proper order; submitting myself first to you and then resisting the devil. In Jesus' Name. Amen.

What is the proper order or the proper way for a Christian to live? First, surrender and submit to the authority of the Holy Spirit in every area of your life. Then resist the devil by agreeing with God in your thoughts, your words and thereby your actions. Satan may try to tempt you but he cannot fight the power of God at work in you.

So, you won your victory over that challenge. However, it is not a onetime deal. You will have other challenges and you will have to repeat the process; surrender to God, resist the devil.

You get the drill!

© By Dr. Sheila Hayford.

July 16
Significance

Luke Chapter 12, verse 15:

And he said unto them, Take heed, and beware of covetousness: for a man's life consisteth not in the abundance of the things which he possesseth.

Prayer: Dear Lord Jesus: you are always teaching us the truth. Help us heed your words at all times. Amen.

A person's significance does not lie in the amount of money or material things they are able to acquire in their lifetime. It lies in the fact that God considered the person worthy of the sacrificial death and resurrection of his Son, the Lord Jesus Christ. The Lord Jesus would have died for you if you were the only individual on this earth who had sinned. However, all mankind has sinned through Adam and are in need of the salvation given to us through the Lord Jesus Christ.

Are material things bad? Is it wrong to be wealthy? Not in and of themselves. God expects you to work with and to increase what God has given you. For indeed, multiplication and replication are God given principles. Using what you have for God, for the betterment of man and the betterment of society is pleasing to God. What you do with what you have is significant to God. Who you are in Christ is where your significance lies.

© By Dr. Sheila Hayford.

July 17
Praying For Each Other

Philippians Chapter 1, verses 10, 11:
That ye may approve things that are excellent; that ye may be sincere and without offence till the day of Christ. Being filled with the fruits of righteousness, which are by Jesus Christ, unto the glory and praise of God.

Prayer: Dear Holy Spirit; help us pray for our brethren in spirit and in truth. In Jesus' Name. Amen.

What a beautiful way to pray for each another. Praying that each of us will approve what is excellent; excellent thoughts, excellent words, excellent actions and that our lives will be sincere, forgiving towards others and bring glory to God. I do not see anything negative about this prayer. Does that mean that this is a perfect world or that there is no negativity in our thoughts? Of course not! It means that when we focus on what is good, what is not good becomes less attractive. And what is good in Christ is what brings God glory. So focus your prayers on the good you want to see happen. Yes, rebuke evil. Yes, shun evil. And yes, keep your focus on what is excellent and brings glory to God.

© By Dr. Sheila Hayford.

July 18
Mercy Is In Abundant Supply

Isaiah Chapter 42, verse 3: A bruised reed shall he not break, and the smoking flax shall he not quench: he shall bring forth judgment unto truth:

Prayer: Dear God, we are so thankful for your mercy, extended to believers and even to those who flaunt their wickedness. Help us to remember that as long as we are alive we are living in your days of grace and mercy for judgement day will come and we want to be ready. In Jesus' Name we pray. Amen.

Some are just wicked. There is no other word to describe it. They would rather the Lord Jesus allow a suffering person to die, than heal the person on the Sabbath day. They can walk right by the widow or the oppressed and not feel any compassion for them. Worse than that, they might even conspire to deprive the orphan of their rightful inheritance.

Not so with our gentle God. The more help you need, the more God is available to you. God has a huge supply of mercy. Note that the end of the verse talks about God's truth. So while God will heal the broken hearted and deliver the oppressed, God will also punish the wicked.

To the wicked God is saying, "Today is a good day to come and experience God's mercy. Acknowledge and confess your sins to God and invite the Lord Jesus to be your Lord and Savior. There are more grace and mercy blessings waiting for you."

© By Dr. Sheila Hayford.

July 19
A Joyful Praise

Psalm 111, verse 1:
Praise ye the Lord. I will praise the Lord with my whole heart, in the assembly of the upright, and in the congregation.

Prayer: Dear God, it is my honor and pleasure to praise you. I worship you for you are truly awesome. In Jesus' Name. Amen.

Have you ever met a person who is so grateful about what God has done that they can't keep it to themselves? You just can't shut us down! We talk and chat about the goodness of God, and then talk and chat some more! So go ahead, give God your praise. Don't be obnoxious, don't be rowdy, be authentic! God loves to be appreciated!

© By Dr. Sheila Hayford.

July 20
It Is A Sure Thing

John Chapter 14, verse 2: In my Father's house are many mansions: if it were not so, I would have told you. I go to prepare a place for you.

Prayer: Dear Lord Jesus, I believe you and am looking forward to the mansions you have prepared for me. As beautiful as they will be, they will pale compared to the joy of being with you face to face. Hallelujah! Amen.

The second coming of our Lord Jesus is a sure thing. This time the Lord Jesus is not coming to die for our sins because he has already accomplished that. The second coming of our Lord will be to receive us to be with him forever.

God prepared mansions are awaiting us. Preparation usually involves excitement and anticipation. So look up, our redemption is a sure thing!

© By Dr. Sheila Hayford.

July 21
Happy! Happy!

1 Kings Chapter 10, verse 8: Happy are thy men, and happy are these thy servants, which stand continually before thee, and hear thy wisdom.

Prayer: Dear God, I am so happy in Christ in God. Happy! Happy! Amen.

I always say that your spouse is the best advertisement for the state of your marriage. When you have a happy wife, she glows and it just shows. The Queen of Sheba was beside herself in admiration for the wisdom of King Solomon. She could not get over the fact that the men in King Solomon's household, even his servants, were so happy.

What is the countenance of your household saying about you?

© By Dr. Sheila Hayford.

July 22
Again And Again

Hebrews Chapter 5, verse 12:

For when for the time ye ought to be teachers, ye have need that one teach you again which be the first principles of the oracles of God; and are become such as have need of milk, and not of strong meat.

Prayer: Dear Holy Spirit, enable us to hear and obey you, submitting to you in everything. We want to grow and become mature Christians, moving forward with God's plans for our lives and for this world. In Jesus' Name. Amen.

As you study the human body, you behold the works of an awesome God who is concerned with the intricate details of every organ. Almost every specialist will tell you that their organ of study is the most amazing organ in the human body. I do not understand everything about the human body but I do know that it needs food. It needs food to grow and thrive physically. This is not a onetime deal. The body needs to be nourished again and again. Healthy eating, therefore, is a good habit.

It is now midyear, and a good time to re-evaluate how you are doing with your New Year's resolutions. What have you accomplished? What adjustments need to be made? What wholesome habits need to be started?

© By Dr. Sheila Hayford.

July 23
Predictable?

Titus Chapter 3, verse 8:

This is a faithful saying, and these things I will that thou affirm constantly, that they which have believed in God might be careful to maintain good works. These things are good and profitable unto men.

Prayer: Dear heavenly Father, we are thankful that your character is constant and dependable. Thank you for the good surprises you give to us. In Jesus' Name. Amen.

We all like good surprises. You get to work and surprise, surprise, you receive a beautiful set of flowers. "How nice!" you say. Then there are times when we want and, in fact, need predictability. If your train is scheduled to leave at nine in the morning, you expect it to leave at that time, or somewhere close to that time. After all, you have other things planned for the day. It is great that we have a predictable, unchanging God. If God said it, God will do it. If God set morning and evening in motion, so it will be as long as this earth remains. We do not have to go to bed and wonder if it will be daytime the next day. And yes, we do love God's surprises. When I wrote this devotional, I had just received a surprise email from my Panera Bread Rewards rewarding me with a free bagel each day for a whole month! How predictable or unpredictable are you?

© By Dr. Sheila Hayford.

July 24
Manufacturer's Instructions

Isaiah Chapter 40, verse 28:

Hast thou not known? hast thou not heard, that the everlasting God, the Lord, the Creator of the ends of the earth, fainteth not, neither is weary? there is no searching of his understanding.

Prayer: Dear God; you are so much more than our finite minds can understand. Thank you for the gift of the Holy Spirit who reveals you to us and for the Lord Jesus Christ who died for the sins of humanity, making it possible for us to become your sons and daughters. In Jesus' Name. Amen.

I do not generally consider myself to be mechanically minded. And I am not enthused about the idea of going through a lot of manufacturer's instructions to figure how a piece of equipment works. I would try to assemble the equipment on my own, only to find a part or two at the end that needed to be somewhere, but where? I would have to take off all the parts I had put in, read the manufacturer's instructions and assemble the parts right. Sometimes I would ask the manufacturer's representative to send someone to do the assembly or installation. Now I look for the instructions before I start the project.

God brought you to this earth with instructions. You are fearfully and wonderfully made and God knows just what you should do to live your fullest life. God's instruction manual for our life is the Holy Bible. However, you cannot just read the Bible once and think you have figured life out. Nor read it twice. This manual should be daily reading for daily living.

Follow the manufacturer's instructions!

© By Dr. Sheila Hayford.

July 25
Strangers No More

Hebrews Chapter 13, verse 2:

Be not forgetful to entertain strangers: for thereby some have entertained angels unawares.

Prayer: Dear God; help us to be hospitable. In Jesus' Name. Amen.

It was going to be a nice warm day. I walked into the lobby with a good attitude and run into a lady and two gentlemen having a conversation. She wished me a "Good Morning!" and I told her it was going to be a wonderful day. Soon I was in the conversation. It turns out they were part of a flight crew. They had flown in from Belgium and would be leaving later for Spain. What a life! I shared with them my passion for writing. As I got up to leave, they said, "Have a nice day, Sheila!" Suddenly we were strangers no more. Make some new friends today. You may be entertaining angels unawares.

© By Dr. Sheila Hayford.

July 26
Her Purple Statement

1 Peter Chapter 2, verse 9:
But you are a chosen people, a royal priesthood, a holy nation, God's special possession, that you may declare the praises of him who called you out of darkness into his wonderful light.

Prayer: Dear Lord Jesus, what an honor to be a part of God's family and to joyfully serve you. Let us share you with others. In Jesus' Name. Amen.

You could tell purple was one of her favorite colors, if not the favorite color. She had on a purple coat, purple clothes, a purple hat, accessorized with a purple bag. And they all were different shades of purple. You could not help but notice her! Her demeanor and words suggested she was comfortable with who she was as she radiated beauty and poise.

We are God's royal children. What statement are we making when we meet others? Are you comfortable in your God given identity? Do you radiate the love of Christ?

© By Dr. Sheila Hayford.

July 27
Profit Or Loss

Mark Chapter 8, verse 35-37:
For whosoever will save his life shall lose it; but whosoever shall lose his life for my sake and the gospel's, the same shall save it. For what shall it profit a man, if he shall gain the whole world, and lose his own soul? Or what shall a man give in exchange for his soul?

Prayer: Dear Lord Jesus, thank you for making the ultimate sacrifice on our behalf. We wholeheartedly give our lives to you. Amen.

It is so like the Lord Jesus to say things exactly the way they are. There is no material wealth that comes anywhere near the price of a soul. For the soul is eternal, material things are temporal. So, first make sure your soul is right with God. Then deal with the secondary matters.

© By Dr. Sheila Hayford.

July 28
If You Don't Give In, You Win!

1 Corinthians Chapter 10, verse 13:
There hath no temptation taken you but such as is common to man: but God is faithful, who will not suffer you to be tempted above that ye are able; but will with the temptation also make a way to escape, that ye may be able to bear it.

Prayer: Dear God, it is reassuring to know that whatever challenge or temptation we may face, you know it is not more than we can handle. We trust you to help us obey you in all things by the power of God the Holy Spirit. In Jesus' Name. Amen.

What did God just say? With God, nothing you are going through is going to be more than you can handle. God will always give you instructions on how to overcome in any challenge or temptation you may face. So don't give in to temptation. God's intention is for you to pass that test. If you do not give in, you win!

© By Dr. Sheila Hayford.

July 29
Samson And That Nagging Woman

Judges Chapter 16, verse 15-20:
And she said unto him, How canst thou say, I love thee, when thine heart is not with me? thou hast mocked me these three times, and hast not told me wherein thy great strength lieth. And it came to pass, when she pressed him daily with her words, and urged him, so that his soul was vexed unto death; That he told her all his heart, and said unto her, There hath not come a razor upon mine head; for I have been a Nazarite unto God from my mother's womb: if I be shaven, then my strength will go from me, and I shall become weak, and be like any other man. And when Delilah saw that he had told her all his heart, she sent and called for the lords of the Philistines, saying, Come up this once, for he hath shewed me all his heart. Then the lords of the Philistines came up unto her, and

brought money in their hand. And she made him sleep upon her knees; and she called for a man, and she caused him to shave off the seven locks of his head; and she began to afflict him, and his strength went from him. And she said, The Philistines be upon thee, Samson. And he awoke out of his sleep, and said, I will go out as at other times before, and shake myself. And he wist not that the Lord was departed from him.

Prayer: Dear God, sin may look enticing but it is never worthwhile. Through the Lord Jesus Christ we have victory over sin and temptation in the power of the Holy Spirit, so help us not yield to sin. In Jesus' Name. Amen.

What is wrong with Samson? What is a man consecrated for the service of God doing with Delilah, a woman working with his Philistine enemies to get him captured? How did Samson get there? It was as a result of Samson's foolish choices, choosing to disobey God's commandment to the people of Israel, even though his parents advised him to reconsider his ways. Samson had gotten away from the Philistines so many times that he despised the grace of God and thought he was invincible. As such, Samson was not aware when God's strength left him. Some think they can serve God in public and the devil in private and ultimately fool God. God is and will never be fooled! Let no man be fooled!

© By Dr. Sheila Hayford.

July 30
Fear Equals Retreat

Judges Chapter 7, verse 3:
Now therefore go to, proclaim in the ears of the people, saying, Whosoever is fearful and afraid, let him return and depart early from mount Gilead. And there returned of the people twenty and two thousand; and there remained ten thousand.

Prayer: Dear God, fear is never a part of your will for our lives. Help us to walk in faith and in your love. In the Name of Jesus we pray. Amen.

Why does satan use fear in the lives of many, even among those who are Christians? It is because satan recognizes this principle; if a person is fearful enough, they will not move forward. Moreover, if they fail to move forward, the work of God in their life is stalled. Gideon was going out to fight the Midianites and initially over thirty thousand people showed up to fight. When Gideon asked those who were fearful to return, two-thirds of the people went back to their "comfortable" ways. God was going to use an unconventional method to bring about Gideon's victory over the Midianites and in the end only three hundred man participated in the battle.

Are you a part of God's battle plan or is fear holding you back?

© By Dr. Sheila Hayford.

July 31
Impress God First

Luke Chapter 12, verses 19-21:

And I will say to my soul, Soul, thou hast much goods laid up for many years; take thine ease, eat, drink, and be merry. But God said unto him, Thou fool, this night thy soul shall be required of thee: then whose shall those things be, which thou hast provided? So is he that layeth up treasure for himself, and is not rich toward God.

Prayer: Dear God, help us to have our priorities right. In Jesus' Name. Amen.

While it is good to do a great job whatever your position, and it is nice to be acknowledged by your peers and others for having done a good job, it is more important to impress God first.

The person in the parable here had several barns, or in today's vernacular, it could be several businesses. He was very successful and had probably impressed many people. However, he had not taken the time to impress God by having a right relationship with God. His focus had been on himself and impressing others, but at the end of his life he had nothing that would be eternally beneficial to him.

Impressing God is not about being perfect. God knows that and that is why God sent the Lord Jesus to die for the sins of humanity. Impressing God involves taking God and God's word seriously. It is taking time to make sure we are in right standing with God by truly repenting of our sins and inviting the Lord Jesus into our heart as Lord and Savior. Remember, your life is not primarily about you, it is not primarily about another person, it is primarily about God and God's plan and purpose.

Impress God first!

© By Dr. Sheila Hayford.

August 1
**Turning Water Into Wine

John Chapter 2, verses 1, 2:

On the third day a wedding took place at Cana in Galilee. Jesus' mother was there, and Jesus and his disciples had also been invited to the wedding. (NIV)

Prayer: Dear Lord Jesus, we are so grateful that you can be implored to work miracles on our behalf. Amen.

**SERMONETTE: What the Miracle of Turning Water Into Wine Tells Me About the Lord Jesus Christ:

**Acronym: RAIN ON US, LORD!!! - Letters underlined in the Sermonette that spell this acronym

Based on St John Chapter 2 verses 1 to 11:

1. The Lord Jesus Christ **R**ecognizes the institution of marriage and celebrates it. And so He was at the wedding in Cana.

2. The Lord Jesus Christ is **A**pproachable – The Pharisees and the Sadducees seemed strict and stern and many did not seem comfortable approaching them, especially if they felt they were "sinners". On the other hand, "sinners" felt comfortable in the presence of the Lord Jesus Christ.

3. The Lord Jesus can be **I**mplored to perform a miracle. He had planned to attend the wedding as a guest but the Lord Jesus' mother, Mary, needed a miracle and begged the Lord Jesus for a miracle. She received her desired miracle.

4. The Lord Jesus Christ will give you specific i**N**structions on what you need to do to receive your miracle. He told the servants what to do.

5. In order to receive your miracle from the Lord Jesus you have to **O**bey His instructions.

6. The Lord Jesus Christ ca**N** do in a short time what it takes years to accomplish.

7. The Lord Jesus can t**U**rn the ordinary into the extraordinary.

8. The Lord Jesus took His disciples to the wedding. It teaches us that a leader has to be willing to **S**hare.

9. The **L**ord Jesus' miracles will cause people to believe on HIM!!!

10. The Lord Jesus' miracles will always bring gl**O**ry to Him.

11. Any time is a good time for the Lord Jesus Christ to perform a mi**R**acle.

12. **D**o not be afraid to have others inspect your miracle. Let the Doctor, the Governor, the Priest or the society at large see what only God could do in your life, whether they choose to receive Him as their Lord and Savior or not.

**Used by permission. Excerpt from the book "Turning Water Into Wine." ©2011 By Dr. Sheila Hayford. All Rights Reserved.

August 2
Give Your Best To Jesus

Romans Chapter 12, verse 1: I beseech you therefore, brethren, by the mercies of God, that ye present your bodies a living sacrifice, holy, acceptable unto God, which is your reasonable service.

Prayer: Dear Lord God, help us to always give you our best. In Jesus' Name. Amen.

It was getting to the end of the year and I received several letters from different organizations asking for money, many for great causes. Some almost equated your blessings from God with the amount of money you donated to their cause. As I reflected on their request, I thought, "giving your best to Jesus cannot be measured in terms of money." <u>The Lord Jesus gave himself for us and so when we give God our best we give God our whole being and all God has entrusted us with.</u> That includes our body, mind, soul, spirit, resources, time and our life. <u>Giving God our best is living a submissive life, yielded to the will of God the Holy Spirit.</u> And that should not only occur at the end of the year, although that is a good time for personal reflection. We should give our Savior, the Lord Jesus Christ, our best every day.

© By Dr. Sheila Hayford.

August 3
All The Tithes

Malachi Chapter 3, verses 10, 11, 12: Bring ye all the tithes into the storehouse, that there may be meat in mine house, and prove me now herewith, saith the Lord of hosts, if I will not open you the windows of heaven, and pour you out a blessing, that there shall not be room enough to receive it. And I will rebuke the devourer for your sakes, and he shall not destroy the fruits of your ground; neither shall your vine cast her fruit before the time in the field, saith the Lord of hosts. And all nations shall call you blessed: for ye shall be a delightsome land, saith the Lord of hosts.

Prayer: Dear God, help us to be faithful in our tithes and offerings to you. In Jesus' Name. Amen.

God will never fail His own test. If God says prove Him in giving Him your tithe, it is because God has good in store for you. Obey God and give Him the pleasure of proving Himself to you.

© By Dr. Sheila Hayford.

August 4
The God Of The Octopus

Genesis Chapter 1, verses 20, 21: And God said, Let the waters bring forth abundantly the moving creature that hath life, and fowl that may fly above the earth in the open firmament of heaven. And God created great whales, and every living creature that moveth, which the waters brought forth abundantly, after their kind, and every winged fowl after his kind: and God saw that it was good.

Prayer: Dear God, you are the all-wise God. I submit to your authority and leadership. In Jesus' Name. Amen.

It was at a book café and we were having a free for all informal discussion. The guy was obviously not pleased with the election results. "You should read this!" he said to me as he pointed to the book he had been reading. It had a picture of an octopus on the front cover. "Octopuses are very wise!" he continued. I figured that if the octopus is very wise, then the God who created the octopus must be wiser. 'What about the God who created the octopus? He must be wiser." I responded. He looked at me, snarled, "I don't believe that!" and walked away. I chuckled. His words did not change the fact that God is wiser than the octopus, for God is all knowing. I am sure the wise octopus would agree!

© By Dr. Sheila Hayford.

August 5
The Memorial

Mark Chapter 4, verses 4-9:

And there were some that had indignation within themselves, and said, Why was this waste of the ointment made? For it might have been sold for more than three hundred pence, and have been given to the poor. And they murmured against her. And Jesus said, Let her alone; why trouble ye her? she hath wrought a good work on me. For ye have the poor with you always, and whensoever ye will ye may do them good: but me ye have not always. She hath done what she could: she is come aforehand to anoint my body to the burying. Verily I say unto you, Wheresoever this gospel shall be preached throughout the whole world, this also that she hath done shall be spoken of for a memorial of her.

Prayer: Dear Lord Jesus, it is commendable what the woman with the alabaster box did for you. Help us to give our best to you. Amen.

Those present despised the woman's action. Yet she had something in her hand so precious that Jesus made her gift a memorial. She brought her very best, her expensive gift and poured it on Jesus' feet as she anointed the body of Jesus in preparation for his burial. What an honor! So how come the religious leaders and those present missed it? They were so focused on the gift that they missed the opportunity to bless the Giver of the gift. Be a blessing to God first!

© By Dr. Sheila Hayford.

August 6
Rejection; Is It Personal?

Luke Chapter 10, verse 16:
He that heareth you heareth me; and he that despiseth you despiseth me; and he that despiseth me despiseth him that sent me.

Prayer: Dear Lord Jesus, as we share the good news of salvation, we may not have the opportunity to see the listener immediately respond to you in faith. The listener may receive you as their personal Lord and Savior at a later time, or they may not. Help us not take their rejection of you personally. Amen.

Some people just do not want to offend anybody. They share the Lord Jesus with their heart and passion and are hurt when the listener does not respond positively to the good news of salvation.

The Lord Jesus does not want you to take such rejection personally. The person is not rejecting you personally; they are rejecting the Lord Jesus. And in turn, those who reject the Lord Jesus are rejecting God the Father who sent the Lord Jesus to save mankind. That is God's problem, not ours.

Relax, and enjoy sharing your faith with passion.

© By Dr. Sheila Hayford.

August 7
God Wants To Forgive You

Isaiah Chapter 55, verses 6-7:

Seek ye the Lord while he may be found, call ye upon him while he is near: Let the wicked forsake his way, and the unrighteous man his thoughts: and let him return unto the Lord, and he will have mercy upon him; and to our God, for he will abundantly pardon.

Prayer: Dear Lord God; help us come to you for forgiveness of sin, through Jesus Christ your Son. Amen.

God wants to forgive you. But you have to say, "I am sorry." We wrong God through sin and deserve the punishment for sin. However, God in his great love and mercy has sent his Son, the Lord Jesus Christ, to take on the punishment for the sins of mankind.

When we come to God, repenting of sin and invite the Lord Jesus to be our Lord and Savior, God will hear us and forgive us. No sin is too great; so come to God, repent and receive God's abundant pardon.

© By Dr. Sheila Hayford.

TEMPLE CE'LESTE BUTTERS

CUSTOM MADE NATURAL FACE, BODY AND HAIR PRODUCTS

Giving Your Body a Heavenly Glow!

We have petroleum free, paraben free, all natural:
- Whipped Shea, Mango and Coconut oil Body Butter
- Emulsified Sugar Scrub
- Whipped Shea, Coconut oil and Essential oils Hair Moisturizer
- Mango Butter and Honey Hair Conditioner and more…

Customized Gift baskets available. Choose your fragrance or keep unscented.

Call (919) 561-1540 to Order or visit www.Templecelestebutters.com

August 8
Longsuffering

Colossians Chapter 3, verses 12-15: Put on therefore, as the elect of God, holy and beloved, bowels of mercies, kindness, humbleness of mind, meekness, longsuffering; Forbearing one another, and forgiving one another, if any man have a quarrel against any: even as Christ forgave you, so also do ye. And above all these things put on charity, which is the bond of perfectness. And let the peace of God rule in your hearts, to the which also ye are called in one body; and be ye thankful.

Prayer: Dear Holy Spirit, help us to live the Holy Spirit led life. In Jesus' Name. Amen.

Wow, what a beautiful description of the fruit of the Holy Spirit, spelled out in practical ways that we can apply. We, the chosen of God, ought to show others the character of God by the way we live. Our elder brother, the Lord Jesus, fulfilled every one of these characteristics and so should we. And that includes longsuffering. How longsuffering and patient is our Lord God towards us? So how longsuffering and patient should we be to our fellow man? We must also apply sanctified common sense with the wisdom the Holy Spirit gives us. A coworker may have some idiosyncrasies that you may have to accept with all longsuffering but that does not mean putting up with verbal abuse in the workplace. Let us allow God the Holy Spirit to lead us for He will always lead us right.

© By Dr. Sheila Hayford.

August 9
All It Takes Is Two

Genesis Chapter 11, verses 3-8:
And they said one to another, Go to, let us make brick, and burn them thoroughly. And they had brick for stone, and slime had they for morter. And they said, Go to, let us build us a city and a tower, whose top may reach unto heaven; and let us make us a name, lest we be scattered abroad upon the face of the whole earth. And the Lord came down to see the city and the tower, which the children of men builded. And the Lord said, Behold, the people is one, and they have all one language; and this they begin to do: and now nothing will be restrained from them, which they have imagined to do. Go to, let us go down, and there confound their language, that they may not understand one another's speech. So the Lord scattered them abroad from thence upon the face of all the earth: and they left off to build the city.

Prayer: Dear God, enable Christians worldwide to help answer Jesus' prayers for the unity of all born again believers. In Jesus' Name. Amen.

It is astounding how much good or evil a united people can accomplish. God was so concerned with the unified defiant building plans of the children of men that God confused their language. Now, they could not work together and abandoned their building project. In the New Testament, the Lord Jesus tells us that if two of us agree on earth concerning anything, obviously within the will of God, it shall be done. What is your project undertaking with God? And with whom are you in agreement for its fulfillment?

© By Dr. Sheila Hayford.

August 10
Passing The Baton

Joshua Chapter 1, verses 5, 16: No one will be able to stand against you all the days of your life. As I was with Moses, so I will be with you; I will never leave you nor forsake you.

And they answered Joshua, saying, All that thou commandest us we will do, and whithersoever thou sendest us, we will go.

Prayer: Dear God, it is an honor to be in your service. We love you. In Jesus' Name. Amen.

Moses, God's prophet, was very humble and yet very powerful in God. There will never be another human being like him. So imagine how Joshua may have felt having to take on the leadership role. Joshua needed great assurance that he would be able to accomplish what God wanted him to do and who best to encourage Joshua than the God who appointed him to the role. Encouragement is a very powerful thing. Sometimes we promote people to positions of authority and then leave them to fend for themselves. Some elect people to leadership roles and then refuse to submit to their authority. Take time to read the entire chapter of Joshua Chapter 1. God told Joshua to be strong and of good courage and to meditate on the word of God. The people needed a leader who would be strong and right. If Joshua obeyed God, God promised Joshua would be successful. And in verse 16, the people declared their submission to the leadership of Joshua.

Leadership without submission creates confusion. In submitting to God given and God led leadership you are submitting to God. So what do you do if a leader is clearly violating the principles of God? Your first allegiance is to God. You must always pray about the situation and then allow God to direct you as to what you should do. And what do you do when God promotes you and asks you to pick up the leadership baton? Submit to God's authority and direction. Go forth with God! His promise is to never leave you or forsake you.

© By Dr. Sheila Hayford.

August 11
Faith Sees

John Chapter 20, verse 29: Jesus saith unto him, Thomas, because thou hast seen me, thou hast believed: blessed are they that have not seen, and yet have believed.

Prayer: Dear Lord Jesus, we believe you. We know you are coming back to earth to receive us, your inheritance, and we are so excited. Hallelujah! Amen.

Thomas gave the Lord Jesus the opportunity to teach believers a very important principle. Faith is to your spirit what the eyes are to your sight. Through faith we receive, by the assurance of the Holy Spirit, the promises God gives us. We see in faith what our natural eyes have not yet seen, before it manifests to our natural eyes. That runs contrary to the 'I have to see it to believe it' mentality. Ask any great inventor, and they will tell you they already saw in their mind the manifestation of their idea before it came to be. Are you looking through the lens of faith?

© By Dr. Sheila Hayford.

August 12
Did You Hear God?

Matthew Chapter 17, verses 5:

While he was still speaking, a bright cloud covered them, and a voice from the cloud said, "This is my Son, whom I love; with him I am well pleased. Listen to him!" (NIV)

Prayer: Dear God; you are speaking to us all the time. Help us to take the time to discern your voice, listen and obey you. In Jesus' Name. Amen.

Oh, goodness! The disciples heard the audible voice of God confirming the Lord Jesus as the Son of God and, as a pleased Father, affirming the work of our Lord Jesus Christ. That was almost more than the mortal bodies of Peter, James and John could handle and the Lord Jesus had to revive them and give them strength. Today, the Lord God is speaking to us in the Holy Scriptures, through his prophets, through his children and through his creation. God says: "This is my Son, whom I love; with him I am well pleased. Listen to him!" (NIV)

Are we listening?

© By Dr. Sheila Hayford.

August 13
Cutting Edge

Hebrews Chapter 4, verse 12:

For the word of God is quick, and powerful, and sharper than any twoedged sword, piercing even to the dividing asunder of soul and spirit, and of the joints and marrow, and is a discerner of the thoughts and intents of the heart.

Prayer: Dear God, thank you for the Holy Scriptures. It is alive and so powerful. We submit to your will. In Jesus' Name. Amen.

We often associate the term "cutting edge" with technology and the rapid developments that accompany it. What might be innovative or cutting edge technology today may be obsolete tomorrow. Not so with the Word of God. The Word of God was before the foundation of the earth. And it will remain forever. The Word of God is alive and powerful. It is able to cut through the chase and penetrate deep through the physical to the deeper soul and spirit issues of our lives. God's Word reveals our sin nature, our motives, our flaws and shows us how to enter into the right relationship with God. It is relevant for every generation, is dependable and will endure forever. In a world that is constantly changing, how reassuring it is for us to have a better than rock solid foundation, the sure foundation of the Word of God.

© By Dr. Sheila Hayford.

August 14
What Did You Say?

Matthew Chapter 21, verses 21, 22:

Jesus answered and said unto them, Verily I say unto you, If ye have faith, and doubt not, ye shall not only do this which is done to the fig tree, but also if ye shall say unto this mountain, Be thou removed, and be thou cast into the sea; it shall be done. And all things, whatsoever ye shall ask in prayer, believing, ye shall receive.

Prayer: Dear Lord Jesus, you teach us the importance of our words. Help us, by the Holy Spirit, not to waste time on idle words. In Jesus' Name. Amen.

It was a packed house and I was in the lobby for a few minutes after the event having conversations. Since I had planned to go grocery shopping afterwards, I headed for the grocery store. Shortly before I arrived at the store, I realized I did not have my wallet. I had left it at the host hotel. I prayed I would find my wallet and remembered the Lord Jesus said you could speak to a mountain and effect change. So I spoke to my wallet and commanded it to return to me, in the Name of Jesus, as I hurried back to the lobby. To my disappointment, there were others sitting where I sat earlier and the seated lady said she had not seen my wallet. I began to walk around looking for my wallet and thought of asking a staff member if anyone had turned my wallet in. Just then, I happened to look down and, lo and behold, there was my wallet. I picked it up and nothing was missing! God's Word works! What did you say?

© By Dr. Sheila Hayford.

August 15
Wholely Living

John Chapter 10, verses 9, 10:

I am the door: by me if any man enter in, he shall be saved, and shall go in and out, and find pasture. The thief cometh not, but for to steal, and to kill, and to destroy: I am come that they might have life, and that they might have it more abundantly.

Prayer: Dear Lord Jesus: we thank you for showing us the way, for your tell us in these verses that you are the door through which we enter and are saved. Amen.

What is the abundant life? It is the Whole Life. By that I mean, wholeness in every aspect of our being; whole physically, whole in our soul (mind, will and emotions), and whole in our spirit (regenerated by the Holy Spirit when we receive Jesus Christ as our Lord and Savior).

Is it possible to live wholly? While we will manifest complete perfection when the Lord Jesus returns, abundant living on this earth is an ongoing process. God wants us to become mature believers in Christ in God by the power the Holy Spirit.

The abundant life in Christ is a victorious life. Live victoriously!

© By Dr. Sheila Hayford.

August 16
The Glory Of God

Exodus Chapter 40, verses 34-35:

Then a cloud covered the tent of the congregation, and the glory of the LORD filled the tabernacle. And Moses was not able to enter into the tent of the congregation, because the cloud abode thereon, and the glory of the LORD filled the tabernacle.

Prayer: Dear God; I am so thankful for your presence in me and throughout my life. Thank you for always being with me. In Jesus' Name. Amen.

How beautiful! The glory of the Lord so filled the tabernacle that the prophet Moses could not enter the tent of the congregation. What we are in desperate need of in this country and in this world is a blanketing of the glory and the presence of God. We need a holy reverence for God, an atmosphere where the glory of God, the ministry of the Holy Spirit and the power of God to save and deliver is manifest.

I am not talking about the "good old days" because truth be told, those good old days were not all good. Sin has always been present in every generation. But where sin abounds, there is always the opportunity for repentance from sin and the opportunity to turn to God and receive the forgiveness and mercy of God.

It begins with born again Christians praying, seeking the face of God and taking a personal and public stand for God. That means forsaking the fleeting temptations of sin and exposing satan as a liar and a thief. Satan's desire is the destruction of humanity. We have the good news and the world needs that good news. May the glorious move of God worldwide manifest here and stay!

© By Dr. Sheila Hayford.

August 17
The Least In The Kingdom Of God

Deuteronomy Chapter 24, verses 10-12:

And there arose not a prophet since in Israel like unto Moses, whom the LORD knew face to face, In all the signs and the wonders, which the LORD sent him to do in the land of Egypt to Pharaoh, and to all his servants, and to all his land, And in all that mighty hand, and in all the great terror which Moses shewed in the sight of all Israel.

Matthew Chapter 11, verse 11: Verily I say unto you, Among them that are born of women there hath not risen a greater than John the Baptist: notwithstanding he that is least in the kingdom of heaven is greater than he.

Prayer: Dear Lord Jesus, thank you for giving us, your disciples, the authority to exert our God give dominion on this earth. Help us by the power of the Holy Spirit to use our God given influence for the glory of God. Amen.

The Lord Jesus is making an astounding declaration. He is saying that among all who have been born there was none greater than John the Baptist. Not the prophet Moses who knew God so intimately and performed so many signs and wonders in the power of God. Amazing! And then the Lord Jesus makes this simple profound true statement. The least in the kingdom of God is greater than John the Baptist. Even more amazing! How can this be?

When was the last time you saw a Christian part the seas in the power of God so that there was a heap of water raised up on either side? If you never saw that, it does not mean that it is not possible. It just means that many do not fully appreciate nor use the power of God the Holy Spirit who resides in them. What the Lord Jesus is saying is that the same Holy Spirit that raised the Lord Jesus from the dead is the Holy Spirit given as a gift to every born again believer. Through the power of

God the Holy Spirit we can do the works that the Lord Jesus did and greater. Live at the level God desires for you!

© By Dr. Sheila Hayford.

August 18
As Deep As Its Roots

Proverbs Chapter 24, verse 10:
If thou faint in the day of adversity, thy strength is small.
Prayer: Dear Holy Spirit, strengthen us by your power. In Jesus' Name. Amen.

It looked strange. A very tall tree uprooted and lying on the ground after what was not really that much rain and wind. Looking at the tall tree and its size you would have thought it was anchored securely. Then I looked at its roots and the reason became obvious. The roots were very shallow and for the tallness of the trees appeared incredibly short. The tree's roots did not run deep! A person may seem to be doing very well and appear to have their life all together. But when adversity comes, that person just falls apart. This verse says that if you fail in the day if adversity or testing your strength is small, in other words, you have shallow roots.

Anchor your faith deeply in the Word of God and you will withstand and remain standing in the tests of life.

© By Dr. Sheila Hayford.

August 19
Give God Something To Work With

1 Kings Chapter1, verses 50-53:
And Adonijah feared because of Solomon, and arose, and went, and caught hold on the horns of the altar. And it was told Solomon, saying,

Behold, Adonijah feareth king Solomon: for, lo, he hath caught hold on the horns of the altar, saying, Let king Solomon swear unto me today that he will not slay his servant with the sword. And Solomon said, If he will shew himself a worthy man, there shall not an hair of him fall to the earth: but if wickedness shall be found in him, he shall die. So king Solomon sent, and they brought him down from the altar. And he came and bowed himself to king Solomon: and Solomon said unto him, Go to thine house.

Prayer: Dear God, we come to you in faith, trusting you to keep your word. Help us to be patient with you. In Jesus' Name. Amen.

Give God something to work with:
- Some Faith
- Some Trust
- Some Words
- And Some Time.

Adonijah feared for his life. He had tried unsuccessfully to usurp King Solomon as king and now he was afraid King Solomon would kill him.

So Adonijah went to God in prayer, grabbing hold of the horns of the altar. Adonijah gave God some faith, some trust, some words and some time. God answered his prayer and Adonojah's life was spared.

© By Dr. Sheila Hayford.

August 20
Talebearers

Proverbs Chapter 26, verse 20:
Where no wood is, there the fire goeth out: so where there is no talebearer, the strife ceaseth.

Prayer: Dear God, I hate gossip! Enable me by the Holy Spirit to apply your wisdom in my words and in my deeds. In Jesus' Name. Amen.

It is disappointing when you find a person who spends his or her time gossiping and criticizing other people. Before you listen to a talebearer ask yourself, "Do I need to know and do I care to know about the situation being discussed?" If the answer is "no" let the talebearer know. I was in charge of the satellite office and from time to time, a "talebearer" would come to my office with a "tale" about a fellow worker. I would ask the talebearer if it was okay for all three of us, the talebearer, the person the talebearer was complaining or gossiping about and myself to sit down together to discuss the situation. "Oh No!" was the usual response, "it isn't that bad." End of conversation! I suspected the talebearer went to the other person and said something negative about me. However, I did not need to know and I did not care to know. Time to move forward!

© By Dr. Sheila Hayford.

August 21
Be Strong And Be Right

1 Chronicles Chapter 28, verses 9, 10:

And thou, Solomon my son, know thou the God of thy father, and serve him with a perfect heart and with a willing mind: for the Lord searcheth all hearts, and understandeth all the imaginations of the thoughts: if thou seek him, he will be found of thee; but if thou forsake him, he will cast thee off for ever. Take heed now; for the Lord hath chosen thee to build an house for the sanctuary: be strong, and do it.

Prayer: Dear God, strengthen us to do all that you have called us to do. May we do so joyfully. In the Name of Jesus we pray, Amen.

Do leaders deserve unqualified support? If God gave commands and put conditions on them and on us, we should do the same. If an elected leader is voted into power because of his or her campaign promises to the electorate, he or she should be held accountable to keep those promises. This does not mean one should always be looking for a reason to criticize leadership. A leader deserves your support but when his or her words or actions are in conflict with what God says, your loyalty to God should come first. Most leaders will appreciate feedback if it is given respectfully and with genuine concern. What if a leader chooses to flagrantly disobey God? Ultimately, he or she will have to answer to God. Pray for the leader and ask God to give you wisdom concerning the situation. God is our Wonderful Counsellor.

© By Dr. Sheila Hayford.

August 22
Looking In The Mirror

James Chapter 1, verses 23-24:
Anyone who listens to the word but does not do what it says is like someone who looks at his face in a mirror and, after looking at himself, goes away and immediately forgets what he looks like. (NIV)

Prayer: Dear Holy Spirit, you reveal ourselves to us, in the way God sees us. As we submit to you, we are transformed to be the persons God intends for us to be. Let us never reject your promptings. Amen.

Looking in the mirror is supposed to be an exercise that shows you where you look good, where you need to make some adjustments or if you just need to change your outfit. If a person looked in the mirror and saw that they had a large obvious stain on their white crisp shirt but then walked out to the Annual Board Meeting without doing anything about the stain you would be concerned. You might wonder if they had a really bad day or even if they were up to the demands of the job. Take the mirror analogy a step further and look at your life. Where you are today is a reflection of your thinking. Yesterday's way of thinking may not solve today's problems. What adjustments or changes do you need to make?

© By Dr. Sheila Hayford.

August 23
Go Forth, Their Wheels Are Falling

Exodus Chapter 14, verses 24-31:

And it came to pass, that in the morning watch the Lord looked unto the host of the Egyptians through the pillar of fire and of the cloud, and troubled the host of the Egyptians, And took off their chariot wheels, that they drave them heavily: so that the Egyptians said, Let us flee from the face of Israel; for the Lord fighteth for them against the Egyptians. And the Lord said unto Moses, Stretch out thine hand over the sea, that the waters may come again upon the Egyptians, upon their chariots, and upon their horsemen. And Moses stretched forth his hand over the sea, and the sea returned to his strength when the morning appeared; and the Egyptians fled against it; and the Lord overthrew the Egyptians in the midst of the sea. And the waters returned, and covered the chariots, and the horsemen, and all the host of Pharaoh that came into the sea after them; there remained not so much as one of them. But the children of Israel walked upon dry land in the midst of the sea; and the waters were a wall unto them on their right hand, and on their left. Thus the Lord saved Israel that day out of the hand of the Egyptians; and Israel saw the Egyptians dead upon the sea shore. And Israel saw that great work which the Lord did upon the Egyptians: and the people feared the Lord, and believed the Lord, and his servant Moses.

Prayer: Dear God, thank you for the awesome demonstration of your power. It led to reverence and faith in you and your word and respect for your chosen leaders. May that be so in our day. In the Name of Jesus we pray. Amen.

If you try to do anything for God, you will face some opposition. So what do you do when God is leading you to your promised land, God has provided a miraculous way for you to cross over and you see and hear your adversaries and enemies pursuing you? They may be well heeled, powerful, vast and defiant of your God. Do you stop in your tracks, look back, or allow fear to delay your momentum? No! God is fighting your adversaries and enemies on your behalf. Their wheels are falling. Go forth in the power of God. When you reach your promised land, those adversaries will be a part of your overcoming testimony. Then get ready for your next adventure with God!

© By Dr. Sheila Hayford.

August 24
Brazen

Isaiah Chapter 5, verse 20:
Woe unto them that call evil good, and good evil; that put darkness for light, and light for darkness; that put bitter for sweet, and sweet for bitter!

Prayer: Dear God, we know there is confusion in society when evil is called good and good is called evil. It was so in the days of the Lord Jesus on earth and persists today. Give us the discernment of the Holy Spirit to distinguish right from wrong, good from bad, holy from unholy and to place our priorities in the right order. In the Name of Jesus we pray. Amen.

It was the weekend of the NASCAR races and, as they would every year, the locals were complaining about the traffic, the cleaning up and all the loud noise that accompanied the NASCAR races. Of course, the businesses loved it, those with homes to rent, parking spaces for RVs to rent and the local NASCAR fans loved it. Well, one of the NASCAR visitors decided to write his opinion. He said the NASCAR fans were coming to town, and those locals who did not want them there should get out of town! Brazen! The rightful homeowners should leave their homes because he was coming to town! Isn't that how satan tries to operate? The born again believer has been given authority over satan in the Name of Jesus. However, for some, when satan tries to wreak havoc in their home they just complain. Then satan acts brazenly and tries to get more of what is rightfully theirs, their health, their wealth and they tolerate him. It is important to use your God given authority in Christ in God. Do not tolerate satan's tactics. Kick the devil off your God given properties. You owe it to yourself and to future generations.

© By Dr. Sheila Hayford.

August 25
Love Does

I John Chapter 3, verse 17:

But whoso hath this world's good, and seeth his brother have need, and shutteth up his bowels of compassion from him, how dwelleth the love of God in him?

Prayer: Dear God, help us to show love in what we say and what we do. In Jesus' Name, Amen.

Love does. How can you show you love someone without doing something? You might show your love by saying, "I love you!" buying roses for your spouse, providing for your family's needs, and so forth.

God, our heavenly Father, is the ultimate lover. We find it easy to love those who are nice to us, kindhearted and share our interests but God loved us while we were sinning against Him, and loved us even when we nailed His Son to the cross.

The powerful thing about love in action is that it never dies. God will always love us. God is fully love and fully just. Therefore, a loving God will only send people to hell not because He does not love them but because they rejected Him by refusing salvation through the Lord Jesus Christ. Love is meant to be a relationship. In other words, love works best when given and received. Let us love God and our fellow man in word and in deed.

© By Dr. Sheila Hayford.

August 26
Mountains In The Sky

Psalm 36, verses 5-7:

Thy mercy, O Lord, is in the heavens; and thy faithfulness reacheth unto the clouds. Thy righteousness is like the great mountains; thy judgments are a great deep: O Lord, thou preservest man and beast. How excellent is thy lovingkindness, O God! therefore the children of men put their trust under the shadow of thy wings.

Prayer: Dear God, your creation is so beautiful! Thank you. As good stewards, help us take good care of this beautiful earth. In the Name of Jesus we pray. Amen.

I love mountains! They are so beautiful, so vast and so reflective of the glorious creation of God. One day, God decided to give me a treat; mountains in the sky! I looked up and there were all these clouds in the shapes of mountains, elegant and different shapes. It was so ... beautiful! I took in the view as I allowed the mountains in the sky cloud arrangement to linger. I have not seen clouds quite like that since.

Thank you, God. I really enjoyed the view!

© By Dr. Sheila Hayford.

August 27
Singing Your Way Through

Judges Chapter 1, verse 2:

And the LORD said, Judah shall go up: behold, I have delivered the land into his hand.

Prayer: Dear God, there is much power in praising you for praise magnifies our God and puts our problems in the right perspective. May our praise be a demonstration of our faith in you. We trust you to intervene on our behalf and grant us victory. In Jesus' Name we pray. Amen.

When faced with challenges I love to sing and praise God. Somehow, as I do that my problem diminishes and my perception of God's power and omnipotence increases. And before I know it, God has given me victory. The people of Israel asked God who would go up against the Canaanites in battle. God's reply was that Judah, or Praise would go up. Judah went up and God gave them victory. Your praises to God go up and God will give you victory, God's way. What do you mean by God's way? It is victory with God having the final word. So rejoice and sing your way through!

© By Dr. Sheila Hayford.

August 28
Keeping It Real

Galatians Chapter 2, verse 20:
I am crucified with Christ: nevertheless I live; yet not I, but Christ liveth in me: and the life which I now live in the flesh I live by the faith of the Son of God, who loved me, and gave himself for me.

Prayer: Dear Lord Jesus, thank you for saving me. Now I am part of the family of God. Help me live the authentic Christian life that is mine through the power of God the Holy Spirit. Amen.

There has been a lot of talk about keeping it real lately. In other words, some feel you should act out your emotions even if it is offensive to those around you. Do your emotions represent the real you? On the other hand, are you a spirit being first with a mind, will and emotions?

Our spirit is the core of who we are, we have a soul and a physical body. Our spirit and soul reside in the physical body God has given us.

We have a responsibility towards God and towards others as to how we act in any given situation. So what should you do when you do not feel like doing what you know God says you should do? Go with God's program. Your reality is who you are in Christ. I find God's way is always the best way.

© By Dr. Sheila Hayford.

August 29
Why I Believe

1 Peter Chapter 3, verse 15:
But sanctify the Lord God in your hearts: and be ready always to give an answer to every man that asketh you a reason of the hope that is in you with meekness and fear:

Prayer: Dear Holy Spirit, help us as we share our faith with others. In Jesus' Name. Amen.

What will you say to someone who asks you the reason why your hope is in Christ? Will you fumble trying to explain your faith? God wants you prepared. <u>Your testimony</u> is about <u>your experience with God</u>, and it authentically yours to share. Share it in meekness, in reverence of God and in the power of God.

© By Dr. Sheila Hayford.

August 30
Which Way?

Matthew Chapter 15, verse 14:
Let them alone: they be blind leaders of the blind. And if the blind lead the blind, both shall fall into the ditch.

Prayer: Dear Holy Spirit, give us wisdom so we do not to fall for deceitful ideologies. In Jesus' name. Amen.

I have asked for directions more times than I would care to admit. These days, we have GPS, Google maps, apps, etc. You can ask your virtual assistant for directions and voila, you got it! Back in those days, I hated the fact that some would give you what sounded like detailed or elaborate, albeit wrong, directions. Turn right, you will see …, go past …, you will see …, shortly afterwards … will be on your right! I would write down what they said, (Don't ask me why I did not take a map!), follow their directions and arrive at the wrong place. Why didn't they just tell me they did not know? I wondered. The Bible warns about the blind leading the blind. It is one thing to lose your way with earthly directions. You can usually find your way back. It is another thing for a person to be spiritually deceived into thinking that all roads lead to God and find out on the other side of eternity that they received wrong directions. At that point, it will be too late because there is no turning back. Whose directions are you following? The Lord Jesus says He is the Way, the Truth and the Life. Will you follow his directions?

© By Dr. Sheila Hayford.

August 31
Color

Genesis Chapter 9, verse 13:
I have set my rainbow in the clouds, and it will be the sign of the covenant between me and the earth. (NIV)

Prayer: Dear God, you are the Almighty God and you keep your promises. Thank you. In Jesus' Name. Amen.

I love the fact that God created color. As humans, we see the major colors of the rainbow but I am told the rainbow has a wide spectrum of so many more colors than we see. Think how bland life would be if everything were in black and white or shades of grey?

However, even though color is a good thing, it has to be appropriate. If you gave someone a lime green carrot they probably wouldn't eat it. And if you went to work with your hair dyed orange, (unless that was your acting job) your boss might have a conversation with you.

Let your good works shine; give them some color! Why? So that your good works may appropriately bring glory to God.

© By Dr. Sheila Hayford.

September 1
Love The Soul

1 John Chapter 4, verse 20:

If a man say, I love God, and hateth his brother, he is a liar: for he that loveth not his brother whom he hath seen, how can he love God whom he hath not seen?

Prayer: Dear God; each person is valuable in your eyes. Help us to see others the way you do. In the Name of Jesus we pray. Amen.

Love the Soul for whom Christ died; Hate the Sin for which Christ died.

© By Dr. Sheila Hayford.

Love God? Love your neighbor!

September 2
Do Unto Others

Luke Chapter 6, verses 44-46:

For every tree is known by his own fruit. For of thorns men do not gather figs, nor of a bramble bush gather they grapes. A good man out of the good treasure of his heart bringeth forth that which is good; and an evil man out of the evil treasure of his heart bringeth forth that which is evil: for of the abundance of the heart his mouth speaketh. And why call ye me, Lord, Lord, and do not the things which I say?

Prayer: Dear Lord Jesus: You hate empty promises. As we relate to others, help us by the Holy Spirit to do unto others as we would like others to do to us. Amen.

Do unto others is a call to action. If we say we belong to God and have the Holy Spirit residing in us, the Lord Jesus expects us to bear fruit consistent with our faith. Treating others with dignity, respect and the sharing of ourselves in service to humanity is a great way to show respect and honor to God. For in placing value on mankind we honor the God who created mankind.

© By Dr. Sheila Hayford.

September 3
And The Praise Goes On!

Ruth Chapter 1, verses 6. 7:
When Naomi heard in Moab that the Lord had come to the aid of his people by providing food for them, she and her daughters-in-law prepared to return home from there. With her two daughters-in-law she left the place where she had been living and set out on the road that would take them back to the land of Judah.

Prayer: Dear God, Thank you for the lives of Ruth and Naomi. What a happy ending to a difficult beginning. Only you could orchestrate the outcome so beautifully and use their story to accomplish your eternal plans for humanity through your Son, the Lord Jesus Christ. Thank you for your good plans in our lives. We trust you, we praise you and we thank you in advance. In Jesus' Name. Amen.

Naomi was in a very difficult place. She had left her home country with her husband and two sons during the famine for better life in Moab.

However, her husband and two sons died in Moab and she was faced with a dilemma. Should she stay in Moab or should she return home? Upon enquiring, Naomi heard that the famine in her hometown was over and set out on the road that would lead her back to Judah, the land of Praise, for Judah is associated with Praise. Naomi left Moab a bitter person and arrived in Bethlehem just as the barley harvest was beginning. In the land of Praise, God turned things around for Naomi and in Ruth Chapter 4 we read: "The women said to Naomi: "Praise be to the Lord, who this day has not left you without a guardian-redeemer. May he become famous throughout Israel! He will renew your life and sustain you in your old age. For your daughter-in-law, who loves you and who is better to you than seven sons, has given him birth. Then Naomi took the child in her arms and cared for him. The women living there said, "Naomi has a son!" And they named him Obed. He was the father of Jesse, the father of David." And through King David we see the genealogy of the Lord Jesus. Moreover, the praise to God continues; through King David, in our generation and in generations to come. Hallelujah!

© By Dr. Sheila Hayford.

September 4
Call Him By His Name

Psalm 107, verse 8:
Oh that men would praise the Lord for his goodness, and for his wonderful works to the children of men!

Prayer: Dear God, we praise and thank you for your goodness to us. You are so nice, so kind and so merciful to us. You take better care of us than we could ever do ourselves. Help us not to take your goodness lightly or for granted and to acknowledge you as our source of all things good. In Jesus' Name we pray. Amen.

The intern had just completed several years of grueling medical education. He was in the patient's room and the patient began to address him by his first name. "Excuse me, my name is Doctor ...., do call me Doctor .... I studied hard for it!" the intern said. If men and women want to be acknowledged by their proper names and recognized for their accomplishments, how much more does God? When God reveals Himself to us through the Holy Spirit, He wants us to acknowledge the personhood of the Holy Spirit. The Holy Spirit is not a "ghost", capital "G" or small "g" and the Holy Spirit is not "it". I would hear some speak and refer to the Holy Spirit and then use the term Holy Ghost when they wanted to express a point. We know some versions of the Holy Bible used the term Holy Ghost in the English language translations at that time and so those who are quoting verbatim from that version are entitled to direct quotes. However, many using the term Holy Ghost do not express themselves in "thou shalt ..., saith ..., etc." in their everyday conversations and are not quoting Scripture verbatim. The Holy Spirit lives in every born again believer and is very much alive. Call Him by His Name!

© By Dr. Sheila Hayford.

September 5
Creation Sings!

Isaiah Chapter 44, verse 23:
Sing, O ye heavens; for the Lord hath done it: shout, ye lower parts of the earth: break forth into singing, ye mountains, O forest, and every tree therein: for the Lord hath redeemed Jacob, and glorified himself in Israel.

Prayer: Dear God, may we join your beautiful creation in worship and praise to you. In Jesus' Name. Amen.

Did you know the trees have a song? Even the rocks can speak! The Lord Jesus declared the rocks would cry out if the people did not acknowledge him. Each of us has many reasons to praise and worship God. So let us join the choir of God's nature in praise and worship of our Creator, God.

© By Dr. Sheila Hayford.

September 6
Do Good

Luke Chapter 6, verse 35:
But love ye your enemies, and do good, and lend, hoping for nothing again; and your reward shall be great, and ye shall be the children of the Highest: for he is kind unto the unthankful and to the evil.

Prayer: Dear God, your agape love extends to all mankind. Help us extend your agape love to our fellow man. In Jesus' Name. Amen.

We all know what it is to do good. And we know it is easy to do good to those who are good to us. But what about doing good to those we feel do not deserve it?

God allows the sun to shine on those who practice good as well as those who practice evil, even when they fail to acknowledge God's goodness. Like God our Heavenly Father, like child! In other words, God's children who are born again and become a part of God's family should represent God well and show others the character of our heavenly Father. Right?

© By Dr. Sheila Hayford.

September 7
Faithful And True

Revelation Chapter 21, verse 5:
And he that sat upon the throne said, Behold, I make all things new. And he said unto me, Write: for these words are true and faithful.

Prayer: Dear Lord Jesus, help us follow your example and speak faith filled and true words. In the power of God the Holy Spirit. Amen.

We know our Lord Jesus is faithful and true. This verse talks about the words of the Lord Jesus as being faithful and true words. You may have heard it said that a person is only as good as their words. God wants our words to be faithful and true, just like Him. So what if you say something that is not in step with what God says? Repent, seek God's forgiveness and renew your mind with the Word of God. As your thoughts line up with God's word, your words will.

© By Dr. Sheila Hayford.

September 8
Excuses Be Gone!

Ecclesiastes Chapter 11, verse 4:
He that observeth the wind shall not sow; and he that regardeth the clouds shall not reap.

Prayer: Dear God, help me to "do" and not to procrastinate or make excuses. In Jesus' Name. Amen.

Have you ever planned to do something and found yourself procrastinating? "The time is just not right", you might say, "when I get more money then I will do it." And if you keep delaying you might even lose the desire for that project. The writer of the book of Ecclesiastes is saying there will not always be a perfect time to do what needs to be done. Tell your excuses to be gone and get it done!

© By Dr. Sheila Hayford.

September 9
Rejoice!

Philippians Chapter 4, verse 4:
Rejoice in the Lord always: and again I say, Rejoice.
Prayer: Dear God, we rejoice in you for through our Lord Jesus Christ we have many reasons to be joyful. Let us share this joy. In Jesus' Name. Amen.

Rejoice! This sounds like a command and it is. In the world we live in, this command is for good reason. It seems like a lot of the news headlines keep emphasizing bad news. Advertisers are always telling you what they think you need and should have. Should you worry about all the bad news? Should you get depressed over what you do not have? No! The solution is to take ownership of your attitude and rejoice in Christ, no matter what. The situation may not be right, but you have a God who hears prayer and who is able to intervene in the affairs of man. God must still have a plan for you because you are still alive. Take heart and rejoice in the Lord Jesus always!

© By Dr. Sheila Hayford.

September 10
Pleasant Words

Proverbs Chapter 16, verse 24:
Pleasant words are as an honeycomb, sweet to the soul, and health to the bones.
Prayer: Dear Holy Spirit, help me say the right words at the right time. In Jesus' Name. Amen.

Wow! This Bible verse implies that what you say and what you hear can affect your physical and mental health. Did you know that words were that powerful? However, if you think about it, it does make sense. I have heard some say they will not let a negative word spoken to them ruin the rest of their day because they realize it has the potential to do so.

Let your pleasant words make a remarkable difference in the life of others.

© By Dr. Sheila Hayford.

September 11
Times Of Refreshing

Acts Chapter 3, verse 19:

Repent ye therefore, and be converted, that your sins may be blotted out, when the times of refreshing shall come from the presence of the Lord.

Prayer: Dear Holy Spirit, we need your refreshing daily. In the challenges of life, lead us to the life giving water of the Lord Jesus Christ. Amen.

Have you ever worked so hard and for so long you got weary? Have you ever been so tired, you were too tired to sleep? If that happens, you know you need a vacation, some time off or maybe, a change of location. Your body is speaking to you and telling you it needs rest and refreshing.

Times of refreshing are not only required physically, but also spiritually. As you pour out into the life of others, you need times of refreshing so the Holy Spirit can refresh and anoint you in greater measure.

Give yourself a spiritual retreat with God. Take the time to relax in God's presence and listen to what God is saying to you. Come away empowered, refreshed and strengthened for your earthly journey.

©By Dr. Sheila Hayford.

September 12
Polls

Numbers Chapter 24, verse 13:

If Balak would give me his house full of silver and gold, I cannot go beyond the commandment of the Lord, to do either good or bad of mine own mind; but what the Lord saith, that will I speak?

Prayer: Dear God, Balaam could not be bought or persuaded to speak contrary to your word, and neither should we. So help us by the power of the Holy Spirit. In Jesus' Name. Amen.

Here in the United States, polling is big business. Companies want to know what you think, advertisers want to know what you like to buy and social media wants to know your preferences. What the polls say influences decisions and policies in many cases. Not so with God. You can choose to agree or disagree with God. However, God's commands, principles or precepts are not decided by popularity contests or polls, they are put in place by a holy, sovereign God. Trust Him!

© By Dr. Sheila Hayford.

September 13
The Majority Rules?

1 Chronicles Chapter 29, verse 9:

And thou, Solomon my son, know thou the God of thy father, and serve him with a perfect heart and with a willing mind: for the Lord searcheth all hearts, and understandeth all the imaginations of the thoughts: if thou seek him, he will be found of thee; but if thou forsake him, he will cast thee off for ever.

Prayer: Dear God, what you say about anything matters more than what anyone else says. So let me keep that in mind in my decision making. Through Jesus Christ, my Lord and Savior. Amen.

The latest United States Presidential elections had people thinking a lot about the voting rules. This is not the first time that a President has won the 270 Electoral College votes needed to win the White House and lost the popular vote. Some began to wonder if the rules should be changed. The question becomes, "Is the majority always right?" History tells us that may not always be so. The more important question should be, "Is the majority in agreement with what God has to say about the situation?" In the long term, that is what really matters. For how we live on this earth is going to affect how we live the rest of eternity.

© By Dr. Sheila Hayford.

September 14
Fleeting

Luke Chapter 5, verse 15:

But so much the more went there a fame abroad of him: and great multitudes came together to hear, and to be healed by him of their infirmities.

Prayer: Dear Lord Jesus, you experienced the fleeting loyalties of the multitudes who came to hear and be healed by you on this earth. Enable us, by your keeping power, to remain faithful to you. Amen.

I remember when Tiger Woods was excelling in his game and on the top of the golf world. Golf got a great boost and many children wanted to grow up just like Tiger. Just the mention of his name was a force to reckon with and he had many company endorsements. As some would say, life for Tiger Woods was very good. Then Tiger had his personal issues to deal with and we saw his fame and influence fleeting. I have always admired Tiger Wood's golf talents and golf abilities and believe he did not get the space or the time to effectively deal with his personal issues. Nevertheless, in the end, does it really matter what people think about Tiger, about you, or anyone else? Is fame or fortune the most important thing in life? No! Fame and fortune may be fleeting. What outlasts these and life on this earth is the solid foundation of the Word of God. Does the Word of God live within you?

© By Dr. Sheila Hayford.

September 15
For Love Of Money

1 Timothy Chapter 6, verse 10:

For the love of money is the root of all evil: which while some coveted after, they have erred from the faith, and pierced themselves through with many sorrows.

Prayer: Dear God, help us not to place our hope or trust in temporal material wealth but to hope and trust in you, the Giver of life eternal. In Jesus' Name. Amen.

Money is a currency tool, to be exchanged for goods and services. You can save money for your needs, goals and aspirations or you can spend money. Having money is not wrong. What you should not do is to love or worship money because God does not want you to have the wrong relationship with money. Some have sold their principles for money. We hear of people accepting bribes of money, people paid to do mischief or paid to keep quiet when they should have spoken out. In the Bible, we read about some who erred because they put more faith in material things than in God. So while we enjoy the goods and services money can buy, let us place our trust in God and not in money.

© By Dr. Sheila Hayford.

September 16
Not For Sale

Acts Chapter 8, verse 18-22:

And when Simon saw that through laying on of the apostles' hands the Holy Ghost was given, he offered them money, Saying, Give me also this power, that on whomsoever I lay hands, he may receive the Holy Ghost. But Peter said unto him, Thy money perish with thee, because thou hast thought that the gift of God may be purchased with money. Thou hast neither part nor lot in this matter: for thy heart is not right in the sight of God. Repent therefore of this thy wickedness, and pray God, if perhaps the thought of thine heart may be forgiven thee.

Prayer: Dear God, we declare in the power of God the Holy Spirit that we have no part in witchcraft or sorcery. In the Name of Jesus. Amen.

Maybe you live in a nice home. Someone stops by and wants to purchase your lovely home. "Sorry!" you say, "it is not for sale." Simon, in this passage, had been involved in witchcraft and sorcery in the past. And when he saw the power of God the Holy Spirit, he thought he could purchase that with money. God the Holy Spirit's anointing cannot be bought. Be careful if you are told that your level of anointing by God is based on the monetary amount of your offering. Yes, you will get God's attention with your tithe and offering if your heart is right towards God. However, God's anointing is not for sale. If perhaps, you have thought otherwise, repent and ask God for forgiveness. God wants rich and poor alike to experience the life transforming power of the Holy Spirit.

© By Dr. Sheila Hayford.

September 17
Why Chance It?

Proverbs Chapter 6, verse 27: Can a man take fire in his bosom, and his clothes not be burned?

Prayer: Dear God, sin is never worth taking a chance on. Enable us, by an act of our will and the power of the Holy Spirit to live holy and acceptable lives for your pleasure and for your glory. In Jesus' Name. Amen.

Why take a chance? Can a man put fire in his bosom and not burn his clothes, and possibly himself, in the process? Of course not! Why commit adultery and take a chance on your marriage? Why get rid of your unplanned baby and risk not having another one? And most importantly, why take a chance on your relationship with God? Make certain you know the Lord Jesus as your personal Savior and Lord for sure.

© By Dr. Sheila Hayford.

September 18
Wonderful!

Psalm 77, verse 14:
Thou art the God that doest wonders: thou hast declared thy strength among the people.

Prayer: Dear God, you do so many wonderful things for us daily. Thank you. Help us share your wonderful works with others as we encourage and minister to others. In Jesus' Name. Amen.

How wonderful! We use that expression when we behold something out of the ordinary that is pleasant, joyful, admirable or inspiring. I attended one of the Summer Olympic Games. At the women's gymnastics event, one of the athletes fell during her routine. That was hard to watch. However, her team rallied and won the gold medal. That was wonderful! Several years ago, a couple at church had been praying for a child for about seventeen years. When his wife conceived, we had to have the baby shower at the church. We were so overjoyed we needed a lot of space to accommodate all those who attended the baby shower celebration. That was wonderful! What are some of the wonderful things God has done for you? Share them. Your experience may encourage someone to hold on a little longer, move past their mistakes and to remain plugged into God's wonderful gift of life.

© By Dr. Sheila Hayford.

September 19
Seasons Change

Isaiah Chapter 50, verse 4:

The Lord God hath given me the tongue of the learned, that I should know how to speak a word in season to him that is weary: he wakeneth morning by morning, he wakeneth mine ear to hear as the learned.

Prayer: Dear Holy Spirit, give us wisdom for each season in our lives. In Jesus' Name. Amen.

It looks beautiful during the autumn season. After the sometimes grueling hot summer weather, it is refreshing to feel the cooler outside temperatures and, in some areas, to observe the beauty of the changing leaves. The constancy of the autumn season is change. Things are not what they used to be and, in some cases, will never be the same. New vibrant leaves will replace the leaves that fall. God has seasons planned for each of our lives, and in many cases, those seasons come with change. So understand that going through a season of testing in your marriage is not reason to change your spouse! However, you may need to change your attitude, your priorities and you might need to spend more time in prayer. We must ask God for wisdom in each season of our lives. For, in each season many are watching God's beauty unfolding in us.

© By Dr. Sheila Hayford.

September 20
Work

2 Thessalonians Chapter 3, verse 10:

For even when we were with you, we gave you this rule: "The one who is unwilling to work shall not eat." (NIV)

Prayer: Dear Lord Jesus, you reprimanded the lazy servant who buried his talent instead of working his talent. Help us to be productive citizens of your kingdom and in the society you have placed us in. Amen.

As we celebrate Labor Day this month, we are reminded of the joy of working. It is one thing if a person is unable to work for good reason. That person may be sick, disabled, in school, lost their job, unable to find a job, pregnant, retired, or may have some other reasonable explanation. It is another thing for an able-bodied person, created by God to be responsible for the abilities and talents God has given him or her, to refuse to work. That is plain LAZY! To those, the Apostle Paul says, if you will not work, go hungry. In other words, do not enable a person to be lazy or slothful. We understand our responsibility to help the poor and needy, especially widows and orphans. However, many times people need more than just a helping hand. They need a job, they need to work, they might need to be taught new skills to be able to work and live independent fulfilling lives.

Do not keep others dependent on the generosity of others; help them succeed in life!

© By Dr. Sheila Hayford.

September 21
Soul Food

Ephesians Chapter 4, verses 22-24:
You were taught, with regard to your former way of life, to put off your old self, which is being corrupted by its deceitful desires; to be made new in the attitude of your minds; and to put on the new self, created to be like God in true righteousness and holiness. (NIV)

Prayer: Dear God, help us to take the time to meditate and study your Holy Scriptures and then apply what we learn for our good and for your glory. In the Name of Jesus we pray. Amen.

When we think of soul food in terms of food cuisine, we usually think of spicy, highly seasoned, maybe hot food. But what about food for our soul, food for our mind? How do we feed our soul? This verse gives us the answer. It is by feeding our mind with the Word of God. As we read and meditate on God's words and study Scripture, we begin to live out what we learn. For the Lord Jesus tells us in Scripture that we live out what we think. As we continually feed our soul with the Word of God, we grow in our understanding, relationship and walk with God. You do not have to like spicy food to enjoy God's soul food. Enjoy!

© By Dr. Sheila Hayford.

September 22
Back To School

Hebrews Chapter 5, verses 12-14:

For when for the time ye ought to be teachers, ye have need that one teach you again which be the first principles of the oracles of God; and are become such as have need of milk, and not of strong meat. For every one that useth milk is unskilful in the word of righteousness: for he is a babe. But strong meat belongeth to them that are of full age, even those who by reason of use have their senses exercised to discern both good and evil.

Prayer: Dear Holy Spirit, I enjoy your school and love learning from you. It is so exciting to see the principles you teach me working and to enjoy the rewards of obeying you. I need your instruction and power to help me make God's grades and I know all you do is perfect. Thank you so much. In Jesus' Name. Amen.

Growing up, we were told to enjoy our days in school because we would look back on them as some of the best days of our lives. Really? Yet how true! We had to study; subjects we liked and those we disliked. We had to do our homework, take tests and pass those tests. We studied hard and played hard. Not playing hard as in getting drunk, nor doing what was illicit, but in making new friends, attending cultural, musical and other events, speaking our mind and understanding the different cultures of those we met. Today, you might ask a person to learn how to use a new piece of technology or learn a new skill and they may be hesitant, even apprehensive. Their attitude may be that if they did not study it back then, they are not going to learn it now. Sadly, they may be left without a job when their current job is gone. So the factory closes and without a new skill, they may be permanently without a replacement job or work at a lower paying job they hate. Not so with the school of the Holy Spirit. You cannot attend the school of the Holy Spirit and expect to make it in life without growing in your relationship with the Lord Jesus and updating your knowledge and understanding of the Holy Bible. You may read the same verse of the Bible several times and each time the Holy Spirit gives you a deeper understanding or revelation of the truth. So do not get stuck in your spiritual growth and do not get left behind when the Holy Spirit is leading you forward. In God's School, the goal is growth and maturity.

© By Dr. Sheila Hayford.

September 23
Accessible

John Chapter 14, verse 6:

Jesus saith unto him, I am the way, the truth, and the life: no man cometh unto the Father, but by me.

Prayer: Dear God, thank you for always being accessible to me. I can call on you at any time, for any reason, to chat, to laugh, to petition, to praise and to worship. And I can hear you speak back to me, laugh with me and encourage me. I am so grateful to have you as my heavenly Father. Through my Lord and Savior Jesus Christ, Amen.

There are several people I respect and admire and Mr. Truett Cathy is one of them. I am so impressed by the work that he did in founding Chick Fil-A, a fast food restaurant with good food. Chick Fil-A continues to grow, even though he is now on the other side of eternity. Mr. Truett took a stand by having his employees off work on Sundays to allow them the freedom to worship God at Sunday church services and to rest and enjoy their day off. That tradition continues to this day. In addition, one of the things I loved about him was his accessibility. I was a tourist visiting their main office, where you could get a tour and learn about the company. To my surprise, Mr. Truett was willing to let us stop by his office for a short time. He was very cordial as he greeted us and we had a short conversation with him. How many C.E.O.'s would do that? Well, our God is <u>All mighty, All powerful, there is no one greater than our God, and yet through our Lord Jesus Christ, God our heavenly Father is very accessible.</u> You can talk to God at any time of the day without needing an appointment, you can laugh with him, smile with him, cry to him, sing to him, serve him and just enjoy him. I say, that is the ultimate in accessibility. I pray you choose to come to God, for if you do not you cannot blame Jesus!

© By Dr. Sheila Hayford.

September 24
What Is The Expiration Date?

Hebrews Chapter 3, verses 13-14:
But encourage one another daily, as long as it is called "Today," so that none of you may be hardened by sin's deceitfulness. We have come to share in Christ, if indeed we hold our original conviction firmly to the very end.

Prayer: Dear God, your Word warns us of the deceitfulness of sin and encourages each person to receive salvation through the Lord Jesus Christ. For as long as a person is alive on this earth, today is the day of salvation. Today and every day we need to come to you. Let us not procrastinate. In Jesus' Name we pray. Amen.

I am always reading labels and checking expiration dates when I go to the grocery store. If the date on the produce or can is past the expiration date, I take it to the manager and ask that it be taken off the shelf, not always to their delight! I also clip manufacturer's coupons to use in the store. I make sure the coupon is not past the expiration date; for if it is, the coupon is no longer good. Yet, some will buy a food item without checking the date, fall sick and find out later the food was past its freshness date. For them, the expiration date was not just a number; it was a matter of life or health. Well, the Bible has an expiration date on when a person can receive salvation through our Lord Jesus Christ and it is a matter of life or death; eternal life with God or eternal death with separation from God. The Lord Jesus came to save lost humanity and gives us the opportunity to receive him as our Lord and Savior while we are living on this earth. After that, the expiration date will be past and your eternal destiny will already be sealed.

Do you know the Lord Jesus as your personal Lord and Savior? If not, as long as you are alive on this earth you have the opportunity to make that wise decision now. Do not delay. Accept the Lord Jesus as your Lord and Savior today.

© By Dr. Sheila Hayford.

September 25
How Small Is Your Faith?

Luke Chapter 17, verse 6:
And the Lord said, If ye had faith as a grain of mustard seed, ye might say unto this sycamine tree, Be thou plucked up by the root, and be thou planted in the sea; and it should obey you.

Prayer: Dear God, let us use our faith to accomplish great things, by the power of the Holy Spirit and in agreement with your holy Word. In the name of Jesus we pray. Amen.

Great things can be accomplished with faith the size of a mustard seed. A mustard seed is a very small seed and yet faith that that size can move mountains. As that faith grows even greater things will be accomplished. The Bible tells us that God has given to each believer a measure of faith. So do not use your small faith as an excuse. Use your mustard seed faith to move mountains. You will be amazed how God will work through you.

©By Dr. Sheila Hayford.

September 26
Did God Answer?

Isaiah Chapter 59, verses 1-3:
Behold, the Lord's hand is not shortened, that it cannot save; neither his ear heavy, that it cannot hear: But your iniquities have separated between you and your God, and your sins have hid his face from you, that he will not hear. For your hands are defiled with blood, and your fingers with iniquity; your lips have spoken lies, your tongue hath muttered perverseness.

Prayer: Dear God, if we confess our sins and come to you in repentance asking for forgiveness, you will forgive us and cleanse us of all sin because of the finished work of the Lord Jesus Christ. So let us come to you in faith, humility and true repentance that our prayers may not be hindered. In the Name of Jesus we pray. Amen.

Sin is always a problem with God. God always hears, and God always wants to give you what is best for you. Sin, however, causes a block or acts as a hindrance to hearing what God is saying. Confess your sins to God and ask God for forgiveness. Then turn away or repent of the sin and allow God to speak to you freely. What did God say?

© By Dr. Sheila Hayford.

September 27
At The Source

John Chapter 4, verses 41-42:

And many more believed because of his own word; And said unto the woman, Now we believe, not because of thy saying: for we have heard him ourselves, and know that this is indeed the Christ, the Saviour of the world.

Prayer: Dear God, let us always come to you first, for you are the source of all truth. In Jesus' Name. Amen.

I like to check things out for myself whenever possible. I will rather listen to what political candidates have to say themselves than hear what someone said the candidates said. In other words, I like to go directly to the source. I remember visiting New England and enjoying spring water straight from the source. The water was so clean and so refreshing. God wants us to experience Him and to study His Word straight from the source. You have to experience salvation through the Lord Jesus Christ personally. You have to take time to read the Holy Bible and allow God to speak to you personally. Is there a place for teaching, Bible study guides and commentaries? Of course! God also speaks to us through others, through situations and through His creation. Yet there are some things about you God only wants to share with you. Allow God to whisper them in your ears!

© By Dr. Sheila Hayford.

September 28
Let It Go!

Hebrews Chapter 12, verses 14-15:
Make every effort to live in peace with everyone and to be holy; without holiness no one will see the Lord. See to it that no one falls short of the grace of God and that no bitter root grows up to cause trouble and defile many. (NIV)

Prayer: My heavenly Father; no one is worth losing sweet fellowship with you because of unforgiveness. And I certainly do not want to give satan any part of me. Enable me to be quick to forgive and to apply the pure wisdom that comes from you in my life. In the Name of Jesus I pray. Amen.

We have all been wronged at one time or another. It does not feel good. Even after the incident, we think of what we could or should have said in our human strength. It seems even worse when the person who did the offending does not or refuses to apologize. And then God says: you forgive them. "I can't on my own", I sometimes reply, "but if you will help me to forgive I am willing." For you see, if you refuse to let things go when God says you should, you set yourself up to develop a root of bitterness. Let that situation go!

© By Dr. Sheila Hayford.

September 29
Who Told You So?

Luke Chapter 6, verses 47-48:

Whosoever cometh to me, and heareth my sayings, and doeth them, I will shew you to whom he is like: He is like a man which built an house, and digged deep, and laid the foundation on a rock: and when the flood arose, the stream beat vehemently upon that house, and could not shake it: for it was founded upon a rock.

Prayer: Dear Lord Jesus, you tell us in Scripture that your sheep know your voice and will not follow the voice of anyone who misleads, speaks lies or words that are contrary to what you say. May the Holy Spirit give us the discernment and direction we need as we live for you. Amen.

Who told you so? God posed that question to Adam and Eve in the Garden of Eden. God had given Adam and Eve specific instructions and carefully explained the consequences that would follow if they disobeyed God. Satan then gave Adam and Eve conflicting, deceitful words that implied that they would not experience the consequences God had spelled out. In their rebellion, Adam and Eve disobeyed God and as a result sin entered the human race, they were expelled from the Garden of Eden and death entered the human race. Thankfully, the Lord Jesus came to rescue lost humanity and to restore those who believe on Him and accept Him as Lord and Savior back into right relationship with God. Today, many still listen to the deceitful words of satan, limiting their growth in Christ and hindering the work that needs to be accomplished in God's kingdom. Go with God's instructions and live!

© By Dr. Sheila Hayford.

September 30
What Is The Cost?

Luke Chapter 14, verse 28: For which of you, intending to build a tower, sitteth not down first, and counteth the cost, whether he have sufficient to finish it?

Prayer: Dear Lord Jesus, thank you for challenging us to count the cost. May we live sober lives to the glory of God. Amen.

If you ask a visionary to explain to you his or her dream or project, he or she will usually be able to explain it to you in elaborate detail. However, the visionary will usually seek out someone more experienced in financial affairs when it comes to the cost of financing their dream or project. Why? It is because they do not want to start their project and have to stop halfway because they run out of money. The Lord Jesus says that it is not enough to know the plan of salvation in elaborate detail. When a person decides to follow the Lord Jesus, that person must count the cost. You must understand that submitting to God's will means you may have to do things your old carnal way of thinking would not do. Things like forgiving your enemies, avoiding foul language, loving everybody. Does that mean you have to be cleaned up before you come to God? No! We come to God to get cleaned up by God. That means we make a conscious decision when we invite the Lord Jesus into our life as

Lord and Savior to repent of and forsake sin. The Holy Spirit, God's gift to us when we receive the Lord Jesus into our heart, enables us to live holy lives that please God. When we sin, we confess our sin to God, repent and ask God for forgiveness. It is an exciting, joyful journey that is not without challenges. So consider the cost and enjoy your faith journey.

©By Dr. Sheila Hayford.

October 1
With The Times

Isaiah Chapter 46, verses 9, 10: Remember the former things of old: for I am God, and there is none else; I am God, and there is none like me, Declaring the end from the beginning, and from ancient times the things that are not yet done, saying, My counsel shall stand, and I will do all my pleasure:

Prayer: Dear God, what you say is what it will be because you have the final word and the ultimate authority. And so, we have confidence in you and trust you with our very lives. In Jesus' Name. Amen.

It is interesting to observe how fashion and food change with the times. In our childhood years we thought the clothes our parents wore were so old fashioned, only to ask them during our teenage years if we could borrow their platform shoes. Then came the tall pointed long heels and the shoes with frills. It used to be you made chicken soup one way. No More! You create your own style of chicken soup and put in whatever you want. Keeping up with the times! Thankfully, the one book that has stood the test of time is the Holy Bible, the Word of God. The God who was, is, and ever will be never changes with time. So, will you place your hopes on what is here today and gone tomorrow, or will you trust the eternal truths of the Word of God? I choose God. I believe you do too!

© By Dr. Sheila Hayford.

October 2
L.E.A.P.

Philippians Chapter 2, verse 5:

In your relationships with one another, have the same mindset as Christ Jesus (NIV)

Prayer: Dear Holy Spirit, thank you for teaching me the L.E.A.P. principle. Help me to practice it as I live authentically for God. In Jesus' Name. Amen.

I developed the L.E.A.P. acronym in my walk with God and my study with God the Holy Spirit that I practice in relationships and I believe it will be a blessing to you.

- **L - Love**: Love as the foundational basis of all authentic relationships
- **E - Empathize**: Listen, Empathize, even if you do not agree with the person by understanding where they are coming from in their experience
- **A - Affirm**: What does God say about the speaker, the hearer, the situation? Affirming what God says gives you the opportunity to share God's perspective.
- **P – Prayer**: Prayer is always appropriate. The more prayer, the greater the results.

Let L.E.A.P. undergird your relationships and watch the hand of God at work.

© By Dr. Sheila Hayford.

October 3
God's Names

Isaiah Chapter 12, verse 2:

Behold, God is my salvation; I will trust, and not be afraid: for the Lord Jehovah is my strength and my song; he also is become my salvation.

Prayer: Dear God, for every need I have, you have a corresponding Name that meets that need. Help me take the time to know you and to receive from you. In Jesus' Name. Amen.

God's character is revealed in His Names. Whatever we need God to be to us, we look to His Name and receive what we need. God is Jehovah-M'Kaddesh. This name means "the God who sanctifies." In a world where sin and the influences of sin are present, we can trust the God who sanctifies to cleanse us of all sin through the blood of Jesus and empower us to live holy lives. What is your need or godly desire? Find out the Name of God that addresses that need. Then go to God in faith, believing that he will take care of you. God always has your best interest at heart and God is always right.

© By Dr. Sheila Hayford.

October 4
It Can Be Done

Matthew Chapter 18, verses 4, 5: And he answered and said unto them, Have ye not read, that he which made them at the beginning made them male and female, And said, For this cause shall a man leave father and mother, and shall cleave to his wife: and they twain shall be one flesh?

Prayer: Dear God, thank you for the sacred institution of marriage. Help us not to take marriage lightly. In Jesus' name. Amen.

The Reverend was praying for his wife to be reconciled to him. He kept praying and believing God that his wife would return to him even though it had been several years since she left. He was a business associate at the time and after he moved on, we lost touch. One day, during church service, the Pastor acknowledged the Reverend who happened to be visiting. Could it be the same Reverend? After service, I went to say "Hello" and there was the Reverend beaming with smiles, his wife by his side. They had been reconciled in marriage for about five years. I was elated as we all introduced ourselves. Who says it cannot be done? God says, "It Can!"

© By Dr. Sheila Hayford.

October 5
Get In The Game

Proverbs Chapter 12, verse 11: Those who work their land will have abundant food, but those who chase fantasies have no sense. (NIV)

Prayer: Dear God, sometimes you ask us to play a part in our prayers being answered. Help us to do so willingly and joyfully. In Jesus' name. Amen.

My favorite sports teams were not playing the football game but I had a tremendous amount of respect for one of the team's coaches so I prayed that his team would win the game. God told me that for that to happen I would have to watch the entire game. I had planned to watch part of the game, do some housework, watch some more of the game, do some more housework and find out the team I prayed for won the game at the end. Now, I realized I would have to sit down and watch the entire game! I sat down and as I watched the game I prayed, watched the game, prayed some more and then, 17 <u>seconds</u> to the end of the game, the team I had prayed for won! God had reminded me of a very valuable lesson; I had to play a part in God answering my prayer. How many people pray and ask God to do something for them but do not want to participate in the answer? They want a pay raise at their job but do not want to take the course or learn the new skills needed to get that pay raise. God wants you in the game. After all, you are the one who prayed. Can we therefore, determine the answer we get to our prayers? Yes, within the sovereignty of God.

© By Dr. Sheila Hayford.

October 6
Is It All About You?

Philippians Chapter 2, verse 4: Look not every man on his own things, but every man also on the things of others.

Prayer: Dear Holy Spirit, help us not to be selfish. We know we should take good care of ourselves and good care of whom and what God has entrusted to our care, but that is not reason to be selfish. I know from experience that sometimes you give me gifts to specifically share with others and I enjoy being a part of your plans. So help me to be faithful, in Jesus' Name. Amen.

Is it all about you, whatever that "it" may be? No! While society often emphasizes the "me, myself and I" way of thinking the Bible encourages us to be concerned about others and not just ourselves.

I remember when I had the realization that some things God gave me were not primarily for me, but for me to give to others, specific others. The testimonies that occurred after those instances were always confirmation. As many givers can attest, there is greater joy in giving than in receiving.

Yes, we love to receive, for we receive from God daily and we sure love to give!

© By Dr. Sheila Hayford.

October 7
You Can't Stop The Harvest

John Chapter 4, verse 36: And he that reapeth receiveth wages, and gathereth fruit unto life eternal: that both he that soweth and he that reapeth may rejoice together.

Prayer; Dear God; it is our time, harvest time! We look forward to the sower and the reaper rejoicing together, on this earth and in the life hereafter. In Jesus' name. Amen.

I love wholesome juicy beefsteak tomatoes and I decided to plant some tomatoes one year. I watered them, fertilized them, cleared the area of weeds and enjoyed taking care of them. It was so relaxing, even though it required work and effort. However, I was totally unprepared for the harvest. I had so many tomatoes I gave them as gifts in **baskets**! I had more than enough fresh tomatoes to enjoy and plenty to freeze for the winter. You just can't stop the harvest. If you plant, fertilize, moisturize, remove the weeds and do the right thing to keep your vegetables healthy and growing, the harvest will come. And you had better be prepared for the harvest so you do not waste what you have worked so hard to reap.

As born again believers, when we spend time with God, pray, study the Holy Bible, fellowship with other Christians and live a life that is willingly submitted to the Holy Spirit, the harvest of the fruit of the Holy Spirit is automatic. That fruit will be attractive to many. They will want to taste and see for themselves what God has done for you. Be prepared for the harvest. How will you share the good news of salvation with others? What will you do to prepare to disciple and mentor a newborn believer who has just invited the Lord Jesus into his or her heart as Lord and Savior? Start making those preparations today.

Your harvest is coming!

© By Dr. Sheila Hayford.

October 8
Take The Beam Out!

Matthew Chapter 7, verse 3, 4:
And why beholdest thou the mote that is in thy brother's eye, but considerest not the beam that is in thine own eye? Or how wilt thou say to thy brother, Let me pull out the mote out of thine eye; and, behold, a beam is in thine own eye?

Prayer: Dear Lord Jesus, you hate hypocrisy. Help us to judge ourselves according to your Word and do what we need to do to become mature disciples in you. That way, we will be a blessing to others. Amen.

I read where a woman at the Nordstrom store called Pastor Omarosa Manigault "Trump's whore" while Pastor Omarosa was out shopping for her bridesmaids' clothes at Nordstrom. I said to myself, "How can this woman say something like that and think she has any moral superiority over Pastor Omarosa or President Trump?" Take the beam out!

Figuratively speaking, every one of us has a beam or beams that may cloud our perspective or judgement. For some it is prejudice, for others it is race, still for some, it is envy and jealousy. And the list goes on. We all need God to continually work on us. And each political party needs God to continually work on their platform. So take the beam out of your eye with the power of God. When the beam is out, you will see better and more fully understand the will of God for you and for God's kingdom. Then yield to the Holy Spirit and walk in love as you strive to obey God, no matter what.

© By Dr. Sheila Hayford.

October 9th:
One Prayer Thought Away

Jeremiah Chapter 29 verse 11; For I know the thoughts that I think toward you, saith the Lord, thoughts of peace, and not of evil, to give you an expected end.

Prayer: Dear Lord Jesus, help me not to take your grace and your goodness for granted. Thank you for loving humankind even when we had sinned in rebellion toward God and for taking the punishment for our sins on the cross. May we walk in obedience to God's plan for our lives by the power of the Holy Spirit, as you showed us in your perfect example. Amen.

I was scheduled to attend a Seminar earlier in the week. I woke up early, decided to snooze a little, woke up late and missed the train. I would now get to the Seminar thirty minutes late instead of an hour early. However, at the station I found out that the printed directions I got the day before were not the most up to date directions. I would have to switch trains to get to my destination and that would mean I would be an hour late. The Seminar was scheduled for two and a half hours before the break-out "one on one" discussions and I hated to miss a whole hour. I had prayed and asked God for forgiveness for waking up late but now I thought in prayer, "Could God somehow have the Seminar start late?" It would be a whisper of a prayer thought because I could not recall a Seminar that short starting a whole hour late.

And so I continued my journey. I found I qualified for an off peak fare now that I was late and was thankful for that. When I got to the Seminar registration desk, the lady asked if I had been caught in the train signal mess up and told me the Seminar had just started! What had happened? Somehow the signal that would bring the attendees to the Seminar had a signal problem and was diverting trains away from the Seminar. One of the Speakers on the Panel of three was affected and so they had to wait. After the Seminar which was extremely productive, I heard the regular commuters on the train complaining about how the trains were VERY LATE that morning because of the signal problem. Even though it was my fault for being late, God in His tender mercy had answered my prayer thought and worked everything for my good. Amazing!

Sometimes we think we have to be in a special place or posture to pray when the truth is that prayer is a spiritual connection between us and God. God hears and answers our prayer thoughts for He loves us and gives us everything that we need for living and godliness through Jesus Christ. The secret is to pray according to the will of God. I had an opportunity to attend a different conference that day but the Holy Spirit led me to the one I attended. It was a seemingly small act of obedience but it mattered to God.

What is God calling you to do?

© By Dr. Sheila Hayford.

October 10th
The Greatest Gift

John Chapter 16, verse 24: Hitherto have ye asked nothing in my name: ask, and ye shall receive, that your joy may be full.

Prayer: Dear Lord Jesus, thank you for giving us the ultimate gift, your very life. Through you, we can come to our heavenly Father knowing that whatever we ask in your name and in agreement with the will of God, we will receive. Help us trust you fully and believe your words entirely that our joy may be complete in you. Amen.

The greatest gift you can give a person is the gift of introducing them to a personal relationship with the Lord Jesus Christ. It starts with the gift of Prayer. Pray for their eternal salvation through the Lord Jesus Christ, their family, their health, their job, and the prayer list goes on.

When we agree with God in our prayer requests and pray in the name of Jesus, the Lord Jesus promises us that prayer will be answered and that our joy would be full. What an honor! We can collaborate with God in prayer to bring about God's will on this earth. What a joy to experience the results of answered prayer!

Ask God now!

© By Dr. Sheila Hayford.

October 11th
Sow Your Seed With Purpose.

Genesis Chapter 8, verse 22: While the earth remaineth, seedtime and harvest, and cold and heat, and summer and winter, and day and night shall not cease.

Prayer: Dear God, you are so kind to us. When we sow kindness, you give us kindness back. You give us love. When we show love, your love grows. You forgive us. When we forgive others, you forgive us. And the principles you established for this earth do your bidding. Thank you. In Jesus' name. Amen.

A farmer sows apple seeds and expects to harvest apples. A farmer plants corn and expects to reap a harvest of corn. Even though that is happening in the natural world, it is part of a general Biblical principle; seedtime and harvest. So why would a person spew out hatred and act surprised when there is animosity in return? Why should a person be kind to another and be surprised that they receive kindness in return?

I struck a conversation with an older woman with her shopping cart by the Shopping Plaza parking lot one time who was en route to the store across the street and had just missed her bus. Understandably, she did not want to cross the highway. I had never met her and I had made other plans for the day. However, that could be changed. I told her I would go with her on a different bus that stopped on the other side of the highway and walk with her to the store. She later told me that her sister usually drove her to the store but her sister had to work that day.

We chatted, took the bus and walked to the store. I had some items I needed anyway so I found the three items I needed and headed to pay at the register. As I pulled out my money, the cashier placed my items in the bag. Before I could pay the cashier I noticed the older lady was right behind me. "I'll take care of that," she said. Surprised, and not wanting to rob her of the joy of giving, I said, "Thank You" and accepted her offer. Unbeknownst to me, she had also come to buy some souvenir mugs to pick up at the register and she asked the cashier to give me three of her fifteen mugs that were heavily discounted and on sale. What a wonderful act of kindness! I would later share two of the three mugs I had just received with others. Wow! Kindness begat kindness! How beautiful is that!

© By Dr. Sheila Hayford.

October 12
Different Destinies, Same Destination

Ephesians Chapter 4, verses 15-16: Instead, speaking the truth in love, we will grow to become in every respect the mature body of him who is the head, that is, Christ. From him the whole body, joined and held together by every supporting ligament, grows and builds itself up in love, as each part does its work.

Prayer: Dear God, you have a unique journey planned for each of your children. Enable us as believers to joyfully yield to the Holy Spirit, recognizing that each of us is required to do our part. In Jesus' Name. Amen.

As children of God we have different destinies. God has pre-destined good works for us on our journey here on earth and gives each of us all that we need to fulfil our destiny through Jesus Christ.

Each one of us in unlike any other person. We bring different personalities, different gifts and talents, different cultures and experiences as we relate to and interact with others. There is no need to be envious or jealous of another person's looks or talents. You probably have strengths in areas others wish they had. Working together in harmony we each fit perfectly when we do our part in God's divine purpose.

As the psalmist says, Oh, how sweet and pleasant it is when brethren dwell in unity.

© By Dr. Sheila Hayford.

October 13
Why Settle For Less?

Daniel Chapter 6, verse 3: Then this Daniel was preferred above the presidents and princes, because an excellent spirit was in him; and the king thought to set him over the whole realm.

Prayer: Dear God, you do everything excellently, no half prayer answers, no half-done provisions for you do all things perfectly. Help us to appreciate excellence and to practice excellence in all that we do in the power of God the Holy Spirit. In Jesus' Name we pray. Amen.

Why do so many people seem to have a problem with excellence? When a manager is doing his or her job they are called "bossy". When an employee is doing the job for which he or she was hired exceptionally well, that employee is made to feel he or she is "making her coworkers look bad" and is resented. When a sports team plays well in the time allotted and routes the other team with a score of 100 to 1 as an example, the coach of the winning team may be fired or investigated as to how his team could win a game by playing so well; instead of finding out what the losing team could do to improve their play. We know sports is not just about winning but true sportsmen value commitment, perseverance and excellence and that is why we have the Olympics and other national and international Championship sports events. If people are willing to settle for less, it not only affects them, it also affects future generations. The U.S. national deficit is over one trillion dollars, and this is debt that is being passed on to future generations. Where is the national outcry?

Sadly, the same kind of apathy may be found in the Christian community when it comes to the Great Commission the Lord Jesus Christ gave us. If a Christian is trying to reach out to those Jesus came to save, and that includes all of us, it goes against the "social club" atmosphere of some and the evangelizing Christian is criticized for being too un-status quo. If we want to hasten the return of our Lord Jesus, we need to be about our father's business of seeking the lost and giving them the good news of salvation. Someone did that for us, whether directly or indirectly. Now is our turn and our time. Go forth in the power and strength of God!

© By Dr. Sheila Hayford.

October 14
Simplicity In Presentation

John Chapter 3, verses 16-18: For God so loved the world, that he gave his only begotten Son, that whosoever believeth in him should not perish, but have everlasting life. For God sent not his Son into the world to condemn the world; but that the world through him might be saved. He that believeth on him is not condemned: but he that believeth not is condemned already, because he hath not believed in the name of the only begotten Son of God.

Prayer: Dear God, the good news of salvation is so simple. We do know that growth in the Christian journey should be the norm in our relationship with you but each person must first receive the Lord Jesus as Lord and Savior. So let us not to burden others by adding to the simple salvation message. May we allow the Holy Spirit to work in and through us. In Jesus' Name we pray, with thanksgiving. Amen.

Salvation is so simple a six-year-old child can understand the message of salvation and invite the Lord Jesus into his or her heart.

God wanted a human family so God sent to earth His only begotten Son, the Lord Jesus Christ, to save lost humankind. However, God respects our freewill and gives us the freedom to accept or reject the Lord Jesus Christ. Those who confess and repent of their sins, ask God for forgiveness, accept and receive the Lord Jesus into their heart as Lord and Savior are saved and born again into the family of God.

Salvation; simply presented!

© By Dr. Sheila Hayford.

October 15
Our Duty

Ecclesiastes Chapter 12, verse 13: Let us hear the conclusion of the whole matter: Fear God, and keep his commandments: for this is the whole duty of man.

Prayer: Dear God, thank you for the gift of your Son, Jesus Christ, to humanity. We could never repay our debt to you. It is our rightful duty to serve you with our whole being. So help us serve you in love by the power of the Holy Spirit. In Jesus' Name. Amen.

When I think of the goodness of God I am filled with gratitude. God did not have to do anything for us. After all, humanity through Adam chose to disobey God and then conspire to kill God's only begotten Son. But God loved humanity enough to allow His Son, the Lord Jesus Christ, to die for our sins on Calvary. If satan had known that was how God would have chosen to save mankind, he would not have instigated the plot for Judas to betray and kill the Lord Jesus. So what should be our rightful response to such a good, loving, great and awesome God? We should reverence God and obey him. That is our rightful duty!

© By Dr. Sheila Hayford.

October 16
Moving With God

Genesis Chapter 1, verse 28: And God blessed them, and God said unto them, Be fruitful, and multiply, and replenish the earth, and subdue it: and have dominion over the fish of the sea, and over the fowl of the air, and over every living thing that moveth upon the earth.

Prayer: Dear God, the authority you give us in Christ to exercise our God given dominion on this earth is astounding. Enable us, by the power of the Holy Spirit, to be faithful in our God given assignments. In Jesus' Name. Amen.

Every one of us has a God given assignment and the assignment carries with it responsibility. We are to be fruitful in what we do and how we live, producing the good fruit of the Holy Spirit and enhancing the betterment of society. We are to teach and mentor others so our good work will be multiplied in the lives of others and fill the earth with things that bring glory to God. And we are to exercise our God given dominion and authority over the planet earth God has given to us rent free. How do we do all that? We do it with the blessing of God. It is the blessing of God, in the person of the Holy Spirit, which empowers us to prosper. And we are to do everything in reverence and humility before God. God is dynamic, God is always moving forward. Move in step with God!

© By Dr. Sheila Hayford.

Eye to Eye Optometry, LLC O.D.

We provide:

Primary Eye Care   **Diabetes Eye Care**

Glaucoma Management   **Contact Lenses**

Cataract Co-Management   **Low Vision Care**

EYE CARE FOR ADULTS AND CHILDREN
CALL 302-678-EYE2

NOW ACCEPTING PATIENTS AT OUR NEWEST LOCATION!

October 17
Serving Others

Malachi Chapter 3, verses 17-18:
On the day when I act," says the Lord Almighty, "they will be my treasured possession. I will spare them, just as a father has compassion and spares his son who serves him. And you will again see the distinction between the righteous and the wicked, between those who serve God and those who do not. (NIV)

Prayer: Dear God, it is a joy serving you. Thank you for the opportunity to serve others for we serve others for your glory. In Jesus' Name. Amen.

There is just something about genuinely taking into consideration the dreams, desires and needs of others. It frees you to become unselfish. You do not have to do that; you choose to do that. And in the process, something interesting happens. While you are helping others, God is helping you. I had an event planned and one of the sponsors was very generous. Many participants benefitted from their generosity and one participant won their beautiful gift basket. After the event, I went to thank the sponsor and give them an update on the winner of their gift basket. To my utter surprise, the sponsor was extremely generous and gave me a wonderful treat! How can we fully serve God without serving others? And how can we truly serve others without God blessing us?

© By Dr. Sheila Hayford.

October 18
Joy In God's Presence

Psalm 16, verse 11: You make known to me the path of life; you will fill me with joy in your presence, with eternal pleasures at your right hand.

1 Chronicles Chapter 16, verse 29: Give unto the Lord the glory due unto his name: bring an offering, and come before him: worship the Lord in the beauty of holiness.

Prayer: Dear Holy Spirit, thank you for the gift of joy. It is much needed in the world today. As disciples of the Lord Jesus Christ, enable us to share and spread the love and joy you give us with others. In Jesus' Name. Amen.

God is such an awesome God! He has given us salvation through our Lord Jesus Christ and, with that, the gift of the Holy Spirit. God the Holy Spirit fills us with love, joy and the fruit of the Holy Spirit and in turn gives us more gifts. Through the power of God, we are blessed eternally. Praise the Lord! Give thanks to the Lord God! Worship the Lord God in the beauty of holiness!

© By Dr. Sheila Hayford.

October 19
God Is So Happy!

Zephaniah Chapter 3, verse 17: The Lord thy God in the midst of thee is mighty; he will save, he will rejoice over thee with joy; he will rest in his love, he will joy over thee with singing.

Prayer: Dear God, thank you for being our loving heavenly Father. We love you and thank you for the gift of our Lord Jesus Christ. In Jesus' Name. Amen.

God is so happy! Really? Yes! God has saved us through the Lord Jesus Christ, has blessed us with heavenly riches in Christ in God, is mighty in acts of deliverance on our behalf and now is rejoicing over us with singing. Listen! Can you hear God singing to you in Scripture? God is so happy! Rejoice in God's love. Sing along with God! Sing back to God! God is so … happy!

© By Dr. Sheila Hayford.

October 20
He Is Coming Again

Mark Chapter 14, verse 62: And Jesus said, I am: and ye shall see the Son of man sitting on the right hand of power, and coming in the clouds of heaven.

Prayer: Dear Lord Jesus, what great news! You are coming to earth again! Help us to be ready and to found faithful. In Jesus' Name. Amen.

As we prepare to enter the Advent season and celebrate the birth of our Lord Jesus, we are reminded of the humble way in which Christ was born. Yes, the angels sang in joyous celebration and the shepherds and the kings from the East came to worship the baby Jesus, but for the most part, there was not much fanfare at that time. How different it will be when the Lord Jesus returns to earth. At the second coming of the Lord Jesus, every eye will see Him for he will come back in authority and with power. Are you ready?

© By Dr. Sheila Hayford.

October 21
The Right Explanation

2 Timothy Chapter 2, verse 15: Study to shew thyself approved unto God, a workman that needeth not to be ashamed, rightly dividing the word of truth.

Prayer: Dear God, help us take responsibility for our personal study of the Holy Scriptures. You reveal yourself to us and instruct us in your Word through the Holy Spirit. Give us understanding that we may correctly interpret and apply your Word. In Jesus' Name. Amen.

We understand the need to study in school and the need to study on the job but when it comes to the Holy Bible some take an apathetic attitude. They choose to depend entirely on someone else studying and explaining the Bible to them. Since they do not take the time to personally study the Bible with the Holy Spirit as their instructor, they may not be able to discern error in the interpretation of Scripture and are spiritually tossed back and forth with every wave of men's tradition. This verse encourages every individual to engage in personal Bible study, approved unto God, rightly understanding and interpreting the Holy Scriptures.

© By Dr. Sheila Hayford.

October 22
Wherefore ...

Matthew Chapter 6, verses 29-31: And yet I say unto you, That even Solomon in all his glory was not arrayed like one of these. Wherefore, if God so clothe the grass of the field, which to day is, and to morrow is cast into the oven, shall he not much more clothe you, O ye of little faith? Therefore take no thought, saying, What shall we eat? or, What shall we drink? or, Wherewithal shall we be clothed?

Prayer; Dear God, when we consider your beautiful creation we know there is no need for us to worry for you will take good care of us. Help us to walk in obedience to you so we will find favor in your sight and our prayers to you will not be hindered, for the fault is never with you. In Jesus' Name. Amen.

What is your "Wherefore"? In the King James Version of the Bible, the word "wherefore" occurs 344 times. When you look at the context where the word "wherefore" is used it is usually used to make a statement in light of the preceding verse. In these verses, the Lord Jesus is teaching about the futility of worry. God clothes the grass of the field that we take for granted with such beauty that even king Solomon with all his wealth could not match the natural beauty of God's flowers. If grass, when gathered by men, is used as hay or thrown away, how much more will God clothe and provide for His children? Wherefore do you worry?

© By Dr. Sheila Hayford.

October 23
Welcome! Or Welcome, Welcome!

Matthew Chapter 10, verse 13:
If that home welcomes you, give it your blessing of peace. If it does not, don't bless it. (NIV)
Prayer: Dear God, thank you for the gift of hospitality. Give us wisdom and direction so that we are discerning. In Jesus' Name. Amen.

People are always welcoming you in the family of God. You are welcomed at church services, Bible study and prayer meetings, church celebrations and church events. Isn't it time you brought a guest? That way they can also experience the same welcome. Welcome! Welcome!

© By Dr. Sheila Hayford.

October 24
Too Comfortable?

Matthew Chapter 22, verse 18:
But Jesus perceived their wickedness, and said, Why tempt ye me, ye hypocrites?
Prayer: Dear Lord Jesus, you lived your live on this earth with your relationship with God and your mission from God as your priority on this earth. Let us learn from you and, in the power of the Holy Spirit, live our lives to our fullest potential. Amen.

One of the things I admire about the Lord Jesus is his straight talk. Yes, the Lord Jesus loves unconditionally and is ultra-compassionate, yet he hates hypocrisy or what some would call "phony living." When the Sadducees or Pharisees tried to trick the Lord Jesus with questions, his answers would shut them up because they realized he was talking the truth directly to them. Of course, many planned to kill Jesus because they hated what he said. However, the Lord Jesus focused on his mission on earth; to die for the sins of all humanity, even his haters.

Sometimes, we can get too comfortable. I mean that collectively individuals and churches can become so comfortable where they are; focusing just on their own needs that they forget or ignore the need to share Christ with others. When a Christian or church group loses their evangelism focus, they begin to focus on less important things like worship styles, personal preferences, personal tastes and idiosyncrasies. Sometimes God will shake things up and allow situations that will lead to more time with God and a re-focus on what should be the main thing, our relationship with the Lord Jesus Christ. Yes, it is okay to be comfortable, for no parent will want his or her child to go through needless pain. The question is: "Are you too comfortable?"

© By Dr. Sheila Hayford.

October 25
Fresh Blossoms

Song of Solomon Chapter 2, verse 12:
The flowers appear on the earth; the time of the singing of birds is come, and the voice of the turtle is heard in our land;
Prayer: Dear God, you make all things beautiful in your time. Thank you for the different seasons and the beauty of each season. In Jesus' Name. Amen.

As we behold the beautiful colors of the autumn season, we know that even though the leaves may look pretty now, most of those leaves will fall with the cooler weather. And that in a matter of time, fresh blossoms will take their place. So we enjoy today. And look forward to the coming spring. So do not say that your best days are behind you, look forward to your fresh blossoms!

© By Dr. Sheila Hayford.

October 26
The Wheat And The Tares

Matthew Chapter 13, verse 30:

Let both grow together until the harvest: and in the time of harvest I will say to the reapers, Gather ye together first the tares, and bind them in bundles to burn them: but gather the wheat into my barn.

Prayer: Dear God, thank you for being patient with us. Help us to remember that when we are required to extend patience to others. In Jesus' Name. Amen.

Sometimes we wonder with our natural minds why God is so patient. Patient with us and patient with others! In this verse God gives us a part of the reason. If God metered immediate justice, some of the wheat (born again believers) in the immediate vicinity of the tares (those who have rejected the Lord Jesus Christ as Lord and Savior) might be uprooted and destroyed. Since we know that it is not the will of God that any should perish, God in his mercy is giving those who have not yet accepted the Lord Jesus as their personal Lord and Savior a little more time or the opportunity to repent and receive the Lord Jesus Christ as Lord and Savior. God always does all things well and so we thank God for his great mercy and patience. For the time will come when the wheat will be separated from the tares; the wheat to everlasting joy in God's presence, the tares to everlasting judgment in hell. If you are wheat (a born again disciple of the Lord Jesus Christ), stay strong in your faith and hope by the power of God. If you are with the tares, you still have time to switch sides while you are on this earth. Let God's patience work for you and not against you!

© By Dr. Sheila Hayford.

October 27
Innovation

Exodus Chapter 35, verses 30-33:

Then Moses said to the Israelites, "See, the Lord has chosen Bezalel son of Uri, the son of Hur, of the tribe of Judah, and he has filled him with the Spirit of God, with wisdom, with understanding, with knowledge and with all kinds of skills - to make artistic designs for work in gold, silver and bronze, to cut and set stones, to work in wood and to engage in all kinds of artistic crafts.

Prayer: Dear God, help us to be the innovative and creative children you have called us to be, in whatever sphere of life. In Jesus' Name. Amen.

Innovation is one of the more recent buzz words that we hear these days. Companies are coming up with innovative products, schools with innovative curriculum and governments with innovative programs. Why? It is because we recognize the need to stay current and relevant for the times we live in. We do not need to fear innovation; we just have to make sure that whatever we are considering lines up with God's Biblical principles. Innovation is not a new word to God. The Lord Jesus already said that knowledge would increase, that is, new ways of doing things would be developed. Let us put God's godly innovations in place.

© By Dr. Sheila Hayford.

October 28
Your Life Is Your Legacy

Psalm 37, verse 18:

The Lord knoweth the days of the upright: and their inheritance shall be for ever.

Prayer: Dear God, thank you for giving us the opportunity to live for you on this earth and to enjoy the rewards of serving you on this earth and throughout eternity. May we leave the lasting legacy of a life well lived, leaving spiritual and material blessings for our generation as well as future generations. In Jesus' Name. Amen.

Ever so often, you will hear that a person has bequeathed thousands or millions of dollars to a charity, school or organization. We hear people describe that as their legacy. But that is only partly true. The gift is only a part of their continuing legacy, beginning with their life. That is why the recipient of the award, scholarship or money is usually given a short lesson or a reminder of the life of the giver and the giver's hopes. Our heavenly Father, God the Almighty has bequeathed a gift to man in the form of our Lord Jesus Christ. The gift did not start when the Lord Jesus came to earth. The Lord Jesus was present with God even before the creation of the human race. The Lord Jesus' birth, death and resurrection on earth are part of the continuing legacy of the Lord Jesus Christ. And as recipients of salvation through Christ, the Holy Bible reveals what the intention of the Lord God is for our lives and what God hopes will be accomplished in our lives. What is your godly legacy?

© By Dr. Sheila Hayford.

October 29
God's Exhibit

Hebrews Chapter 11, verse 6: But without faith it is impossible to please him: for he that cometh to God must believe that he is, and that he is a rewarder of them that diligently seek him.

Prayer: Dear God, you are a loving Father who desires your children come to you in faith and expectation for you will never fail us. Let us be encouraged by the faith and fortitude of men and women of faith and trust the Holy Spirit to enable us live victorious lives on earth. In Jesus' Name. Amen.

I have had the opportunity to visit Madame Tussauds, a place where the figures of men and women who have contributed in significant ways to society are displayed. It is inspiring to walk through. Each figure represents a different era, a different struggle, but for most a deep desire for the betterment of society. God has his exhibit in Hebrews Chapter 11 and in God's exhibit are men and women in God's Hall of Faith. We see Abraham, known as the Father of faith, David, who later became King David, Rahab the harlot and countless others commended for their faith. As with Madame Tussauds exhibit, some of those depicted have long departed this earth. Figures are continuously added as events unfold. And as with Madame Tussauds, God's exhibit in the Hall of Faith is ongoing. There will be a large multitude of believers, washed in the blood of Jesus who overcame their life challenges with faith in God and the Word of God. What joy awaits us then!

© By Dr. Sheila Hayford.

October 30
Affirmations

Job Chapter 19, verse 25-26: For I know that my redeemer liveth, and that he shall stand at the latter day upon the earth: And though after my skin worms destroy this body, yet in my flesh shall I see God:

Prayer: Dear God, I know the power of affirming your Word. Your Word is true and as we agree with you in our words, your word accomplishes what you desire for us. And so we thank you. In Jesus' Name. Amen.

Affirmations, or what some call declarations, are very popular these days. There is a lot of truth to the fact that what you hear repeatedly can affect what you do and how you live. With that in mind, let us look at positive and negative affirmations. God declares that you are created in the image of God, that you have value in God's sight. God has a good plan for your life and God wants to you to prosper. Meditating on God's promise to you in Jeremiah Chapter 29, verse 11 is a great reminder that God is for you and not against you. Contrast that with satan, the accuser of the brethren. Satan went to God wrongfully accusing Job of having wrong motives. Then satan tried to use others to cause Job to give up on God. Nevertheless, Job kept his affirmations strong. Even if God should slay him, he would still serve God, Job declared. And Job affirmed that not only did his Redeemer, the Lord Jesus live, but that the Lord would resurrect Job also. So what happened? God restored Job to health, gave Job twice as much as Job had before, added 140 years to Job's life and welcomed Job into His presence when Job's life here on earth was completed. What affirmations do you know for sure? Speak them in your hearing. Reject those declarations that are contrary to what God says about you. Then watch God's hand at work as you walk in your God appointed destiny.

© By Dr. Sheila Hayford.

October 31
Correction - How Do You Handle It?

Matthew Chapter 7, verse 6: Give not that which is holy unto the dogs, neither cast ye your pearls before swine, lest they trample them under their feet, and turn again and rend you.

Micah Chapter 6, verse 9: The Lord's voice crieth unto the city, and the man of wisdom shall see thy name: hear ye the rod, and who hath appointed it.

Prayer; Dear Holy Spirt, you are so poignant as you gently correct us. Help us to be sensitive to you and to be obedient to your promptings. In Jesus' Name. Amen.

You can tell whether a person is wise or foolish by the way they handle correction and by this I mean correction that is given sincerely, genuine and true. A wise person will thank you for the correction and take the steps needed to rectify the situation. A foolish person will hate you for it. Do you smear or bad mouth your boss after he or she has offered constructive criticism? When the Bible says we should not to cast our pearls before swine, that includes the giving of correction. If you realize that the person will not be able to handle the correction you are about to give, it may be better to hold your correction for another time. In Scripture, we read of instances where God gave people up to their evil ways. Why? It was because they persisted in doing evil, even though God tried to woo them, correct them and appeal to them to turn from their wicked ways. Your free will is very important to God, so God will not force his will on anyone. How do you handle God's correction?

© By Dr. Sheila Hayford.

November 1
Thanksgiving

1 Chronicles Chapter 16, verses 8-9: Give thanks unto the LORD, call upon his name, make known his deeds among the people. Sing unto him, sing psalms unto him, talk ye of all his wondrous works.

Prayer: Dear heavenly Father, even if we had a thousand tongues we could not praise and thank you enough. Blessing, glory and thanks be unto you, now and forevermore. We so love you! In Jesus' Name. Amen.

As we prepare to celebrate Thanksgiving Day this month with family, friends and strangers, let us remember to thank the Lord God first and foremost, for He is the One who gives us so freely in life all good things to enjoy.

And let us not only share the turkey and the trimmings with others, but also share the good deeds of God and His wonderful works. Let us share how God sent His only begotten Son, the Lord Jesus Christ, to die for the sins of humanity. Let us share God's faithfulness towards us in myriad ways all year long. All let us call upon God for His continued guidance, protection and provision in the years to come.

© By Dr. Sheila Hayford.

November 2
What Do You Expect?

Matthew Chapter 6, verse 8: He hath shewed thee, O man, what is good; and what doth the Lord require of thee, but to do justly, and to love mercy, and to walk humbly with thy God?

Prayer: Dear God; humility is an absolute requirement for us to come to you for we have no righteousness of our own, only the righteousness we receive when we invite the Lord Jesus into our heart as Lord and Savior. Help us to serve you in humility. In Jesus' Name. Amen.

One of the youth members was reading the program for the church service. When it came to the "Passing of the Peace" she said, "Now is the time for the passing of the peace." She continued, "This is when you say God Bless You! Welcome to the church! Good to see you!" What had she just done? She had given the congregation her expectations of what we should do during that time. What do you expect of God? And what does God expect of you?

© By Dr. Sheila Hayford.

November 3
As Far As The East Is From The West

Ecclesiastes Chapter 7, verses 8, 9:
Better is the end of a thing than the beginning thereof: and the patient in spirit is better than the proud in spirit. Be not hasty in thy spirit to be angry: for anger resteth in the bosom of fools.

Prayer: Dear God, many bad things have been done in what some wrongly ascribe to as love, for true love and abuse do not go together. Help us to do unto others as we would want others to do unto us. In Jesus' Name we pray. Amen.

Domestic violence and domestic abuse have generated a lot of discussion lately. How can you truly love a person and beat them until they become bruised or battered? If the individual doing the beating is that angry, that individual needs help to control his or her anger and the person receiving the beating needs to be out of that violent situation until a peaceful solution can be reached. Husbands are told in Scripture to love their wives as the Lord Jesus loved the church, for marriage is to be a foreshadow of the relationship between the Lord Jesus and his bride, the church body of believers. Wives are to respect their husbands. Sarah, Abraham's wife, referred to her husband as "lord" out of respect. And that did not diminish Sarah. If you love or respect a person or something you will not abuse the person or the object. If you respect money, you will not waste it. If you respect hard work, you will not be lazy. If you respect your body, you will take care of it. Love and respect for a person go with caring and sharing. And so I say, "As far as the east is from the west, so is true love and abuse."

© By Dr. Sheila Hayford.

November 4
Controversial

Galatians Chapter 5, verse 19-21:

Now the works of the flesh are manifest, which are these; Adultery, fornication, uncleanness, lasciviousness, Idolatry, witchcraft, hatred, variance, emulations, wrath, strife, seditions, heresies, Envyings, murders, drunkenness, revellings, and such like: of the which I tell you before, as I have also told you in time past, that they which do such things shall not inherit the kingdom of God.

Prayer: Dear God, let us not compromise the truth of God's Word. And when we speak, let us speak your truth in love. In Jesus' Name. Amen.

Differences can be okay. During civil discussions, it is respectful to hear what others have to say, even if you disagree with them. You might even find some common ground you can both agree on. Sometimes you cannot help but be controversial. In other words, there are some things that are plain black or plain white. What God lists as sin is sin. That does not change with time. What God lists as the fruit of the Holy Spirit does not change with time because God's character does not change.

What fruit are you bearing?

© By Dr. Sheila Hayford.

November 5
Satan's Lost Opportunity

Galatians Chapter 6, verse 7:
Be not deceived; God is not mocked: for whatsoever a man soweth, that shall he also reap.

Proverbs Chapter 14, verse 9:
Fools make a mock at sin: but among the righteous there is favour.

Prayer: Dear God, give us discernment so that we may rightly answer those who are seeking and searching for you and the truth of your Word and avoid pointless arguments with those who choose to mock you or deride your Word. In Jesus' Name. Amen.

God does not have time for foolishness. It is one thing to genuinely desire to know the truth about the Christian faith and to come to God with your heartfelt questions and concerns. On the other hand, it is entirely foolish for a person to attempt to ridicule God, the Creator of their life. Unless they repent, those who mock God are setting themselves up for God's judgment. Satan found that out the hard way. He had an excellent job on God's angelic choir, with excellent benefits until he allowed pride to enter his heart and wanted to be worshipped like God. That was satan's downfall. Satan was thrown out of heaven and fell to earth. When the Lord Jesus was out in the wilderness fasting and praying, satan tried to mock the Lord Jesus by taunting the Lord Jesus and asking the Lord Jesus to fall off the mountain. Jesus responded with a poignant quote from the Bible when he said, "Get thee hence, Satan: for it is written, Thou shalt worship the Lord thy God, and him only shalt thou serve."

King David refused to be in the company of those who mocked God. Do you?

© By Dr. Sheila Hayford.

November 6
Life Played Out

Matthew Chapter 23, verse 26:
Blind Pharisee! First clean the inside of the cup and dish, and then the outside also will be clean. (NIV)

Prayer: Dear God, we come to you through your Son, the Lord Jesus Christ. Help us live our lives in submission to the Holy Spirit who is within us. In Jesus' Name. Amen.

Your life is being played out from the inside out. So you might ask, "What do you mean by that?" The Lord Jesus said that what is inside a person is what comes out of the person. If a person's heart is in right standing with God, you see the results displayed. If a person's heart is not right in right standing with God, you see the results displayed as well.

What is the movie of your life playing out for all to see? Let us allow God to cleanse us inside, for God's service and God's good pleasure as we live our lives on the outside.

© By Dr. Sheila Hayford.

November 7
Canned Goods

Psalm 92, verse 10:

But my horn shalt thou exalt like the horn of an unicorn: I shall be anointed with fresh oil.

Prayer: Dear God, fill us to overflowing with the refreshing anointing of the Holy Spirit. In Jesus' Name. Amen.

I enjoy wholesome fresh vegetables and fresh fruit. At times I will use canned fruit or vegetables. However, no matter how fresh it was when the fruit or vegetables were packed, canned fruit just does not have the same taste. For one, the canned fruit or vegetables have to be preserved so additives are generally added to the canned fruit.

Some Christians accept canned goods by default. They do not take time for personal Bible study and quiet time with God so they do not hear what God has to say to them directly. As a result they go to others for advice, depending on others to find out what God is saying. While godly counsel in commendable and we must encourage and mentor our fellow believers in Christ, there is nothing comparable to the refreshing anointing of the Holy Spirit. Spend personal time with God!

©By Dr. Sheila Hayford.

November 8
Custom Tailored

Genesis Chapter 37, verse 3:
Now Israel loved Joseph more than all his children, because he was the son of his old age: and he made him a coat of many colours.

Prayer: Dear God, thank you for your custom made destiny for my life, designed to fit me perfectly. May I walk in that custom made suit, by the power of the Holy Spirit. For then I will be my truest self, fulfilled and joyful in Christ. In Jesus' name. Amen.

You can go to the department store and buy that beautiful suit. You may buy it at the regular price, on sale or at a huge discount. However, if you desire a custom tailored suit, that is an entirely different matter. You have to buy the right material, look for the right tailor, the tailor has to take your measurements and create a custom suit designed just for you. It may take longer, and will probably cost you more, but at the end of the day, you take joy in your one of a kind custom fit suit. God is the precise tailor we each need to be properly clothed in this life. When God created you, he gave you talents, abilities, desires, dreams, projects, relationships that are custom tailored for you. Yes, you can go to the store and do well with what you purchase but wouldn't it be better to meet with the God who created you and discover his wonderful plan for your life?

© By Dr. Sheila Hayford.

November 9
Do Not Begrudge God

Matthew Chapter 18, verses 32-33:
Then his lord, after that he had called him, said unto him, O thou wicked servant, I forgave thee all that debt, because thou desiredst me: Shouldest not thou also have had compassion on thy fellowservant, even as I had pity on thee?

Prayer: Dear God, help us extend compassion and forgiveness to our fellow man. In Jesus' Name. Amen.

Since he had been forgiven so much, you would think the man in the parable would have mercy on someone who owed him far less than he had been forgiven. Instead he was merciless to his fellow man and beat him up severely. It is easy, especially when as a born again believer you have walked with the Lord Jesus for a while, to forget how much we were forgiven. Our sins were stench to God, but through our Lord Jesus Christ, they were washed in the blood of Jesus and we were given God's clean slate. I remember saying that I would never begrudge anyone God's mercy since I receive so much from God. Then I read about Rahab in the book of Hebrews. God lists Rahab in God's hall of faith and the godly lineage that followed her. Somehow, it seemed to me like being a prostitute was a greater sin. To man it may be, but to God all sin is sin. God's halls of faith are filled with stories of sinners, saved like us through the death, burial and resurrection of the Lord Jesus Christ. And so, I had to repent for judging Rahab more harshly. Let us extend God's mercy to others for God will show mercy to the one who extends mercy.

© By Dr. Sheila Hayford.

November 10
Understanding The Times

1 Thessalonians Chapter 5, verse 1:

But of the times and the seasons, brethren, ye have no need that I write unto you.

Prayer: Dear Holy Spirit, give us discernment of the times and seasons, and enable us to live for God. In Jesus' Name. Amen.

Have you heard the expression that opportunity knocks? Why is that? Sometimes you are given the chance or opportunity to do, receive or experience something within a limited period of time. If a person misses that opportunity and the time period is past, they may never have that same opportunity. It is the same with understanding the times. God gives individuals, peoples and nations grace periods to get things right with God. It is meant to be a time of personal, corporate and national repentance towards God for sin, and towards our fellow man. It is to be a time to consecrate ourselves to the principles, plan and purpose of God and to seek God earnestly to heal us and our land. It is a time to take seriously the God ordained people, projects and resources assigned to us. If Christians miss this opportunity and focus on divisions, politics and strife, instead of focusing on God, the lost opportunity may never be regained in their lifetime. That is serious business. Do not let your God given opportunities pass you by!

© By Dr. Sheila Hayford.

November 11
Veterans

1 Thessalonians Chapter 5, verses 12, 13:

Now we ask you, brothers and sisters, to acknowledge those who work hard among you, who care for you in the Lord and who admonish you. Hold them in the highest regard in love because of their work. Live in peace with each other. Honor those who labor among you.

Prayer: Dear God, help us honor those who deserve our honor, in our homes, in the church body of believers, in the community and in our government. In Jesus' Name. Amen.

A veteran is one who has a long history of service or experience, in his or her profession, company, church, or in military service. And so, on this Veteran's day, as we thank and salute our veterans, let us also recognize, respect and honor the veterans of the faith.

© By Dr. Sheila Hayford.

November 12
Learning from Tom Brady

I Corinthians Chapter 9, verse 24:

Know ye not that they which run in a race run all, but one receiveth the prize? So run, that ye may obtain.

Prayer: Dear God, help us remember that our Christian journey on this earth is a marathon and not a sprint. Give us the ability by the power of the Holy Spirit to run with patient endurance the race that you have set before us. In Jesus' Name. Amen.

I have great respect for football quarterback Tom Brady and his Head Coach, Bill Belichick of the United States New England Patriots football team. They have shown courage, determination, fortitude and team spirit in the face of numerous challenges. It is therefore, no surprise, that the New England Patriots have participated in the football Super Bowl seven times and that Tom Brady has won the MVP award four times. Was it easy? Of course not! Tom Brady is known for his diet, discipline and work ethic. He is a great example of setting goals, working hard to achieve them, sacrificing when needed for the greater cause and winning the game despite all the odds. Can we apply these principles to our Christian walk? Yes! As Christians we are athletes participating in the marathon race of life. What we do and how we live counts for eternity. How do we live?

©By Dr. Sheila Hayford.

November 13
Rosa Parks: A Lesson In Courage

Deuteronomy Chapter 31, verse 6:

Be strong and of a good courage, fear not, nor be afraid of them: for the Lord thy God, he it is that doth go with thee; he will not fail thee, nor forsake thee.

Joshua Chapter 1, verses 8-9:

This book of the law shall not depart out of thy mouth; but thou shalt meditate therein day and night, that thou mayest observe to do according to all that is written therein: for then thou shalt make thy way prosperous, and then thou shalt have good success. Have not I commanded thee? Be strong and of a good courage; be not afraid, neither be thou dismayed: for the Lord thy God is with thee whithersoever thou goest.

Prayer: Help us, dear God, to always stand for your truth. As born again believers, we are seated in heavenly places with the Lord Jesus, your Son to whom you have given all authority. Enable us to walk in our God given authority. In Jesus' Name. Amen.

How dare you remain sitting? Don't you know your place or your position? Rosa Parks did. She knew who she was in Christ in God and so she sat. And the rest is history. Sometimes you may be right. You stand for the right cause and your cause is in line with the principles of God.

Then you discover there are those who are bent on trying to discourage you, intimidate you or taunt you into giving up on your cause or your principles. Do you give in to them? God forbid! Let Rosa Parks inspire you to stand for your godly stance.

You may be pleasantly surprised by the lives that will be positively impacted by your courageous decision.

© By Dr. Sheila Hayford.

November 14
A Spectacular Supermoon

Psalm 8, verses 3, 4: When I consider thy heavens, the work of thy fingers, the moon and the stars, which thou hast ordained; What is man, that thou art mindful of him? and the son of man, that thou visitest him?

Prayer: Dear God, your awesome creation is so amazing! And yet you are so mindful of mankind. What an honor! Thank you. In Jesus' name. Amen.

It was going to be the largest Supermoon since 1948, and there would not be a Supermoon like the one on November 14, 2016 till the year 2034. I put the date on my calendar to be sure I observed this event that evening. In the course of the business of that day I forgot about the Supermoon. Around 3am, the Holy Spirit reminded me of the Supermoon. I was lying in bed and walking downstairs at that time was not very attractive to me. I thought, "I can watch it later in the morning." But no, the sun would be rising from the east at that time. I went downstairs, pulled the kitchen curtains aside, did not see the moon and came back to bed. "I'm sorry, Holy Spirit" I said as I lay back down in bed. Then I pondered the opportunity that would be missed. More importantly, I figured that if the Holy Spirit had prompted me to take a look at the Supermoon wonder that was reason enough to look. I went back to the kitchen and opened the back kitchen door. I looked up at the sky and in between the trees was the most beautiful, bright moon I have ever seen. It seemed so very close and seemed to have more 'detail' than I had ever seen. "This is so beautiful!" I kept saying as I took in the spectacular view. I went upstairs to get my mobile smartphone and take a picture to remind me of this special event. As I walked back upstairs, I thought, "I must be special to God." I sat on my bed and found myself raising my hands in worship to God.

How many times has a person said, "I'm sorry, Holy Spirit, I know you want me to start this business or ministry but I am so comfortable where I am right now"? Or someone might say, "I'm sorry, Holy Spirit. I know I can have healing from sickness or disease through Jesus Christ on this earth but I will wait till the Lord Jesus comes for my glorified body." Sometimes the excuse may sound pious, "I'm sorry Holy Spirit, I know I should stop and help this person but I am on my way to church and don't want to be late." I am so thankful God looked past my initial foolishness and allowed me to experience the spectacular beauty of His creation. Thank you, dear Holy Spirit. I really enjoyed the show!

© By Dr. Sheila Hayford.

B.C.P. SMYRNA

19 S. DuPont Blvd, Smyrna, DE 19977

302-653-8521

Chrysler. Jeep, Dodge.

BUY HERE, PAY HERE: Financing Options Available!

Serving Our Customers for over 70 years!

Buy Local; It's Worth THE DRIVE!

November 15
Protected In The Blood Of Jesus

Isaiah Chapter 54, verse 17:

No weapon that is formed against thee shall prosper; and every tongue that shall rise against thee in judgment thou shalt condemn. This is the heritage of the servants of the Lord, and their righteousness is of me, saith the Lord.

Prayer: Dear God, you always keep your promises. Thank you for the protection that is ours in Christ, for satan's plans against us will not prosper. In Jesus' Name. Amen.

Every born again believer understands the salvation that we enjoy through the blood of Jesus, when the Lord Jesus died on the cross at Calvary as punishment for our sins. But did you know that we are protected by God as part of that same covenant? Salvation in and through the Lord Jesus Christ includes deliverance and protection by God. God does not want us to be anxious or fearful. God, our heavenly Father, wants what is best for us. And God has given his holy angels power and authority to war with our adversaries on our behalf. Trust God! God has you covered!

© By Dr. Sheila Hayford.

November 16
G.P.T. – A Godly Heritage

Malachi Chapter 2, verse 15:

Has not the one God made you? You belong to him in body and spirit. And what does the one God seek? Godly offspring. So be on your guard, and do not be unfaithful to the wife of your youth. (NIV)

Prayer: Dear God, thank you for the institution of marriage and for your desire for godly offspring. Help us, as Christ's disciples, to leave a godly heritage to all you entrust us with the responsivity of caring for. In Jesus' Name. Amen.

Having a godly heritage is one of the greatest blessings in life. There are special blessings and God given anointings that are passed down from godly parents to their descendants. When I look at Pastor Joel Osteen I say that if satan had known how much trouble Pastor Joel would give him satan would have left his father alone. It is so refreshing to see the godly influence Pastor John Osteen had on his son, Pastor Joel. And just like Pastor John's son, the anointings of God are supposed to increase through the generations. Each child has the giftings God gives them and, in the case of godly parents, additional special promises given by God to their parents. King David was very much loved by God. King Solomon, King David's son, was also very much loved by God. God would speak to King Solomon and remind him of the blessings that were his because of his father, King David and likewise, King Solomon would remind God of the promises God made to his father concerning King Solomon. So what if you did not grow up with godly parents? Do not fret. Be the first in your family to start what I call the "G.P.T.", that is, the Godly Parent Tradition. Future generations will thank you!

©By Dr. Sheila Hayford.

November 17
Happy, Happy, Happy!

Psalm 35, verse 9:
And my soul shall be joyful in the Lord: it shall rejoice in his salvation.
Prayer: Dear God, my heart rejoices in you and in my salvation in Christ. Thank you! In Jesus' Name. Amen.

It had been a busy morning. So busy I had skipped breakfast. So I decided to treat myself to lunch. I went into the restaurant and the service of my waiter was impeccable. I have always had a disdain for paying waitresses minimal wage because it is expected they will make up the difference in tips received, but that is a different subject for a different day. And so, after the meal I decide to give almost 20% of the total bill for the tip instead of the customary 15%. The Holy Spirit said to increase the tip to almost 30% of the total bill. I knew God was up to something greater in my life and with the great service I received I was happy to oblige. The waiter was very happy with his tip. "Thank you!" he said, "Come back and see me anytime." He was happy, I was happy. But God was not done. I had a work related item I needed to purchase and had planned to purchase it right after lunch. It would cost me over one hundred dollars but I was prepared for that expense since I needed it. Somehow, I decided to check my inventory just before I made that purchase. To my surprise, I had one more of that item left and since that would last a long time I did not need to make that purchase. God had immediately put over one hundred dollars back into my pocket. God was happy, the waiter was happy, I was happy. Happiness without compromising your values is a good thing.

© By Dr. Sheila Hayford.

November 18
Prayer is Productive

Psalm 66, verses 19-20:

But verily God hath heard me; he hath attended to the voice of my prayer. Blessed be God, which hath not turned away my prayer, nor his mercy from me.

Prayer: Dear God, we are so grateful that when we pray you hear us. And we have the confidence that when we pray according to your will, you will honor your word. Through our Lord and Savior, Jesus Christ. Amen.

Prayer is always an answer to any problem. So why do some try everything else before they decide to pray to God? There are many reasons. Some may think they are capable of handling the situation by themselves only to find out they were wrong. Others have not been taught to pray and do not know how to pray or what to expect. Contrary to what some may have been taught, prayer is not supposed to be complicated. Prayer, simply put, is having a conversation with God. However you choose to talk to God; silently, loudly, in song, using Scripture verses, a cry for help, a desperate call for God's intervention and so forth. Your prayer is one on one time with God and it is productive. You can pray productive prayers on your own and God will hear you. However, the effect of godly prayers are compounded so the more prayer, the greater the results. Now is the time to see the results of prayer, in our lives, in the nations and across the world. Pray, the world is depending on you!

© By Dr. Sheila Hayford.

November 19
Who Says "No" When God Says "Yes"?

James Chapter 1: verses 2, 3: Consider it pure joy, my brothers and sisters, whenever you face trials of many kinds, because you know that the testing of your faith produces perseverance. (NIV)

Prayer: Dear God; it is easy to look back and see your hand at work in our lives, not so easy during the challenging situation. We thank you for peace and joy, fruit of the Holy Spirit, which are ours through Jesus Christ. Accomplish your perfect will in us. In the Name of Jesus we pray. Amen.

"No, No, NO!" is what our enemies and adversaries will be saying because they never imagined our future would be so spectacular and so bright to which our God will respond, "Yes, Yes, YES!"

If satan had known that the very method he used in wrongfully killing the Lord Jesus would be the way God would free mankind from the clutches of satan and the stronghold of sin, satan would not have crucified the Lord Jesus.

Remember, the Lord Jesus willingly gave up His spirit and died on the cross, believing that God would raise Him up and honor Him for all eternity. What God did in what looked like a dire situation for the Lord Jesus on the cross is proof that God can work all things out for our good. So count it, or consider it to be, joyful when you face difficult or challenging situations, trusting God to work all things out for our good.

© By Dr. Sheila Hayford.

November 20
Your Heavenly Crown

Acts 5, verses 38-42: And now I say unto you, Refrain from these men, and let them alone: for if this counsel or this work be of men, it will come to nought: But if it be of God, ye cannot overthrow it; lest haply ye be found even to fight against God. And to him they agreed: and when they had called the apostles, and beaten them, they commanded that they should not speak in the name of Jesus, and let them go. And they departed from the presence of the council, rejoicing that they were counted worthy to suffer shame for his name. And daily in the temple, and in every house, they ceased not to teach and preach Jesus Christ.

Prayer: Dear Lord Jesus, help me to make my earthly decisions with my heavenly future in mind. Amen.

If living for God will cost you an earthly crown, remember the heavenly crown that awaits you and make the eternally correct decision.

© By Dr. Sheila Hayford.

November 21
Let The Children Come

Mark Chapter 10, verses 13-14:

People were bringing little children to Jesus for him to place his hands on them, but the disciples rebuked them. When Jesus saw this, he was indignant. He said to them, "Let the little children come to me, and do not hinder them, for the kingdom of God belongs to such as these. (NIV)

Prayer: Dear Lord Jesus: I look at your beautiful children and I am amazed. I see their little fingers and smiling faces and watch them grow. They come with enthusiasm for life, worry free, carefree, trusting their parents for their need. Their energy seems boundless, their creativity limitless. What happens in life that causes many adults to exchange these wonderful qualities for a life filled with fear, worry and regret? Help us to come to you as little children and trust you for every need. Forgive us where we allowed doubt, fear or worry to limit our potential and enable us to move forward, empowered by your Holy Spirit. In Your Name I pray. Amen.

While on a business trip I would meet these eight-year-old twin girls in the lobby from time to time. I am fascinated with twins and the miracle of life they represent and we would talk and laugh together. One day they came to the lobby with a young boy about their age who needed help connecting his mobile device to the Wi-Fi. One of the twins brought him to me. "That's my buddy", she told him as she introduced me, "we hang out together." I was old enough to be her mother! Honored and somewhat flattered, I smiled as he handed me his device to work on. Soon his Wi-Fi was working perfectly. I thought about our Lord Jesus Christ. Children were always comfortable with him. Indeed it was the Lord Jesus who said that we must come to him as children, in childlike trust, as we acknowledge our total dependence on him. Take the Lord Jesus at His Word and let the children come. © By Dr. Sheila Hayford.

November 22
Put The "Class" Back In Classy

Proverbs Chapter 8, verse 6:
Hear; for I will speak of excellent things; and the opening of my lips shall be right things.

Prayer: Dear God, your words are always appropriate, given at the right time and for your intended purpose. May the Holy Spirit enable our speech to be excellent, spoken at the right time, with the right attitude and for your glory. In Jesus' name. Amen.

It was around the holidays and a client wanted to do something special for those who had advance ordered her book. After the book was printed she did not just send them the printed book, she sent them a book package which included the book as well as elegant and unique gifts. I was so impressed I said to her, "you have put the 'class' back in classy!" Give God your best FIRST and see what follows.

© By Dr. Sheila Hayford.

November 23
A Taste Of Heaven

Luke Chapter 2, verses 41-42:
Now his parents went to Jerusalem every year at the feast of the passover. And when he was twelve years old, they went up to Jerusalem after the custom of the feast.

Prayer: Dear God, we thank you that our life here on earth is preparation for our life with the Lord Jesus on the other side of eternity. Help us to make the most of this time. In Jesus' name. Amen.

As we celebrate Thanksgiving, we are first grateful to God for being God. We thank God for the gift of life, for family and friends and for all the wonderful food we are blessed to enjoy; mouthwatering dishes, grandma's sweet potato pie, delicious desserts and so on. As we celebrate Thanksgiving, let us also remember that as Christians our life on earth is designed by God to give us a foretaste of heaven where we will be with our heavenly Father and our Lord Jesus Christ forever, sealed with the Holy Spirit.

And so we look forward to the wonderful feasting at the Marriage Supper of the Lamb with our bridegroom, the Lord Jesus Christ. There will be singing, laughing, chatting and much rejoicing.

Mmm, mmm, mmm!

© By Dr. Sheila Hayford.

November 24
Quilted; From The Inside Out

Romans Chapter 8, verse 28: And we know that all things work together for good to them that love God, to them who are the called according to his purpose.

Prayer: Dear God, we can rejoice in you because we know that you are working everything in our lives for our good. We chose to trust you with the end result of your finished quilt of our lives. In Jesus' name. Amen.

Have you seen a quilt project in the making? Each person has their share of the quilt to work on. Then all the different parts are put together and at the end you have one beautiful quilt. During the process the different sections look haphazard, out of place and disjointed. However, when they come together and fall in place, you admire the genius of the creator.

Your life is a quilted masterpiece designed by the Almighty God. What you may be going through now, or may have experienced in your past, may look out of place. However, God is working all things out for your good.

Stay in God's will and watch the beauty of your life unfold. God the Almighty, the Creator of all life, has an exquisite quilt planned for your life that stretches from this life to eternity.

If you stay with God's plan, you are going to like God's finished results!

© By Dr. Sheila Hayford.

November 25
At Your Word

Luke Chapter 5, verse 5: And Simon answering said unto him, Master, we have toiled all the night, and have taken nothing: nevertheless at thy word I will let down the net.

Prayer: Dear God, there have been many instances when I chose to obey your word and have been pleasantly amazed at the results. I have thanked you many times for enabling me to obey you when I consider what I would have missed if I had not. May we always put you and your Word first, no matter the circumstances, what others may think or how we may be perceived because we are your children and desire to please you first and foremost. In Jesus' Name. Amen.

Has God ever asked you to do something that seemed ridiculous to you at the time? Your mind told you it would not work but you knew in your heart that if God said it, you would be wise to obey God. I desired a special project but did not have the finances for it. However, I knew God wanted me to do it. Two weeks before the deadline, it seemed I would not make it. Then the Holy Spirit told me if I would pray and do a partial fast for seven days I would get what I wanted. So I did. It was now one week to the deadline and it seemed nothing was happening. Was I supposed to do another fast? I asked the Holy Spirit if I was supposed to do another seven day fast. He said no! So I began to rejoice and thank God because I knew that meant God had given me my desire, even though it seemed nothing had changed. Three days to the deadline, I received a surprise, unsolicited gift and it was for the exact amount that I needed. God had come through! During the project, as I reflected on God's miraculous provision, I would tell myself, "remember, you are on God's time."

Nevertheless, at Thy Word; obey God!

© By Dr. Sheila Hayford.

November 26
Project Earth

Luke Chapter 11, verse 2:
And he said unto them, When ye pray, say, Our Father which art in heaven, Hallowed be thy name. Thy kingdom come. Thy will be done, as in heaven, so in earth.

Prayer: Dear God, help us take responsibility for being good stewards of this earth and all the resources you have blessed us with. In the name of Jesus we pray. Amen.

If a person paid the gym membership fee, went to the gym, used the gym equipment and then trashed the equipment, left their belongings strewn on the floor and showed total disregard for the gym, the owners of the gym would obviously be upset. And suppose the attitude of the person doing the trashing was "I paid my dues!" Yes, you paid your dues, but not to mess things up. After you are done exercising at the gym, you are supposed to leave the gym in a respectable condition.

How different is that from project earth? By virtue of our humanity, God has given each human being the opportunity to live on this earth. God told Adam to take care of the earth God had place under Adam's authority. And God expects us to take good care of the territory God has given us dominion over.

Be a good steward of God's Earth Project!

© By Dr. Sheila Hayford.

November 27
Celebrating Our Youth!

Psalm 71, verse 17:
O God, thou hast taught me from my youth: and hitherto have I declared thy wondrous works.

Prayer: Dear Lord Jesus, how you love the little children! They are so trusting and teach us so much. And they grow so fast. As we celebrate our youth we pray that we will come to you in humility and childlike faith and be a godly example that the youth can emulate. Thank you for the Holy Spirit who empowers us to live for God. Amen.

How quick some are to forget their youthful days! They complain about the style of the sometimes loud music, the clothes, the movies, anything that has to do with the youth! I am not referring to inappropriate or ungodly lyrics, provocative clothes or trash movies, because we know there are some of those out there. I am talking about those who are stuck in nostalgia about the "good old days" even though all that took place then was not good!

Celebrate the youth! They are God's handiwork, created to continue the good works of the Lord God. They are strong, eager to learn, smart, respectful when they have been taught right and are entitled to be able to learn from the wisdom and experience of others. If you have only criticism and nothing good to say to a young person, say nothing at all. If the youth need encouragement, encourage them; if they need help, help them; if they need mentoring, mentor them. Use God's wisdom as you mentor and teach the youth. Celebrating our youth includes leading them to a personal relationship with the Lord Jesus Christ. Each one of us is blessed that God would honor us with relationships with our youth.

Let us play our part in proclaiming God's wonderful plan for the youth through the Lord Jesus Christ!

© By Dr. Sheila Hayford.

November 28
Where Are You Looking?

Luke Chapter 24, verse 5:
And as they were afraid, and bowed down their faces to the earth, they said unto them, Why seek ye the living among the dead?

Prayer: Dear Holy Spirit, give us direction so we know where to look for what we need. That way we will not waste time or resources looking in the wrong place. In Jesus' Name. Amen.

Have you ever lost something and set about trying to find it? You take the time to remember where you last saw it or where you last used it so that you will know where to look. The Lord Jesus had told his disciples he would rise again from the dead. Yet the disciples went to the grave, expecting to find his body even though the Lord Jesus was already alive and no longer in the grave. The angel of God had to remind them that the Lord Jesus was risen, just as he said.

The Lord God tells us that the Lord Jesus is God's beloved Son and that we should listen to Him. The Lord Jesus says he is the way to a right relationship with God and that he will come back to earth again, this time in all his power and authority. He spoke the truth when he said he would rise from the dead and he speaks the truth to us today, whatever we face in life. Where are you looking? And to whom are you looking? Look up, for the times may be closer than you may think.

© By Dr. Sheila Hayford.

November 29
Thank Those Christians!

Acts Chapter 9, verse 36:

In Joppa there was a disciple named Tabitha (in Greek her name is Dorcas); she was always doing good and helping the poor. (NIV)

Prayer: Dear God, thank you for the power of the Holy Spirit manifest on this earth and for the delegated power you have given us as born again believers to influence this world for good. Have mercy on us! In Jesus' Name we pray. Amen.

What do you mean? Thank those Christians? Yes, thank those Christians. Why? It is because they are the restraining force holding back evil in this world. Satan is a wicked master and if satan had his way, people would always be hurting themselves, each other and wrecking much havoc following satan into hell. Christians pray thereby restraining the powers of evil, have started schools, fed the poor, visited the sick, taken in widows, orphans, immigrants and continue to do so many good works. So why does it seem that Christians get such negative press? It is because many have taken their good works and influence for granted. A time is coming when the Lord Jesus Christ will return and born again believers will be caught up to meet him in the air. The influence of those Christians on this earth will be no more. Mayhem and panic will ensue as born again believers from all works of life are called off the job to meet the Lord Jesus in the air. Appreciate your fellow believers today. And thank them for the work they are doing!

© By Dr. Sheila Hayford.

November 30
I Will Show You What...

Acts Chapter 9, verses 4-5:

And he fell to the earth, and heard a voice saying unto him, Saul, Saul, why persecutest thou me? And he said, Who art thou, Lord? And the Lord said, I am Jesus whom thou persecutest: it is hard for thee to kick against the pricks.

Prayer: Dear God, thank you for the unique way you relate to each one of us through the Lord Jesus Christ. Amen.

The Apostle Paul was faced with a difficult choice. Stop preaching about Jesus and enjoy a temporary reprieve from all the physical beatings for Christ's sake, or spread the Word of God and endure more tribulations. Not everyone will experience the trials of Paul. Remember, a part of Paul's trials were the result of his persecution of the Christian church before he received Jesus Christ into his life. However, the Apostle Paul, counted everything secondary to his relationship with the Lord Jesus Christ and kept on preaching God's Word with the anointing of the Holy Spirit.

When Jesus said we would have trials and tribulations in this world, it is to different degrees or levels for each person. Each of us has a unique life to live - one unlike any other. We can encourage each other with our testimony of God's faithfulness but we cannot expect everyone to handle their experiences the way God worked things out for us. Let God show us His plans for us and enable us to each live faithfully for God.

© By Dr. Sheila Hayford.

December 1
The Power Of Discipleship.

Mark Chapter 4, verses 33, 34:
With many similar parables Jesus spoke the word to them, as much as they could understand. He did not say anything to them without using a parable. But when he was alone with his own disciples, he explained everything. (NIV)

Prayer: Dear Lord Jesus, we are your disciples and yet you regard us as friends. Thank you for revealing our heavenly Father to humanity and for teaching us and empowering us by the power of the Holy Spirit. Being your disciple can be tough, costly and sacrificial at times. But you gave your life for us and we love you. Thanks for the opportunity to serve you. Amen.

I have heard some companies say they hire attitude and not necessarily qualifications presented on a resume. This is because a person with a good attitude can be trained to align themselves with the company's mission, vision, goals and work on the implementation of the plans to achieve the goals. A person who has all the qualifications for the job but is not willing to learn anything new will not be a "good fit" for their organization. What is the principle here? Companies are looking to "make disciples."

The Lord Jesus chose twelve men who did not look like the ideal group to start his earthly outreach ministry. But when we look at the work God used the disciples to accomplish and consider the fact that their work continues to this day, by the Holy Spirit, we see the power of discipleship. Judas, one of the twelve disciples, chose to betray Jesus. This shows us that discipleship is voluntary. The disciple must trust his or her leader and willingly submit to the leader's mission, vision, goals and the ways of implantation to bring their goals to pass. A disciple learns what his leader is doing and why. The disciple can then explain and teach others the principles of his leader and continue the work even if the leader is not physically present. A follower may not understand what the leader is doing, nor necessarily be in agreement with the leader. Some of the crowds followed Jesus because they wanted something to eat or a specific need addressed. We are born again believers, saved through our Lord Jesus Christ. God is not looking for followers, but disciples.

© By Dr. Sheila Hayford.

December 2
Filters

Luke Chapter 8, verses 11-12:

Now the parable is this: The seed is the word of God. Those by the way side are they that hear; then cometh the devil, and taketh away the word out of their hearts, lest they should believe and be saved.

Prayer: Dear Holy Spirit, empower us to guard our eye gate, our ear gate, our speech gate and our associations gate so that we can effectively filter out what does not need to enter. Help us to hold fast to the truths of the Holy Scriptures and to submit ourselves fully to you. In the Name of Jesus we pray. Amen.

A filter lets some things in and keeps other things out. A tightly knit filter will keep more things out than it lets in. All through life we are faced with situations that involve our physical senses. However, our relationship with God through our Lord Jesus Christ is spiritual. So how do live a life that pleases God on this earth? By filtering what you see, hear and speak through the eyes, ears and words of God, that is, from God's perspective. If God would look at the situation, would God be pleased? If God would listen to the lyrics of that song, would God be pleased? If Jesus was carrying on that conversation with you, would He be pleased? While it is impossible for us to live a life without sin in our own human strength, God the Holy Spirit will empower us to live holy.

© By Dr. Sheila Hayford.

December 3
He Is Risen Indeed

Romans 8:34:

Who is he that condemneth? It is Christ that died, yea rather, that is risen again, who is even at the right hand of God, who also maketh intercession for us.

Prayer: Dear Lord Jesus, we are forgiven in you. Help us not listen to satan, described in your word as the accuser of the brethren. As our Savior, you are risen indeed and interceding for us and that is always great news. Hallelujah! Thank you so very much! Amen.

He is Risen Indeed! Wait a minute; I thought that is an Easter salutation. It is, but why limit it to Easter? It should be an everyday reality. When the challenges of life come your way, remember that because the Lord Jesus is risen indeed you can make it and live victoriously. When satan tries to tempt you, remind yourself that satan could not hold the Lord Jesus in the grave and through the Lord Jesus Christ, satan has no hold on you. It may be the month of December but your Risen Lord is presently seated at the right hand of God the Father, interceding for you. Rejoice!

© By Dr. Sheila Hayford.

December 4
Many Have Not Bowed To Baal

1 Kings Chapter 19, verse 18:
Yet I have left me seven thousand in Israel, all the knees which have not bowed unto Baal, and every mouth which hath not kissed him.

Prayer: Dear God, when we are look around and are discouraged or disappointed with the state of society, we may be tempted to think we are the only ones on your side. Help us keep our focus on you and remember that those with us on God's side are always more than those on the side of satan. We know that satan and satan's accomplices are no match for your awesome power and authority. In Jesus' Name. Amen.

The prophet Elijah was so depressed. He had just proven to the people that the false god, Baal, was no match for the Almighty God. Elijah had the prophets of Baal killed by the people. Elijah should have been elated! However, after all the emotions Elijah had gone through, he was exhausted. I am the only prophet of God left, he complained to God, and they even want to kill me! He was so tired it clouded his perceptions. No! God assured him, there were seven thousand in Israel who did not worship the false God, Baal.

You see, God will always have those in the earth who will follow and obey God in the power of the Holy Spirit. God leaves the choice to follow God and to obey God with us, but when we choose to be on God's side, God will enable us and equip us for service to him. God knows our human frame and expects us to take good care of our physical body. Elijah was tired and needed rest. As we give to others in the service of God, let us take the time needed to rest and be refreshed by God. Do not give satan the opportunity to cause you to sin because your body is physically tired. Remember, satan tried to tempt the Lord Jesus while the Lord Jesus was fasting in the wilderness when satan knew the Lord Jesus was hungry. On whose side are you?

© By Dr. Sheila Hayford.

December 5
Speaking Truth To Power

2 Kings Chapter 1, verses 3-4:
But the angel of the Lord said to Elijah the Tishbite, Arise, go up to meet the messengers of the king of Samaria, and say unto them, Is it not because there is not a God in Israel, that ye go to enquire of Baalzebub the god of Ekron? Now therefore thus saith the Lord, Thou shalt not come down from that bed on which thou art gone up, but shalt surely die. And Elijah departed.

Prayer: Dear God, we look to you first for you have all authority and all power. Enable us to speak your word with boldness, compassion and love. In Jesus' Name. Amen.

The prophet Elijah had a tough assignment from God. He was sent by God to tell the king of Samaria that the king was going to be punished by God. This was because the king sought to consult Baalzebub, the god of the Philistines, instead of going to the Lord God in prayer and seeking counsel from God's prophet. What was Elijah to do? Obey God and risk man's displeasure or keep silent and disobey God? The prophet Elijah made the wise choice and immediately departed to do what God had asked him to do.

The prophet Elijah knew God well enough to know that God would always have the final word in any situation. What do you do when God asks you to do something that involves speaking truth to those in authority? Will you obey God or will you let the fear of man cause you to disobey God? Remember, God has the final say in the eternal destiny of each individual. When God gives you an assignment, he not only equips you for the task, God will direct you on how to do it. In 2 Kings Chapter 20 we read that when King Hezekiah was told by the prophet Isaiah that King Hezekiah would be punished for displeasing God, King Hezekiah immediately repented towards God. God immediately sent the prophet Isaiah back to tell King Hezekiah that God was going to add fifteen years to King Hezekiah's life. So go ahead and trust God. You may find that the assignment, though uncomfortable, results in the saving of a life. What if you are treated unfairly for speaking God's truth to those in power? Always trust God. God knows you did your part. The rest is up to God.

© By Dr. Sheila Hayford.

December 6
Where Are You?

Revelation Chapter 1, verses 9, 10, 11:
I John, who also am your brother, and companion in tribulation, and in the kingdom and patience of Jesus Christ, was in the isle that is called Patmos, for the word of God, and for the testimony of Jesus Christ. I was in the Spirit on the Lord's day, and heard behind me a great voice, as of a trumpet, Saying, I am Alpha and Omega, the first and the last: and, What

thou seest, write in a book, and send it unto the seven churches which are in Asia; unto Ephesus, and unto Smyrna, and unto Pergamos, and unto Thyatira, and unto Sardis, and unto Philadelphia, and unto Laodicea.

Prayer: Dear God, help us to be willing to be used by you in whatever way, in whatever place and by whatever means you choose. In Jesus' Name we pray. Amen.

The Apostle John was in a very specific place, an uncomfortable place, when he wrote the book of Revelation. To the natural man, it seemed that John had been banished to the isle of Patmos but to God, John was where he needed to be, free from distractions, able to hear and see distinctly what the Lord Jesus wanted John to see, hear and write. This was so John could reach out and communicate God's words to multitudes, many of whom were not yet born. Did John know all of that at that time? Probably not! But in his humility and surrender to the good heart of God, John was willing to be used of God, no matter where, no matter how and no matter what. Where are you? Are you in a place where God can speak to you? Are you putting aside distractions so you can hear clearly from God? Are you willing to be used by God in whatever way and by whatever means God chooses? If so, enjoy the benefits and intimacy of a life yielded to God. There is no way you can know the full extent of your obedience. Suffice it to know that God knows, and God's got you covered.

© By Dr. Sheila Hayford.

December 7
I Understand

Hebrews Chapter 4, verse 15:
For we have not an high priest which cannot be touched with the feeling of our infirmities; but was in all points tempted like as we are, yet without sin.

Prayer: Dear Lord Jesus, thank you for truly understanding the challenges of this earthly life. Through the power of the Holy Spirit, you enable us to live as overcomers in this earthly realm. We know we will live and rule with you forever. We bless you, we honor you and we love you. Glory to your holy name! Amen.

"I understand" is a powerful phrase. When sincere, it gives one a sense of comfort or relief that the experience they face is not unique to them. Unfortunately, it can also become a smug cliché when you want to put a "nice" touch to a conversation that might be going nowhere. When the Lord Jesus says, "I understand" He means it; not as a license to disobey God but as an encouraging way of saying, you too can obey God. For the Lord Jesus lived on this earth, was tempted as a human being and resisted sin in the power of the Holy Spirit. Jesus is saying to each of us, "I overcame and so can you."

© By Dr. Sheila Hayford.

December 8
Glory, Glory!

Revelations Chapter 22, verses 3, 4:
And there shall be no more curse: but the throne of God and of the Lamb shall be in it; and his servants shall serve him: And they shall see his face; and his name shall be in their foreheads.

Prayer: Dear Lord Jesus, I know I am a sinner and deserve the punishment of death. For the Bible says that the wages of sin is death but the gift of God is eternal live through the Lord Jesus Christ. I repent of all my sins, those that I know about and those that I do not and ask you to forgive me of all sin. Thank you for dying on the cross on my behalf and paying the punishment for my sins. I invite you now into my heart to be my Lord and Savior. Fill me with your Holy Spirit and enable me to live for you. I believe that you are preparing a wonderful place for me in your presence and I am honored to be a part of your family. Enable me to share this good news with others. Amen.

Glory! Glory! It's a wonder! It's a wonder! Living in the presence of God in a place where there is no curse, where the throne of God and the Lord Jesus, the Lamb of God, dwells. And we get to participate in this wonder. For the former things on this present earth will have passed away. We will see our Lord Jesus face to face and we will serve him. There is a requirement though. You have to have the Name of the Lord Jesus in the forehead of your glorified body. How so? The Lord Jesus has made it simple. You have to be born again, not by entering a second time into your mother's womb as Nicodemus asked, but by receiving the Lord Jesus into your heart as Lord and Savior while you are on this earth. If you are ready to make that commitment now, pray the prayer above. I would very much love for you to be a part of that wonder, the wonder of being a part of the family of God!

© By Dr. Sheila Hayford.

December 9
Love Is A Series Of Actions

Hebrews Chapter 6, verse 10:
For God is not unrighteous to forget your work and labour of love, which ye have shewed toward his name, in that ye have ministered to the saints, and do minister.

Prayer: Dear God, sometimes we perform acts of kindness motivated by your love and those efforts are unappreciated or misjudged. Help us remember, in those times especially, that you are watching our works and labors of love and you are the one who will reward us at the right time. May we remember that we should be God pleasers first, and not primarily men pleasers. In Jesus' Name we pray. Amen.

True love always expresses itself. Indeed, love is always looking for opportunities for expression. "I think my spouse would love this …" and so you surprise him or her with a gift. God's love is revealed to us in so many ways each day; new mercies, loving kindness, provision, protection and of course, through the ultimate gift of our Lord Jesus. Love without any corresponding action is secret love. If a person only wants to love you from a distance, and by that I do not mean love separated by distance, but love that does not say or do anything loving, that should be a red flag.

God's agape love, which should be our example of genuine love, never ends.

© By Dr. Sheila Hayford.

December 10
Love Motivated Or Fear Motivated

1 John Chapter 4, verse 18:
There is no fear in love; but perfect love casteth out fear: because fear hath torment. He that feareth is not made perfect in love.

Prayer: Dear God, help us to walk in love, love for you and love for our fellow man. As we walk in your perfect love, we will not fear. In Jesus' Name. Amen.

As I meditated on the title of today's devotional I thought about how many people live their lives motivated by fear. They are afraid of being poor so they work hard. They are afraid of losing their home so they stay at a job they know in their heart they should have left years ago. While their actions may be good, and providing decent provision for your family is commendable, a fear motivated life is an oppressive way to live.

Consider the reverse, what I call the "Love Motivated Life." You do something because you genuinely desire to do it. It may be hard work, it may cost more, but you enjoy it and are fulfilled as a result.

Outwardly the end results may appear to be similar, but the two are diametrically opposed. How so? <u>There is no torment in true love, neither can there be the full expression of love where there is fear.</u>

© By Dr. Sheila Hayford.

December 11
The Proper Way

Ruth Chapter 4, verses 5-6, 13-15:

Then said Boaz, What day thou buyest the field of the hand of Naomi, thou must buy it also of Ruth the Moabitess, the wife of the dead, to raise up the name of the dead upon his inheritance. And the kinsman said, I cannot redeem it for myself, lest I mar mine own inheritance: redeem thou my right to thyself; for I cannot redeem it. So Boaz took Ruth, and she was his wife: and when he went in unto her, the LORD gave her conception, and she bare a son. And the women said unto Naomi, Blessed be the LORD, which hath not left thee this day without a kinsman, that his name may be famous in Israel. And he shall be unto thee a restorer of thy life, and a nourisher of thine old age: for thy daughter in law, which loveth thee, which is better to thee than seven sons, hath born him.

Prayer: Dear God; thank you for the example of Ruth, through who you show us that your proper way is indeed the right way and that satan ought not win for your destined plans for us are good and great. Help us to be patient and trust your process, always keeping our focus on you. In Jesus' Name. Amen.

Ruth, the delightful daughter-in-law of Naomi was in for a pleasant surprise. Her mother-in-law was happy to do some match matching for Ruth and gave Ruth specific instructions. Ruth followed her mother-in-law's advice and Boaz was ready to marry Ruth. There was an initial obstacle though, because there was a proper way for Boaz to marry Ruth. There was a kinsman closer to Naomi than Boaz who had first right of refusal when it came to Naomi's land and marriage to Ruth. Boaz wanted to do things the proper way. So Boaz went and sat at the city gate. As God would have it, that nearer kinsman passed by and Boaz asked him to have a seat by him. Boaz then asked ten of the elders of the city to witness his offer. Naomi's land was up for sale but whoever bought the land had to marry Ruth, in order to continue the family name as was the common practice at the time. If the kinsman refused, Boaz would buy the land and marry Ruth. The nearer kinsman initially wanted to accept the land but when he realized that he would have to marry Ruth, he began to consider his own inheritance and declined to accept the offer. As confirmation of his refusal, the kinsman took off his shoe, another common practice at the time. Boaz was now free to marry Ruth. Boaz and Ruth had a child and the name of their child was Obed. Obed was the father of Jesse and Jesse was the father of King David.

When Ruth decided to leave Moab with Naomi and serve the God of the Israelites she had no idea how greatly God would honor her. Her words to us today would probably be, "God worked things out for me in the proper way!"

© By Dr. Sheila Hayford.

December 12
Hibernating Or In The Game

Matthew Chapter 11, verse 28:
Come unto me, all ye that labour and are heavy laden, and I will give you rest.

Prayer: Dear Lord Jesus, we come to you with all our cares and concerns and cast them on you. Thank you for being willing to take those cares and concerns and replace them with faith and trust in God, the God who promises to meet our needs. In so doing, we experience your peace and can rest, assured of your goodness. We love you and we trust you. Amen.

Many have heard of groundhogs and bears that hibernate in the winter. In the winter, the ground hog goes underground and does not come out until the weather gets warmer. Unfortunately, some Christians act that way when their faith walk gets a little challenging. They focus on the challenge and get so depressed they essentially check out on life. As a result, they do not attend church services or fellowship events, do not call their fellow Christians, they might not even talk to God. God wants you in the game of life. He already knows what challenges you will face before you get there. The Lord Jesus invites you to come to him first with your burdens and challenges. When you give the Lord Jesus your heavy burden, you take the pressure off you and allow God to take care of the situation in God's way and in God's time. In exchange, you receive God's peace, which passes all understanding, while trusting God to meet your needs and address your cares and concerns as he sees fit. As a result, you experience the rest that comes from a life at peace with God.

© By Dr. Sheila Hayford.

December 13
Where Is Your Faith?

Mark Chapter 11, verse 22:
And Jesus answering saith unto them, Have faith in God.

Prayer: Dear God, forgive me for the times I have had doubts when your word and your instructions to me were clear. Help me to walk in faith, trusting you and your words, confident that you always keep your word. In Jesus' Name, I pray. Amen.

It was Super Bowl 51 and I wanted Tom Brady and the New England Patriots to win. The New England Patriots had won many Super Bowls, although they were not my favorite team. However, in my opinion, Tom Brady had not been treated right in the "Deflategate" saga and so I wanted him to win. I prayed and asked God for the Patriots to win and God said okay. At half time the New England Patriots were trailing the Atlanta Falcons by 25 points. The score was 28-3 with the Patriots having scored only 3 points. I had seen one of my favorite football teams come back from a 10 point deficit to win the Super Bowl, but I had never seen a team come back from a 25 point deficit to win the Super Bowl. I went back to God and asked if I could change my prayer. "Sure!" He replied. And so I said that I knew I had prayed for the Patriots to win but if God wanted it otherwise, He could do so. I rationalized in my thoughts that maybe God was trying to tell me something. Well, the Patriots came back to tie the game at 28-28 at the end of the fourth quarter. That put the game into overtime, the first overtime in Super Bowl history. Within four minutes of overtime, the Patriots had a touchdown for a 34-28 win. The New England Patriots had won Super Bowl 51 with a game for the history books! And Tom Brady was now a five-time Super Bowl champion and a four-time MVP!

When God said okay to my prayer request the first time, He meant it. Nevertheless, when the Patriots got so far behind I began to have my doubts. Moreover, I clothed those doubts in "Maybe that is not the will of God." God used Tom Brady and the New England Patriots to remind me to stay focused in my faith in God and in the Word of God, no matter the obstacles or odds that make what God said look impossible. God wants us to muster the resolve and fight to run life's race in the power of the Holy Spirit until the victory manifests, a testimony for all to see.

Where is your faith?

©By Dr. Sheila Hayford.

December 14
SMART?

Proverbs Chapter 21, verse 30:
There is no wisdom nor understanding nor counsel against the Lord.
Prayer: Dear God, our heavenly Father; you are the All-wise God, the All-knowing God. We thank you for revealing yourself to us in the person of our Lord Jesus Christ, through whom we become a part of your family. May we come to you with all our challenges for you have the perfect answers to any challenge we face. In Jesus' Name. Amen.

We live in an era of smart cars, smart homes, smart phones and smart appliances. However, these smart devices are only as good as the one who created them, for the purpose for which they were created. From time to time, you read about a manufacturer recalling a part, updating an existing model or creating new models to increase efficiency. Not so with God. God created men and women perfectly; no recalls ever needed to update the efficiency of, for example, a particular human organ. Even before Adam and Eve sinned, God had set the plan for the Lord Jesus to die on the cross for the sins of humanity.

So in this era of smart this and smart that, you can entrust your life to the precise God, the perfect manufacturer of your spirit, soul and body.

© By Dr. Sheila Hayford.

December 15
Keep Calm And Trust God

Psalm 81, verse 2:
I will say of the Lord, He is my refuge and my fortress: my God; in him will I trust.

Prayer: Dear God, thank you for your keeping power. We bless you and magnify your Name for you do all things excellently. We thank you for yesterday, and ask that you help us trust you today and forevermore. In Jesus' Name we pray. Amen.

We are approaching the end of another year and are extremely grateful for God's love, faithfulness and provision. We could not have made it this far without the Lord and we know He has more in store for us in the coming year.

As we enter the hustle and bustle of the Christmas season, with busy shoppers pushing their way, gift giving at its peak, and as we prepare to celebrate the birth of our Lord Jesus on earth, let our motto for the coming year be: Keep Calm and Trust God!

© By Dr. Sheila Hayford.

December 16
Confidence

John Chapter 15, verse 5:

I am the vine, ye are the branches: He that abideth in me, and I in him, the same bringeth forth much fruit: for without me ye can do nothing.

Prayer: Dear Lord Jesus; we find our true identity in you, for without you life would be futile. Help us to be authentic as we share you with others, trusting the Holy Spirit's leading and ability to transform our life and the lives of others. Amen.

There is something compelling about a person who is confident in what they are saying. That person has studied or has knowledge of what he or she is talking about and is not intimidated when asked about their subject or project. In fact, they welcome questions because it gives them the opportunity to explain their subject or project more fully and to share their passion with others. Although a confident person may not necessarily be right, they might still command respect because of their knowledge. God wants us to be confident in our faith but he wants our confidence to be in God. The Lord Jesus tells us that he is the vine and we are the branches. His power, the Holy Spirit, flowing in and through us enables us to live a life confident in the God we serve. Our personal relationship with God, study of the Scriptures and the enabling of the Holy Spirit gives us the power and confidence we need to share our faith.

Is your testimony for God compelling? It does not have to be the wordy, the most exciting or the one with the most transformation. Your most compelling testimony is your most authentic testimony; sharing God with others from your heart. So go ahead and confidently share Jesus, knowing that God who began the good work in you will keep you on this earth and throughout eternity. You are impacting lives for eternity.

© By Dr. Sheila Hayford.

December 17
The Power Of Your Choice

Deuteronomy Chapter 30, verse 19:
I call heaven and earth to record this day against you, that I have set before you life and death, blessing and cursing: therefore choose life, that both thou and thy seed may live:

Luke Chapter 15, verses 18-20:
I will arise and go to my father, and will say unto him, Father, I have sinned against heaven, and before thee, and am no more worthy to be called thy son: make me as one of thy hired servants. And he arose, and came to his father. But when he was yet a great way off, his father saw him, and had compassion, and ran, and fell on his neck, and kissed him.

Prayer: Dear God; help us to choose you and to choose life in every area of our lives. In the Name of Jesus we pray, Amen.

If a person repeatedly and persistently chooses to live a life in rebellion towards God, God will watch that person go down because God respects every person's free will. It is only when the prodigal son decided to return from his erroneous ways that the Father ran towards him. Your choices are powerful for they shape the direction of your life. Choosing God's way is not always the easiest, convenient or the most logical way but it is always the best choice.

Choose life!

© By Dr. Sheila Hayford.

December 18
Live Forever – It's God's Idea!

John Chapter 4, verses 50-51:

Jesus saith unto him, Go thy way; thy son liveth. And the man believed the word that Jesus had spoken unto him, and he went his way. And as he was now going down, his servants met him, and told him, saying, Thy son liveth.

Prayer: Dear God: As your children, we are thankful for salvation through your Son, our Lord and Savior, Jesus Christ. Thank you for the life we have with you now and forever. Hallelujah! Amen.

When God created Adam and Eve, God created them with eternity in mind. Adam and Eve disobeyed God and sinned against God. In turn, sin entered the human race and led to death and separation from God. Thank God for sending the Lord Jesus! The Lord Jesus came to rescue humanity from sin by taking on himself the punishment for the sins of all humanity. Whoever believes on the Lord Jesus and invites the Lord Jesus to be their Lord and Savior is saved and will live forever more with God. Eternal life; that's God's idea. Eternal hell; that's the devil's destination. Do not let the devil take you to the wrong eternal destination.

© By Dr. Sheila Hayford.

December 19
Bow; Now Or Later

Romans Chapter 14, verses 11-12:

For it is written, As I live, saith the Lord, every knee shall bow to me, and every tongue shall confess to God. So then every one of us shall give account of himself to God.

Prayer: Dear Lord Jesus, we willingly and lovingly acknowledge you as our Lord and Savior. Help us to share you with others, for you desire the best for mankind and desire that we live with you forever. Amen.

It is very interesting that evil spirits and demons recognized and acknowledged the authority and Lordship of Jesus Christ while some of the religious leaders in Jesus' day did not. Sadly, the same could be said about some today. The question is not whether every knee will bow to the Lord Jesus Christ. The question is "when?" A time is coming when every knee will bow and every tongue will declare the Lordship of Jesus Christ, to the glory of God the Father. Will you willingly bow to the Lord Jesus today? Those who refuse to do so on this earth will make the acknowledgement that the Lord Jesus is Lord in the most unpleasant way; before they go to an eternal hell where satan and those who choose to follow satan will inhabit. No one should want to have to go through that!

© By Dr. Sheila Hayford.

December 20
Short Cuts

Jeremiah Chapter 6, verse 16:

Thus saith the Lord, Stand ye in the ways, and see, and ask for the old paths, where is the good way, and walk therein, and ye shall find rest for your souls. But they said, We will not walk therein.

Prayer: Dear God, you lead us in the paths of life as we submit to the Holy Spirit. Enable us to choose your way every day. In the Name of Jesus we pray, Amen.

It was before the age of Google maps and there was a lot of traffic so I decided to take what I thought would be a short cut to my destination. Well, I got lost and it ended up taking me longer to reach my destination. The Lord Jesus Christ came to show us the way to reach God and our heavenly destination. The Lord Jesus' directions are simple but there are no short cuts. Here they are:

1. Acknowledge you are a sinner, confess your sins to God and repent of your sins.

2. Then invite the Lord Jesus Christ into your heart as your Lord and Savior. You will immediately receive God's gift of the Holy Spirit.

3. Allow the Holy Spirit to help you live the Christian life.

4. Read the Word of God, the Holy Bible, pray to God, submit to and obey the Holy Spirit.

5. When you sin, confess your sins, ask God for forgiveness and continue your Christian journey.

6. Trust God always. God has an eternal future for you.

It is that simple. Living the Christian life is a journey that requires faith. Sometimes you just have to obey God when you do not have all the answers. In those times when you are tempted to take short cuts in your faith journey by doing what you think is right instead of what God has told you to do, consider the consequences. What seems like God's longer route is actually the shortest route to your heavenly destination.

© By Dr. Sheila Hayford.

December 21
It Is Warm Inside

Matthew Chapter 25, verse 40:

And the King shall answer and say unto them, Verily I say unto you, Inasmuch as ye have done it unto one of the least of these my brethren, ye have done it unto me.

Prayer: Dear Lord Jesus; it is very sobering to think that when we serve the least among us in your Name, we are serving you. Help us to serve you in love, remembering that you came to earth to serve and to save a lost humanity. Thank you. Amen.

Imagine how Joseph and Mary must have felt. Mary, due to deliver her first-born child and having to embark on this long journey. This was probably not what she envisioned when the angel Gabriel announced the coming birth of her Son, the Lord Jesus Christ. We do not read about Mary complaining, even though it would have been nice to be inside where it was warm. And so Joseph dutifully knocked on doors until he found an innkeeper who was willing to let them stay in his stable. There, in that humble place, our Lord and Savior Jesus Christ was born.

So how did so many people miss it? I mean those whom Joseph asked for a place to stay who said "No!" Had they known it was for the Son of God, they might have given up their bed. Today we do not have to worry about missing Jesus. He says if we give a child a cup of water in Christ's name, we will not lose our reward. The Lord Jesus says whatever we do to help the least of his brethren we are doing unto him. If we feed the hungry, visit the sick, visit those in prison, take care of the stranger, clothe those who need clothes, we will be acknowledged on that day when the Lord Jesus separates what He calls the sheep from the goats; those who helped the least of their brethren and those who did not. May God help us to be on the Lord Jesus' right side!

© By Dr. Sheila Hayford.

December 22
Wicked Herod

Matthew Chapter 2, verses 16, 19, 20:
Then Herod, when he saw that he was mocked of the wise men, was exceeding wroth, and sent forth, and slew all the children that were in Bethlehem, and in all the coasts thereof, from two years old and under, according to the time which he had diligently inquired of the wise men. But when Herod was dead, behold, an angel of the Lord appeareth in a dream to Joseph in Egypt, Saying, Arise, and take the young child and his mother, and go into the land of Israel: for they are dead which sought the young child's life.

Psalm 139, verses 23-24:
Search me, O God, and know my heart: try me, and know my thoughts: And see if there be any wicked way in me, and lead me in the way everlasting.

Prayer: Dear God: How utterly wicked satan is; using King Herod to massacre all those children! Lest many be quick to judge King Herod, we still read of many atrocities that continue to take place against unborn babies, women and children. May we, as Christians, be vigilant in our prayers and in our civil responsibilities. You are the perfect judge and Scripture tells us in Romans Chapter 12, verse 19 that revenge is yours to mete. We entrust ourselves to you and to your care. In the Name of Jesus we pray. Amen.

Not only was King Herod insecure, he was also very wicked. He was so threatened by a baby boy that he planned to kill Jesus, even before the baby grew up. When Herod found out that the wise men did not return to him with the whereabouts of baby Jesus, he calculated the time period that had passed since he spoke to the wise men and had all the children who were two years of age and under massacred. He foolishly thought that would prevent King Jesus from assuming authority. King Herod did not know that Joseph, Mary and Baby Jesus were already in Egypt and that there was nothing the wicked King Herod could do that would change or thwart God's plans. When you receive the Lord Jesus Christ in your heart, you are born again and are a new baby in Christ. Now satan hates you because you are now on God's side. Satan may try to harm you but God has a good plan for you. Like Joseph, you must listen to God and obey God as God leads and directs you in life. With God on your side, your obedience to God will give you victory over sin and satan. When your life on this earth is over, you will be singing, "Praise God, in Jesus Christ I won!"

© By Dr. Sheila Hayford.

December 23
20/20 Vision

1 Corinthians Chapter 13, verse 12-13: For now we see only a reflection as in a mirror; then we shall see face to face. Now I know in

part; then I shall know fully, even as I am fully known. And now these three remain: faith, hope and love. But the greatest of these is love. (NIV)

Prayer: Dear God; we trust you and we trust your process. In Jesus' Name we pray. Amen.

God, who knows the end from the beginning, sees each life today and every day with 20/20 vision. He knows the challenges we will face before we get there and has the answers and solutions to our challenges. Someday we too will have 20/20 vision as we look back from the other side of eternity.

In the meantime, trust God and trust God's process.

© By Dr. Sheila Hayford.

December 24
Joy Now, Joy Later

Luke Chapter 2, verse 10: And the angel said unto them, Fear not: for, behold, I bring you good tidings of great joy, which shall be to all people.

Prayer: What great news! God came to earth to live among men, die for our sins and rise to reign forevermore. Hallelujah! Embolden and empower us, dear Holy Spirit, as we share this good news with others. May many rejoice at Christ's birth. In the name of Jesus we pray. Amen.

"Good tidings of great joy!" the angel said. For to us, the Savior of mankind, the Lord Jesus Christ is born. The Savior who died on the cross for our sins, rose from the dead and is seated in glory at the right hand of God the Father. **All** who confess their sins, repent of sin, ask God for forgiveness and invite the Lord Jesus Christ into their heart as Lord and Savior will be born again, this time into the family of God. No matter your walk in life or your estate, no exclusions. This Lord Jesus Christ is coming again to receive all believers. There we will experience eternal joy in his presence. That is very good news. Like the angel, let us proclaim the good tidings with great joy. Hallelujah!

© By Dr. Sheila Hayford.

December 25
A Child Is Born

Isaiah Chapter 9, verse 6:

For unto us a child is born, unto us a son is given: and the government shall be upon his shoulder: and his name shall be called Wonderful, Counsellor, The mighty God, The everlasting Father, The Prince of Peace.

Prayer: Hallelujah! The Lord Jesus Christ came to earth and we rejoice exceedingly. We bless you dear Lord Jesus, honor you and thank you for coming to save a lost humanity. We pray that all who hear the good news of salvation will respond to you with love and appreciation and personally accept you as Lord and Savior. Amen.

Unto us, humankind, a child is born! This child, the Son of God, is given to us for our salvation.

Children are usually helpless at birth and must be nurtured so they will grow to become mature responsible adults. With the baby Jesus Christ, it is different. The government of all the nations will be on his shoulder. He is the mighty God for he came to earth from his position in divinity as God the Son. He is the Prince of Peace; a commodity very much needed in this world and that we all desire in our personal lives.

As we celebrate the birth of our Lord Jesus, let us remember that he is the Risen Lord and Savior, seated at God's right hand of authority, interceding on our behalf. And, he is coming back again in His glory to receive us to Himself.

Hallelujah!

© By Dr. Sheila Hayford.

December 26
Longevity

Luke Chapter 1, verses 32-33:

He shall be great, and shall be called the Son of the Highest: and the Lord God shall give unto him the throne of his father David: And he shall reign over the house of Jacob for ever; and of his kingdom there shall be no end.

Prayer: Dear God, the God who inhabits eternity; we look forward to the second coming of our Lord Jesus with great joy. Help us to live, love and serve you with our eternal destination in mind. In Jesus' Name. Amen.

Queen Elizabeth II has reigned as Queen of Great Britain for 65 years. The beloved Queen Elizabeth II is 91 years old and has the longest reign of any queen of Great Britain. Royalty has its privileges. We know maintaining the monarchy can be expensive, a cost the Britons are happy to bear. And so we rejoice when royal marriages take place, are sorry to hear of a royal divorce and wish the monarchy the best in their endeavors. As we celebrate the birth of our Lord Jesus, let us remember that His reign has the most longevity. For the Scriptures tell us that the reign and kingdom of our Lord Jesus Christ is forever. And that is cause for joyous celebration!

© By Dr. Sheila Hayford.

December 27
Prosper In Every Way

3 John Chapter 1, verse 2:

Beloved, I wish above all things that thou mayest prosper and be in health, even as thy soul prospereth.

Prayer: Dear God, it is your will that your children prosper in every part of our being; spirit, soul and body. As we do so, we will have healthy wholesome relationships and enjoy prosperity in the spiritual, emotional and temporal areas of life. Let us not be misled into thinking that prosperity is a bad word for you are a good God, our heavenly Father who does not enjoy seeing children neglected. In Jesus' Name. Amen.

What is the Apostle John talking about when he uses the word "prosper"? He is talking about prosperity in the soul, physical and spiritual areas of life. That is prosperity in every aspect of life. It is easy to understand that we must prosper spiritually. However, some do not heed the words of the Lord Jesus when He says that as a man thinks, so is he. In other words, where you are today is a reflection of your thoughts. And the way you think affects how you take care of your body physically. Let us resolve to grow every year in every area of our life, as we yield to God's power at work in us.

© By Dr. Sheila Hayford.

December 28
Fresh Paint

Philippians Chapter 2, verse 13:
For it is God which worketh in you both to will and to do of his good pleasure.

Prayer: Dear God, we need you for without you we can do nothing. Thank you that were are your handiwork, created by you for your purpose, plans and pleasure. Thank you for continuing the good work you began in us. Enable us to be patient with you and with ourselves as you mold us into the image of your Son and our Lord, Jesus Christ. Amen.

Fresh paint gives us a sense of newness. It may be the fresh paint of a new house or of a new car. Even in an old house, applying a fresh coat of paint seems to make the walls come alive! However, the application of fresh paint can be a messy process. It can also be inconvenient. For example, the application of fresh paint on the roads delineating the different lanes can be inconvenient for those driving to and back from work. In the end, it benefits most, if not all of us. So now, apply this thought to our salvation. When we receive the Lord Jesus as Lord and Savior of our lives, we are new creatures in Christ. We are born again and given a fresh coat of paint. However, we still have old ways of doing things that need to be changed. We continually need fresh paint as the Holy Spirit does His work in us. It may be messy at times and we may find it inconvenient at times. In the end we bring forth productive lives in God's kingdom, to the glory of God and the betterment of society.

© By Dr. Sheila Hayford.

December 29
Chosen To Serve

Ephesians Chapter 6, verses 7, 8:

Serve wholeheartedly, as if you were serving the Lord, not people, because you know that the Lord will reward each one for whatever good they do, whether they are slave or free. (NIV)

Prayer: Dear God; what a joy and a privilege to be chosen by you! We love you and are honored to be in your service. Empower us to serve you and others in the power of the Holy Spirit so that our service will be pleasing to you. For we want to hear your "Well Done!" In Jesus' Name, Amen.

Some Christians separate their profession or vocation from their Christian faith as if the two are mutually exclusive. In fact, they are both part of one continuing spectrum.

The same God who gifted you with intellect, passion and the abilities to do the job you do so well is the same God who chose you to be His child. Your service to God involves your service to man. So serve God in every area of your life. Remember, you get double pay; pay for your earthly work by your employer or clients and pay for your earthly service by your God.

© By Dr. Sheila Hayford.

December 30
Prayer: A Gift And A Responsibility

Matthew Chapter 7, verse 7:

Ask, and it shall be given you; seek, and ye shall find; knock, and it shall be opened unto you:

Prayer: Dear God, our heavenly Father, thank you for inviting us into your presence and giving us the opportunity to present our requests to you. Thank you for answering our prayers through your Son, Jesus Christ. Amen.

Prayer is both a gift and a responsibility. Use it wisely! As we approach the end of the year it is natural to look back and see areas where we could have done better. Prayer frees us from the limitations of our human self and puts us in connection with the All-powerful God who loves us so much he sent his Son to die for us. This is the God who invites us to partner with Him in prayer. A good resolution for each year would be to start a Prayer Journal. Write down your prayer requests and the date, then find Scriptures that confirm that your prayer request is in agreement with the will of God and write down when and how God answers those prayers. We do the praying and believing, walking out our faith in love and God honors His Word. You are more powerful in prayer than you imagine. Use prayer wisely!

© By Dr. Sheila Hayford.

December 31
The Fourth Man

Matthew Chapter 24, verse 13:
But he that shall endure unto the end, the same shall be saved.

Prayer: Dear Lord Jesus, You are the author and finisher of my faith, my perfect example. As long as I have breath on this earth, my earthly race is not over. Help me to finish my race strong. Thank you for the gift of the Holy Spirit, my enabler. I commit myself to do the will of our heavenly Father with joy and bless you for the year to come. In Your Name I pray, Amen.

It was the week of the Summer Olympics in Rio, Brazil and I watched some of the world's greatest athletes perform and display their talents. The personal stories were almost unbelievable; stories of overcoming personal challenges, dedicated daily practice and discipline in their sport in order to achieve that Olympic medal. Two events I watched had a profound impact on me. They both involved the track events, one was in the women's event and the other was in the men's event. As the men's track event neared the end of the race, the person who was in third position to get the bronze metal looked back. At that moment, the fourth man snuck up into third position and claimed the bronze medal prize. By a single careless act, the person looking back was distracted and lost his medal. In contrast, there were three women from the United States racing in the track event. It looked as if the first three women running were about to clinch the gold, silver and bronze medal. Somehow, the woman in fourth place suddenly found the strength to sprint to the finish line and clinch that third bronze medal. What made her victory even sweeter was that by her action, all three women in that race from the United States made a clean sweep of the medals by winning the gold, silver and bronze Olympic medals.

So it is in life. The devil is looking for ways to distract us in the race of life. Satan wants us to look back at our past, waste time rehearsing past mistakes and try to cause us to lose our crown. On the other side is the Holy Spirit, our enabler. No matter what happened in the past, the Holy Spirit gives us the sprint we need in life to finish well and claim our reward. As I saw the Olympic medalists drape themselves in the flag, smiles on their faces as they held onto their hard won medals, I was sure they would say that all they went through was worthwhile because of what they accomplished at the end. God has shared a lot with us in this book as we continue to strive towards perfection. The Holy Scriptures tell us that he who endures to the end will be saved. Your brothers and sisters in Christ are cheering you on. Get your sprint on!

© By Dr. Sheila Hayford.

A Celebration of Book Writing

What A Word Publishing and Media Group is on a mission to promote Book Reading, Writing and Publishing nationally and globally.

We believe that everyone has a story to tell; each story as varied as our life experiences. We believe that each story can have a positive benefit and, in some cases, a life changing effect on another person's life. We also recognize the barriers to book writing and publishing that may confront an individual. To this end, What a Word Publishing and Media Group offers Book Writing Seminars and Workshops.

Our Book Seminars are designed to demystify the Book Writing and Publishing process and our workshops are designed to provide hands-on experience in initiating the book writing process. We also offer Book Writing Seminars and Workshops "ON LOCATION" so your group can experience our book writing Seminars and Workshops at their location.

We also offer individualized Book Coaching, Editing, Resume, Promotion and Publicity Services and work with varying budgets. To request information on hosting a Book Seminar and Workshop, or to inquire about our Private Book Coaching and other Services please email: info@whatawordpublishing.com or fill out the contact page at www.whatawordpublishing.com

What A Word Publishing & Media Group: Published Book Titles include:

- ❖ L.E.A.D. - The Truth About Raising High Achieving Kids
- ❖ Heart to Heart Connections
- ❖ Miya - Caring and Sharing
- ❖ Alisha - The Dog Rescuer
- ❖ God's Sound Bites
- ❖ Snatched From The Fire - One Man's Compelling Story
- ❖ I Love My Family - Liberian Literacy Series

Coming Soon:

- ♦ Brian's Journey: A Novel
- ♦ Miatta Goes To School

Isn't it time **you** published your book?
Let's talk!
Email: info@whatawordpublishing.com
Visit www.whatawordpublishing.com/contact us

Thank You!